MORTUARY DIALOGUES

ASAO Studies in Pacific Anthropology

General Editor: Rupert Stasch, Department of Social Anthropology, University of Cambridge

The Association for Social Anthropology in Oceania (ASAO) is an international organization dedicated to studies of Pacific cultures, societies, and histories. This series publishes monographs and thematic collections on topics of global and comparative significance, grounded in anthropological fieldwork in Pacific locations.

Volume 1
The Anthropology of Empathy: Experiencing the Lives of Others in Pacific Societies
Edited by Douglas W. Hollan and C. Jason Throop

Volume 2
Christian Politics in Oceania
Edited by Matt Tomlinson and Debra McDougall

Volume 3
The Death of the Big Men and the Rise of the Big Shots: Custom and Conflict in East New Britain
Keir Martin

Volume 4
Creating a Nation with Cloth: Women, Wealth, and Tradition in the Tongan Diaspora
Ping-Ann Addo

Volume 5
The Polynesian Iconoclasm: Religious Revolution and the Seasonality of Power
Jeffrey Sissons

Volume 6
Engaging with Strangers: Love and Violence in the Rural Solomon Islands
Debra McDougall

Volume 7
Mortuary Dialogues: Death Ritual and the Reproduction of Moral Communities in Pacific Modernities
Edited by David Lipset and Eric K. Silverman

Mortuary Dialogues
Death Ritual and the Reproduction of Moral Community in Pacific Modernities

Edited by
David Lipset and Eric K. Silverman

First published in 2016 by
Berghahn Books
www.berghahnbooks.com

© 2016, 2019 David Lipset and Eric K. Silverman
First paperback edition published in 2019

All rights reserved. Except for the quotation of short passages
for the purposes of criticism and review, no part of this book
may be reproduced in any form or by any means, electronic or
mechanical, including photocopying, recording, or any information
storage and retrieval system now known or to be invented,
without written permission of the publisher.

Library of Congress Cataloging-in-Publication Data

Names: Lipset, David, editor. | Silverman, Eric Kline, editor.
Title: Mortuary dialogues : death ritual and the reproduction of moral community in
 Pacific modernities / edited by David Lipset and Eric K. Silverman.
Description: New York : Berghahn Books, 2016. | Series: ASAO studies in pacific
 anthropology : vol. 7 | Includes bibliographical references and index.
Identifiers: LCCN 2015045924| ISBN 9781785331718 (hardback : alk. paper) |
 ISBN 9781785331725 (ebook)
Subjects: LCSH: Pacific islanders—Funeral rites and ceremonies. | Funeral rites and
 ceremonies—Pacific Area. | Mourning customs—Pacific Area. | Death—Social
 aspects—Pacific Area.
Classification: LCC GN663 .M67 2016 | DDC 306.90995—dc23
LC record available at hip://lccn.loc.gov/2015045924

British Library Cataloguing in Publication Data

A catalogue record for this book is available from the British Library

ISBN 978-1-78533-171-8 hardback
ISBN 978-1-78920-506-0 paperback
ISBN 978-1-78533-172-5 ebook

In Memory

of

Eugene Amen Ogan (1930–2015)

Teacher, Mentor, Colleague, Pacific Scholar, Friend

Contents

List of Figures and Tables	ix
Foreword by Shirley Lindenbaum	xii
Acknowledgements	xvii
Map	xviii
Introduction. Mortuary Ritual, Modern Social Theory, and the Historical Moment in Pacific Modernity *Eric K. Silverman and David Lipset*	1

PART 1. Tenacious Voices

Chapter 1. Fearing the Dead: The Mortuary Rites of Marshall Islanders amid the Tragedy of Pacific Modernity *Laurence Marshall Carucci*	25
Chapter 2. Into the World of Sorrow: Women and the Work of Death in Māori Mortuary Rites *Che Wilson and Karen Sinclair*	47
Chapter 3. Death and Experience in Rawa Mortuary Rites, Papua New Guinea *Doug Dalton*	60
Chapter 4. The Knotted Person: Death, the Bad Breast, and Melanesian Modernity among the Murik, Papua New Guinea *David Lipset*	81
Chapter 5. Mortuary Ritual and Mining Riches in Island Melanesia *Nicholas A. Bainton and Martha Macintyre*	110

PART 2. Equivocal Voices

Chapter 6. Finishing Kapui's Name: Birth, Death, and the Reproduction of Manam Society, Papua New Guinea — 135
Nancy C. Lutkehaus

Chapter 7. Transformations of Male Initiation and Mortuary Rites among the Kayan of Papua New Guinea — 159
Alexis Th. von Poser

Chapter 8. Mortuary Failures: Traditional Uncertainties and Modern Families in the Sepik River, Papua New Guinea — 177
Eric K. Silverman

Chapter 9. Everything Will Come Up Like TV, Everything Will Be Revealed: Death in an Age of Uncertainty in the Purari Delta, Papua New Guinea — 208
Joshua A. Bell

Afterword. Mortuary Dialogues in Pacific Modernities and Anthropology — 234
David Lipset, Eric K. Silverman, and Eric Venbrux

Index — 241

Figures and Tables

Figures

0.1.	Sites in this volume.	xviii
1.1.	Young men carry a casket to the extended family cemetery, Enewetak Atoll. Photo: Laurence M. Carucci, 2009.	36
1.2.	With the extended family looking on, young men lower a casket into a grave at Na'alehu cemetery, Hawai'i. Photo: Laurence M. Carucci, 2014.	40
1.3.	A grieving husband/elder, standing behind headstone, is surrounded by extended family. Photo: Laurence M. Carucci, 2014.	41
1.4.	Jemej gives a commemorative speech at Na'alehu cemetery, Hawai'i. His own grave site is now nearby. Photo: Laurence M. Carucci, 2010.	43
3.1.	Village graveyard with ceramic bowls on wooden crosses. Photo: Doug Dalton, 1983.	72
3.2.	Ancestor shrine within village. Photo: Doug Dalton, 1999.	74
4.1.	Two senior men bind an outrigger boom to a hull. Photo: David Lipset, 1981.	85
4.2.	Murik canoes docked at rural market. Photo: David Lipset, 2012.	86
4.3.	Sheltered grave. Photo: David Lipset, 2012.	92
4.4.	Men tie knots over a corpse in an open canoe-coffin. Photo: Louis Pierre Ledoux, 1936.	94
4.5.	A grieving husband on his way to the cemetery with knotted headband, Darapap. Photo: David Lipset, 1982.	97
4.6.	Moru's body, her daugher clinging to her bier, is carried from the Death House. Photo: David Lipset, 1982.	98
4.7.	Knotted property marker tied onto the shaft of a canoe paddle prior to the "attack." Photo: David Lipset, 1982.	99
4.8.	Members of the Female Cult take turns jumping over Rhiana's coffin beneath a canopy of knotted strips of fabric. Photo: David Lipset, 2010.	102

4.9.	Rhiana's brother cried (l.) while her father consoled her *nabran*-spirit. Photo: David Lipset, 2010.	103
4.10.	A prayer is said at Rhiana's grave. Photo: David Lipset, 2010.	104
5.1.	Lihirian dancers. Photo: Simon Foale, 1998.	120
5.2.	Lamatlik clan members performing on the roof of the men's house during the *tuntunkanut* feast. Photo: Nicholas Bainton, 2011.	123
6.1.	Manam men decorate canoe-coffin. Photo: Nancy Lutkehaus, 1978.	140
6.2.	Manam women cook pork for *bobola* mortuary feast. Photo: Nancy Lutkehaus, 1978.	142
6.3.	Men eating shelled nuts at *kangari rokoaki* mortuary celebration. Photo: Nancy Lutkehaus, 1978.	145
6.4.	A pig decorated as a chief with dog's teeth necklace and bird-of-paradise plume. Photo: Nancy Lutkehaus, 1978.	148
7.1.	Questioning the "wandering coffin." Photo: Alexis von Poser, 2008.	164
7.2.	A grave-house for the night-spirit. Photo: Alexis von Poser, 2008.	165
7.3.	Bamboo pincers for cigarettes and betel nuts. Photo: Alexis von Poser, 2008.	165
7.4.	A procession of initiated men. Photo: Alexis von Poser, 2005.	167
7.5.	The symbolic death. Photo: Alexis von Poser, 2005.	168
8.1. and 8.2.	The *melu* effigy of Freddy in the living room of his widow in Wewak town. Photos: Eric K. Silverman, 2010.	179
8.3.	The mortuary snake. Photo: Eric K. Silverman, 1989.	186
8.4.	The "bone" of the mortuary snake is decorated so thoroughly that it disappears. Photo: Eric K. Silverman, 1989.	188
8.5.	Mourning widow beside effigies. Photo: Eric K. Silverman, 1989.	190
8.6.	The mortuary snake awakens. Photo: Eric K. Silverman, 1989.	193
8.7.	*Melu* effigies are burned by the riverbank and their ashes are swept into the river. Photo: Eric K. Silverman, 1989.	196
8.8.	A mother tends a homestead grave. Photo: Eric K. Silverman, 2010.	200
8.9.	The grave of John Gawi. Photo: Eric K. Silverman, 2010.	201

9.1.	Mailau Aneane Ivia (1932–2002) on his veranda. Photo: Joshua Bell, 2002.	209
9.2.	Sketch of the grave of Inaua Noko (Robert Francis Maher Papers, Box 1; courtesy of the National Anthropological Archives, Smithsonian Institution).	215
9.3.	A body in a canoe-coffin is wrapped in plastic; mourners place clothes and personal effects around a nipa mat. Photo: Joshua Bell, 2001.	219
9.4.	Woven nipa, underneath a piece of tarp, covers the burial mound while a taboo marker has been placed before the grave. Photo: Joshua Bell, 2001.	220
9.5.	Sleeping shelter around grave. Photo: Joshua Bell, 2001.	224
9.6.	Cement cross marking the grave of Aivei's son located next to his house. Photo: Joshua Bell, 2010.	225
9.7.	Relatives carry the coffin of Koivi Kunu to a yard in Baimuru. Photo: Joshua Bell, 2002.	226
9.8.	Koivi Kunu's refurbished homestead grave included a photograph of him and the inscription "In loving Memory of Late Mr. David No'o Y.O.B. 1959 D.O.D. 20.06.02 RIP." Photo: Joshua Bell, 2006.	229

Tables

7.1.	Ritual status in time (time: horizontal axis, social status: vertical axis)	166
7.2.	Modern status in time (time: horizontal axis, social status: vertical axis)	171

Foreword

SHIRLEY LINDENBAUM

In the Pacific, as elsewhere, postcolonial communities strive to assert their own beliefs and practices as they fashion relationships with modern forces, institutions, and cultural knowledge. The chapters in this volume show that mortuary rituals provide a vital setting for individuals and communities to challenge the view that the rituals speak with a unified voice to repair the social fabric caused by death.

The editors' introduction offers a detailed account of the ways in which anthropologists have misunderstood the dynamic and changing nature of the rituals associated with death. They begin with a discussion of a school of thought associated with the journal *L'Année Sociologique*, which viewed mortuary rites as performances counteracting the grief and social disruption caused by death, contributing to the restoration of a collective moral order, a theoretical position associated with functionalism. Legendary figures from Durkheim to Malinowski and more contemporary descendants of the functionalist school are shown to have added some new theoretical elements, but one way or another, anthropologists seem to have maintained the view that mortuary rituals support sociopolitical order. The editors propose a refinement of this framework. They accept the idea that death creates a moral problem for individuals and collectivities, asserting instead that rituals in the Pacific convey different, historically derived messages that shape the experience of moral personhood in collective life. Attention to historical context allows the editors as well as the authors to write against the vision of self-contained, self-reproducing populations that recreate self-stabilizing systems.

The editors adopt Bakhtin's concept of discourse, used creatively here to identify official and unofficial voices in mortuary debates about Christianity, capitalism, and the state, the three modern forces said to have changed the lives of people in the Pacific. The multivoiced and contested mortuary debates, which they call dialogical, establish a framework that avoids portraying local encounters with modernity in simple, binary terms. The dialogic framework leaves the contributors free to adopt their own theoretical and interpretive orientations which provide the ethnographic foundation for the volume's innovative shift in perspective.

Recent studies in the Pacific have directed our attention to the importance of regional similarities among often-neighboring communities based on language, material culture, cultural heritage, and genetics. Although seven of the nine communities discussed in this volume come from Papua New Guinea, the inclusion of Marshall Islanders and Māori in New Zealand/Aotearoa underline the editors' statement that geographic proximity is not the main focus of attention. They ask us to look instead at how people in different Pacific communities engage with modernity in mortuary dialogues that assert the cosmological autonomy of the ancestors and themselves in ritual practices that stress continuity, a pattern that suggests a persisting moral coherence in the region.

Despite the many variations in ritual practice, the chapters also convey a sense of coherence that stems from the charge to examine the rituals in historical context. The authors look back to published accounts of mortuary rituals by earlier observers, review field notes for rituals and ancestral histories that people remember, and describe in detail ceremonies they have observed. This time lapse method confirms that mortuary rituals have been changing for many years. Going beyond a conventional sense of the ethnographic past, the chapters provide a cumulative understanding of the ways in which encroaching entities from outside interact with local institutions and collectivities, each reshaping the other in continuously shifting relationships.

The contributors present a close-up view of transformations of concept and practice, some of them associated with the influence of Christianity and capitalism in Europe. The Kayan concept of cyclical time, for example, is shown to have been displaced by a linear view introduced in Christian rituals that proclaim the finality of death, as well as by Kayan participation in the marketplace. The infrequent staging of male initiation is also said to have interrupted the sequence of life cycle rituals that once provided a circular vision of the death and rebirth of the world.

Local concepts of sorcery have also been transformed as a result of European political and economic penetration. Among I'ai descent groups, the prospect of unevenly distributed royalties from capitalist ventures have led to increased antagonism, accompanied by a sense of the pervasiveness of sorcery and its newfound lethal nature. The historical transformation of occult beliefs documented in many of the chapters illustrates the modernity of sorcery, providing further evidence to discount the assumption that sorcery and witchcraft will disappear with the increasing presence of imported religion and the rationality of scientific education.

The chapters reveal the different and uneven experience of modernity in Pacific communities, as the editors indicate by dividing the volume in two sections. In the first, local cosmologies are said to assume an assured, even dominant voice in the mortuary dialogue. The second section includes case studies that offer pessimistic appraisals of the fate of both the living and the dead.

Communities are shown to vary in the way they assess their historical experience with the many dimensions of modernity; the multi-voiced rituals of death in the modern Pacific accommodate unresolved points of view. In the legally bicultural world of New Zealand/Aotearoa, Māori dialogues with the state and church unfold with dignity and assurance, as mourners affirm the power and privilege of Māori customs. Māori women perform important ritual work as guardians of the dead, and in the case of a large mortuary rite, the army may be called on for assistance in supervising the number of visitors. For a century and a half, Marshall Islanders experienced disastrous encounters with colonialism, during which they created new ritual forms that confirmed their cosmological beliefs. As new immigrants to Hawai'i, they have once again reframed their rituals, this time to meet state regulations about how and where to bury their dead, while retaining Marshallese concepts of the moral person.

In Papua New Guinea, where the state has a light imprint, mortuary dialogues sometimes arise in urban settings, where state and medical bureaucracies may delay funerals: the corpse of a Murik woman was kept in a morgue until a postmortem had established an official cause of death. Back home, however, the jural authority of the community took charge of the funeral, based in local mortuary practices as well as in Murik conceptions of moral personhood. In some places, burial rites are also performed to establish claims over land, whether this be land occupied in the past, as on Manam Island; disputed I'ai territories; or, as among the Rawa, lands that may not have been included in a government register.

The chapters portray Christian and local cosmologies incorporated rather seamlessly into Pacific mortuary rites. In New Zealand/Aotearoa, a Catholic mass, the final event before burial, is held on Māori ceremonial space. Christianity in Papua New Guinea has acquired an image of modernity based in part on its link with global Christian denominations, as well as its status as a national symbol. The authors describe Christian rites absorbed into local ceremonies and mortuary rituals followed by Christian burial. The spiritual essence and life force of the individual, however, is thought to remain vital, beyond biomedical and Christian conceptions about the end of life. The Rawa relatives of a deceased person watch the corpse for a sign that a sorcerer might have caused the death. Bodies also "speak" ambiguously about guilt and the cause of death during Murik, Kayan and Eastern Iatmul ceremonies, in which the corpse directs pallbearers toward the houses of certain residents. Local spirits are a forceful presence in communities where a Christian identity is also meaningful.

The encounter with capitalism, the third form of modernity, is shown to be more problematic. Several chapters in the second section of the volume depict the woes of economic marginalization and failures of development that have resulted in cultures of unfulfilled desire. Case studies of the I'ai and

Eastern Iatmul offer despairing expressions of collective and personal loss. I'ai convey deep concern about the destabilizing impact of money on community life. Individuals speak about a sense of moral decay in their increasingly commoditized relationships with close kin. Eastern Iatmul mortuary rites are described as failing to bring about significant psychosocial closure, in keeping with ongoing changes to the family, marriage, and personhood. The image of a husband's endless grief following the death of his wife is a poignant addition to the history of changing Melanesian sensibilities.

As the chapters document, mortuary rituals are now the largest remaining ceremonial events in the Pacific. They are also the most expensive, and many communities have begun to express concern about the proper use of money and commodities in mortuary rites. With the closing of the Misima mine, and the cost of death now greater than available resources, Misima mortuary exchanges in the post-mining era have continued in an abbreviated and contested form. Manam Islanders have adopted a different solution. Money cannot be substituted in Manam mortuary rites for the baskets of Pacific almonds given as gifts to exchange partners, but it can be used to purchase these key items. The huge influx of money from mining presented Lihirians with a more complex problem. Lihirians are reported to have introduced market goods into the exchange system, which are converted into cultural gifts as if they embodied traditionally valued attributes. Their rituals provide the illusion of cultural continuity, even as new wealth from the unequal allocation of mining money has begun to destabilize the cyclical nature of the exchange. Drawing on ritual to link the seemingly unbridgeable realms of custom and capitalism, they convert goods into gifts. As a performative mode of communication that does not depend on verbal discourse, its meaning is rendered unverifiable. More than reflecting reality, Lihirian mortuary rituals bring new meanings into existence.

The authors in this volume provide detailed accounts of mortuary practices in Polynesia, Micronesia, and Melanesia, along with a range of theories and interpretations. The emphasis on the particular ethnographic characteristics of individual cases provides a touchstone against which their theories may be tested. The essays put to rest the assumption that mortuary rituals assert an eternal sociopolitical order. Ritual dramas of psychological complexity, theatrical flamboyance, and measured grace illustrate the way innovation is woven into customary practice. In vividly-documented arguments the authors show that mortuary rites offer solace and assurance, but also express anxiety and despair. The volume is a significant contribution to the ethnography of Pacific modernity.

Shirley Lindenbaum is a professor emerita at the Graduate Center, City University of New York. She has carried out anthropological research among the Fore in the Eastern Highlands of Papua New Guinea and also in

Bangladesh. Her published works include *Kuru Sorcery. Disease and Danger in the New Guinea Highlands* (updated 2013), and two coedited books in medical anthropology.

Acknowledgements

This book has taken some time to do. It began as a session that the editors organized at the 2009 meetings of the Association for Social Anthropology in Oceania (ASAO) in Santa Cruz, California.

It subsequently received editorial and intellectual support from Rupert Stasch, the ASAO book series editor, as well as from Tierney Brown, Robert Foster, Roger Lohmann, James Weiner, and former colleagues and students at the University of East Anglia's Sainsbury Research Unit of Joshua Bell.

Several universities and granting agencies generously provided research funds for the fieldwork from which the book draws. We list them alphabetically: Australian Research Council, Brown University, DePauw University, Eastern Michigan University Graduate School, Firebird Foundation for Anthropological Research, Fulbright Foundation, the German Academic Exchange Service, Gender Studies Program at the University of Southern California, Institute for Intercultural Studies, Institute for Money, Technology, and Financial Inclusions at the University of California at Irvine, National Endowment for the Humanities, National Science Foundation, the New Zealand History Group of the Ministry of Culture and Heritage, the Graduate School and Department of Anthropology at the University of Minnesota, the University of California at San Diego, the Volkswagen Foundation Wenner-Gren Foundation for Anthropological Research, Wheelock College, and the Wilford Fund for Anthropological Research at the Anthropology Department at the University of Minnesota.

Not least, we are grateful to Enewetak/Ujelang, Lihir, Manam and Misima Islanders as well as Eastern Iatmul, I'ai, Kayan, Murik Lakes, Ngati Rangi and Rawa peoples who shared their lives and losses with us. Laurence Carucci would like to express appreciation to the following individuals: Sato, Enok, Luta, Benjamin, liMeyer, Joniten, and Bilimon. Martha Macintyre and Nick Bainton are particularly grateful to Luke Kabariu of Masahet Island for the time he spent with them over the years in discussions of Lihirian culture and history. They would also like to acknowledge the late Mesulam Aisoli and the late Emma Zanahien with whom they talked about changes in feasting customs. In addition, Nancy Lutkehaus thanks Kapui's son, the late Sila Watakapura, for hosting her and Sarina Pearson on Manam Island in 1994. She also thanks Norbert Sono for reading her chapter. Alexis von Poser is grateful to Blasius Jong, Philip Apa, Jordan Yor, Raphael Manabum and Venantius Mbapai as well as the following women, Clara Madac, Lena Biag, Caroline Karong, Regina Mairong, and Bertha Yambu. Joshua Bell also would like to add his appreciation to the residents of the Mapaio and Baimuru villages.

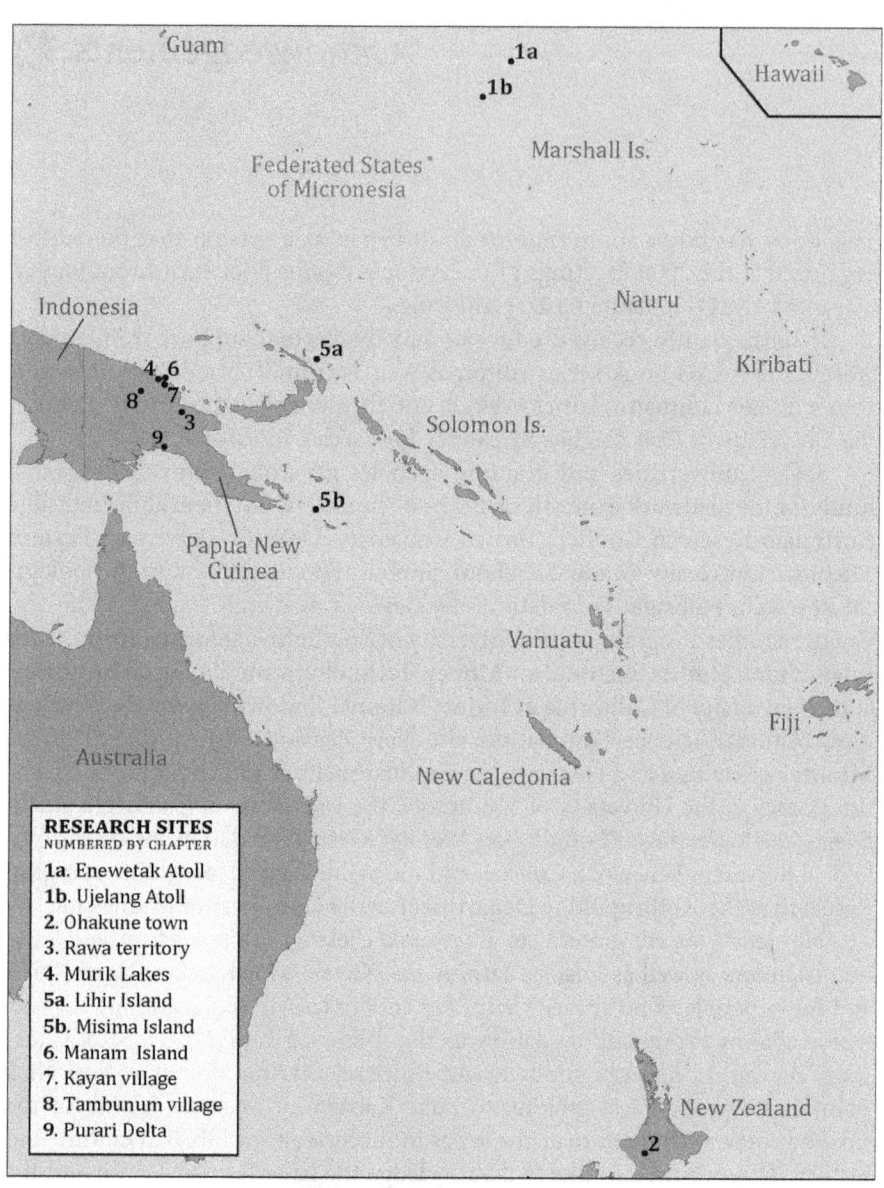

Figure 0.1. Sites in this volume.

Introduction

Mortuary Ritual, Modern Social Theory, and the Historical Moment in Pacific Modernity

ERIC K. SILVERMAN and DAVID LIPSET

Death and the Triumph of Moral Community

In the latter nineteenth century, two analytical approaches to death and mortuary ritual developed in social theory. The one had a broad "intellectualist" orientation that probed ideational aspects of death such as fertility symbolism or the nature of the soul (e.g., Frazer 1933). In part, this paradigm promised to solve a great puzzle in *fin de siècle* European thought, namely, the explanation of prelogical "primitive mentality" (Lévy-Bruhl 1975). The second, and far more influential approach, saw death rites as a mechanism in the maintenance of collective order. This school, known as L'Année sociologique, which was also the name of its flagship journal, came to dominate the anthropology of mortuary ritual.

Our introductory chapter is meant to develop a theoretical framework for the ethnographic chapters that follow. Basically, our position is that while we agree with the classic perspective of the L'Année sociologique school that death calls moral community into question, where we differ is with respect to the consequences of mortuary ritual, which we see as ambiguous, restorative yet inconclusive, rather than functional. Moreover, we will also argue that not only do mortuary rituals in the contemporary Pacific express personal loss, but they also reflect the fluctuating positions of moral communities in global modernity. In other words, as we will elaborate, Pacific mortuary rites comprise open-ended dialogues about loss as well as about the world, changing and shifting as it is.

Foundational for the L'Année sociologique circle was a premise we call "the triumph of moral community." By "moral community," we refer to an autonomous, largely static system of normative institutions and "collective representations" that prevail over individual experience and communal disarray (Durkheim 1965: 16). In this view, transgressive rites or subversive practices do not undermine solidarity and threaten moral order. There was, as we might say today, no agency. Nor did any subaltern speak. Dissonance during ritual was both temporary and authorized and was ultimately harnessed to reinstate the *status quo ante*. Even suicide, as Durkheim (1951) so famously argued, a seemingly consummate act of antisocial individualism, affirmed that society was the basis for understanding behavior. The moral community always triumphed. Its "social facts" reigned supreme (Durkheim 1982: 52).

In *The Elementary Forms of Religious Life* (1965), written on the eve of the first horrific collapse of modern Europe, Durkheim understood death as an individual, hence, immoral violation of normative order. In consequence, mortuary rites, like all religious ceremonies, met this threat to social harmony by renewing "collective sentiments … which then lead men [sic] to seek one another and to assemble together" (1965: 399). We mourn, in this view, not to assuage personal grief, but, duty bound, to renew our commitment to and membership in moral community. Any society that "allows one of its members to die without being wept for," Durkheim declared, "shows by that very fact that it lacks moral unity and cohesion: it abdicates; it renounces its existence" (1965: 400). And any individual who rejects attending a funeral breaks "the bonds uniting him to the group … [thus] contradicting himself." The terror of death is bested only by the horror of what might happen if a community refuses to come together to weep for its loss.

It was left to Durkheim's student Robert Hertz to formulate fully the classic anthropological statement on death and mortuary ritual (1960).[1] Focusing on what he called "secondary burial" rites (1960: 75) among the Dayak or Olo Ngaju of southeastern Borneo, Hertz argued that death was a prolonged, multistaged process, culminating in rebirth, rather than an instantaneous biological moment of destruction and finality.

Hertz parsed death into the corpse, its spirit/ghost, and the survivors. All three components—somatic, cosmological, and social—run the same course during death because they are all part of one body (see Metcalf and Huntington 1991). The cadaver decomposes, becoming impure and polluted; the ghost, now "pitiful and dangerous" (Hertz 1960: 37), lingers between the living and the ancestors; and mourners vacate everyday moral life. This tense and uncertain interlude goes on, essentially, until the end of corporeal desiccation, at which time a "final feast" restores and celebrates moral order (Hertz 1960: 75–76).

The body, now reduced to bones, is permanently interred in a secondary burial; the ghost is dispatched to the ancestral realm, where it can assist, rather than haunt, the living; and mourners, now shaven and cleansed, rejoin society anew (see Metcalf 1982: 95). Death begins with the disintegration of body, self, and society yet concludes with the values of purity, closure, and the reintegration of moral community. In this way, Hertz avowed, "society, its peace recovered, can triumph over death" (1960: 86).

Similarly, van Gennep (1960) argued that ritual sustained order during times that might otherwise collapse into chaos and dystopic, Hobbesian violence. As individuals moved across indeterminate moral spaces, ritual protected society by affirming the continuity of collective values. Famously, van Gennep divided what he called "*rites de passage*" into three phases. Actors were, first, separated from ordinary moral status, then, second, isolated into a liminal or transitional phase for education, and, last, reincorporated back into moral life.

van Gennep's tripartite schema was anything but subject to improvisation. Predictability and repetition were its essential features. Thus mortuary ritual adhered to conventional scripts and symbols that solved the ambiguities death posed. The new ghost must be forced out of the world of the living and sent off to the afterlife, while mourners, disposed as they are to follow the deceased into the netherworld, must cease grieving and return to the community. For van Gennep, as for Hertz and Durkheim, these challenges were moral, not biological, existential, or psychological. And so they required a moral solution: a collective funeral.

The broad L'Année sociologique perspective on death and mortuary ritual exemplified the self-confident convictions of that phase of modernism often identified with so-called grand theory. For one, its single, analytic vision, namely, functionalism, would assuredly expose the essences of sociocultural phenomena. For another, moral community always triumphed over social and psychological conflict. That this confidence persisted through two world wars, including the Holocaust, remains an enigma of modern social thought. But persist it did.

The L'Année sociologique perspective entered Anglophone anthropology through Radcliffe-Brown (Stocking 1984). In his framework, each person "occupies" a specific role in a "network of social relations" (Radcliffe-Brown 1922: 285). Consequently, death disrupts "social cohesion" whereupon "society has to organize itself anew and reach a new condition of equilibrium." Funerals compensate for the loss of the deceased's "social personality," that is, "the sum of characteristics by which he [*sic*] has an effect upon the social life … of others." Funerals also promote "sentiments" that align the individual's "conduct" with "the needs of the society" (Radcliffe-Brown 1922: 275). Last, the funeral engulfs participants in the "moral force" of community—what, in regard to dance among the Andaman Islanders, Radcliffe-Brown described as "unity and harmony" (1922: 252). Otherwise, things fall apart.

Malinowski offered a similar, somewhat more psychological perspective (1916). The anguish of death, he argued, unless contained, might burst into overwhelming feelings of horror and abandonment, leading to flight and wanton destruction. Thus mortuary ceremonies soothe mourners by offering the prospect of an afterlife and immortality and by detaching the spirit/soul from the Shakespearean "mortal coil."[2] The funeral denies the finality of death to prevent individual and collective psychosis. Additionally, the performance of the rite, per the reigning paradigm, renews moral cohesion.

Despite his Durkheimian orientation, Malinowski also conceded another important, albeit neglected, point about death. In the Trobriand Islands, the "actual feelings" of mourners *clashed* with "the official display of grief" and "the conventional sentiment and idea" pertaining to death (1929: 161–62). But few anthropologists, Malinowski included, followed up on this insight. As a result, analysis of mortuary ritual remained encumbered by the value of regenerating the *status quo ante*.[3]

Malinowski's view of death was likely influenced by Freud (see Stocking 1986). Normal mourning, Freud (1964) theorized, can turn into pathological melancholia, leading even to suicidal thinking. "In mourning," as Freud stated, "it is the world which has become poor and empty; in melancholia it is the ego itself" (1964: 246). In successful mourning, the desire to remain alive eventually leads to the withdrawal of attachment from the deceased. In melancholia or depression, however, the ego remains forever attached to loss and so is destroyed (see Robinson 1990).[4] Malinowski likely projected Freud's view of bereavement onto society as the ego writ large. In the absence of moral and psychological integration during mourning, then, it was not just the ego that would suffer annihilation, but community itself. Subsequent anthropologists often offered a similar argument.[5]

For much of twentieth-century anthropology, moral views of mortuary ritual took on two forms. One side, initiated by Malinowski, argued that funerals protected moral community by calming and containing individual anguish (e.g., Wilson 1939; Powdermaker 1931: 43; LeVine 1982). As Monica Wilson put it succinctly, the funeral prevented "madness," allowing the Nyakyusa of Tanzania to "express their grief and put it all behind them" (1954: 239). The bereaved were thus reintegrated back into society (Reid 1979)—or, as in Jewish traditions, never allowed entirely to depart the community (Heilman 2001). The funeral was therapeutic. The other side attributed the efficacy of mortuary ritual to the restoration of "social morphology" (e.g., Gluckman 1937; Firth 1951: 63–64). Thus Goody (1962) highlighted the ritual representation of political order among the West African LoDagaa and the orderly transmission of property. Other anthropologists saw the funeral as a "kind of climax" of the deceased's life (Powdermaker 1966: 313) or an idealized image of personhood (Hogbin 1970: 160; Pearson 1982). But whether viewed through psychology or sociology, both sides of this debate committed to a moral vision: the primary function of mortuary ritual was to enclose the individual within collective order, restore normative categories, and reintegrate society.

Within this broad theoretical dichotomy, anthropologists over the past half century or so also argued that mortuary ritual resolved key sociocultural tensions. Belief in the afterlife among the LoDagaa, for example, discharged the opposition between the mortality of the human body and the perpetuity of the body politic (Goody 1959). Among the Bara of Madagascar, the desiccation of female flesh leaves only masculine bones, resulting in an imbalance between "order" and "vitality." The funeral responded with a bacchanal, as a classic "rite of rebellion" (Gluckman 1954), to restore the "polar continuum of reality" (Huntington 1973: 82) Similarly, Danforth (1982) adopted a structuralist framework to analyze rural Greek funerals as mediating the contradiction between life and death. In all of these studies, funerals answer dilemmas that would otherwise subvert the solidarity and continuity of moral order.

We read a similar view of the funeral in Bloch and Parry's introduction to their 1982 volume *Death & the Regeneration of Life* (see also Bloch 1982). We acknowledge the contributions of this work toward rethinking and reviving the relationship between death and fertility that had long been consigned—unjustly, in our view—to the Frazerian dustbin of anthropological theory. Still, Bloch and Parry, following the lead of Goody (1962), also argued that mortuary ritual dissolves individuality and temporality in order to assert the primacy of an eternal, often masculine sociopolitical order. The funeral, in other words, responds to death by reinstalling normative canons of gender and leadership.

Among other ethnographic examples Bloch and Parry (1982) reinterpreted was Andrew Strathern's (1982) analysis of mortuary rites in Highland New Guinea. They saw these ceremonies as abrogating the deceased's exchange relationships, thus promoting the autonomy of corporate groups. Lévi-Strauss phrased this utopian eschatology or regression best: "Mankind has always dreamed of seizing and fixing that fleeting moment when it was permissible to believe that the law of exchange could be evaded, that one could gain without losing, enjoy without sharing ... a world in which one might keep to oneself" (1969: 497). But this ritual message could never prevail, since moral life throughout the Pacific Islands and elsewhere pivots on reciprocity and marriage. At best, then, the funeral offers a compromise between everyday reality and ideology, thus subsuming anguished grief, despite Lévi-Strauss's infantile desire, under the imperative to uphold moral and political order.

Earlier, we made a brief reference to the "rite of rebellion" paradigm, a mode of ritual, said Max Gluckman, in which expressions of discontent about "particular distributions of power and not about the structure of the [political] system itself" are allowed (1954: 3). Our point is this: ritual was viewed to authorize moments of cathartic disorder but only for the purpose of restoring "social cohesion" (Gluckman 1954: 231). Ritual never seriously calls moral and political foundations of society into question. This view, with just a few exceptions (e.g., Helander 1988), has pervaded the anthropology of mortuary ritual (e.g., Corlin 1988: 73).

In this view, the funeral is provoked by a teleological vision Evans-Pritchard termed the "sociologistic metaphysic" (1956: 313). The funeral creates moral solidarity and largely speaks with one authoritative voice in support of what Ortner and Whitehead (1981) once termed the "prestige structure" of society. Hence, funerals that fail to foster moral order and emotional equanimity are ethnographically exceptional (e.g., Geertz 1959; Harris 1982). The funeral becomes a salvation, staunching the inevitable decline of the cosmos (Jorgensen 1985).

Death, Modernity, Dialogue

Today, perhaps, the cosmos is less becalmed. But neither is it in decline. Bloch's (1989) analysis of the Merina *famadihana* ceremony is a justly famous case in point. In the mid-1960s, the festival stressed culturally specific forms of disorder such as decomposition, individuality, and women precisely to strengthen the moral status quo that privileged continuity, corporate groups, and men (see also Dureau 1991). Today, one can view the *famadihana* ceremony on hundreds of YouTube clips; dozens of websites use the rite to promote tourism in Madagascar. Indeed, the ceremony is listed by Lonely Planet, the popular travel guide publishing house, as one of the "world's best festivals." All this suggests that, whatever the *famadihana* rite communicates about moral order, it now does so within a thoroughly globalized context. No longer are its meanings exclusively local.

In addition to acknowledging emerging references of mortuary ritual to modernity, we join a few anthropologists and social theorists who have also sought to refine the "triumph of moral community" view of mortuary ritual that we traced to L'Année sociologique. Particularly in societies, as in Melanesia, where exchange is central both to mortuary ritual and to what Fortes called the attainment of the status of "full personhood" (1987: 257), death rites do not so much as uphold ideology as provide a public arena for actors—again, usually men—to compete for prestige (e.g., Lincoln 1989; see also Goldschmidt 1973; Volkman 1985; Kan 1989). Or, as Roseman (2002) argued for rural Galicia, the sharing of personal memories of the deceased helps mourners move beyond "the loneliness and fear of solitude." But the constant public voicing of these memories also serves to critique the dominant classes by affirming that everybody dies. Death rites become as politically and ideologically divisive as they are solidary.

We agree with the L'Année sociologique that death promotes moral order. But we disagree that mortuary rites only result in collective and psychological closure. Instead, we argue that their complexity may resist any reduction to moral community, whether to sustain the status quo or to challenge it, as we have argued elsewhere (Lipset and Silverman 2005). Equally important, we see contemporary mortuary rites as composed of contrary voices. Thus our key theoretical claim is that voices in these rites do not necessarily reach moral resolution. Mortuary rites *may* reproduce order in terms of local cosmologies, social processes, and concepts of moral community. But modernist voices asserting capitalism, Christianity, the state, and development are also heard. That is to say, the subjectivities of multiple stakeholders, situated in particularistic values amid global histories, find inconclusive and ambiguous expression.

To be sure, the crisis into which the moral community must succumb at the death of one of its members provokes impassioned expressions of grief. But the tears, dirges, chants, and oratory are plural—contradictory and disputed. Here, we adopt a Bakhtinian concept of "dialogue" among both official and unofficial voices into an egalitarian framework in which no single voice holds sway (Bakhtin 1984: 18). Mortuary rites do not necessarily move forward to synthesis or resolution. No chaos, psychological or social, is necessarily soothed. Rather, the ritual performances of personhood and moral community—we hesitate to label the ritual a "restoration"—remain "unfinalized," which is to say, open ended, amid a globalized polyphony (Bakhtin 1984: 53). Death provokes arguments, quarrels, and juxtapositions, but no last word.

Death in the Contemporary Pacific

In taking the measure of Pacific Islanders' mortuary ritual with regard to modernity, perhaps there is no better place to start than with Sahlins's reference (1985) to Frazer's famous image of the "dying god" (1900). Sahlins of course invokes it in connection with the arrival of Captain Cook on the big island of Hawai'i during the New Year's rite in 1778.[6] Interwoven, self-evident concepts of life and death that drove the meaning of the ceremony were sufficiently powerful to negate the utter distinctiveness of Cook's first contact and recast him as Lono, the spirit of fertility and object of annual commemoration. The avatar of mercantile capitalism was incorporated into Hawai'ian cosmology in terms of which the world was renewed by "a kind of periodic deicide" (Sahlins 1985: 113). Cook qua Lono represented a unified Polynesian body politic that was at once moral and timeless, triumphant and defeated, impenetrable yet very much part of global history.

In Melanesia, death finds no less of an indissoluble relationship with the regeneration of the modern, moral world. Such is the regional vitality of this ambivalent unity that James Weiner (2001: 56) eschewed the opposed categories "life" and "death" and preferred the single term, "lifedeath." Or, as Mimica put it in his peculiar Jungian voice: the "primordial, ouroboric unity of libido and mortido constitutes the ontological core of many New Guinea life-worlds"

(2003: 280). But kindred existentialist tropes remain underutilized in Melanesian anthropology. Instead, since the 1970s, most Melanesianists have followed the lead of Annette Weiner's restudies of Trobriand Island culture (e.g., 1976, 1980) and have looked more pragmatically to exchange theory (see Lutkehaus, this volume).

In the Trobriands, as we learned from Weiner, death rites were part of long-term exchange sequences that reproduced moral relationships. Not only men, Weiner pointed out, but women as well seek to expand their prestige during funerals by giving wealth to various kin. In fact, women were primary agents in this exchange process. Trobriand prestations, as throughout Melanesia, conclude the deceased's relationships while they also disperse and deconstruct his or her identity. Gifts, in other words, remove the deceased from moral life (see also Mosko 1985: 221; Strathern 1981).[7] Society in Melanesia does not regenerate through deicide. But mortuary exchange still transforms the individuality of loss into a model of personhood that repairs, rather than calls into question, moral community.

Melanesian mortuary exchanges are also often said to compensate kin for assisting the deceased during his or her lifetime and to formally declare their innocence from accusations of sorcery or neglect. Funerary gifts, too, are seen to restore normative gender and to thwart cosmological decay by celebrating fertility rather than decomposition.[8] In all these instances, however, mortuary rites, as Hertz theorized, complete a life so that the dead, the mourners, and the community as a whole can move forward (see Macintyre 1983; De Coppet 1981; Lindstrom 1988; Wagner 1989; Battaglia 1990; Barraud et al. 1994; Foster 1995; Aijmer 2008). Melanesian mortuary rites, as a function of the theoretical framework that makes sense of them, privilege the maintenance of moral community.

Anthropologists who study the southwestern Pacific agree on the supreme importance of death in local experience (e.g., Stasch 2009: 208; Damon 1989: 3). But they have not adequately situated or conceptualized mortuary rites either in colonial histories or the postcolonial present—with the exception, really, of the impact of Christianity (e.g., Brison 1998; Lohmann 2005; Schram 2007; Tomlinson 2007).[9] However, even in the context of missionization, it is fair to generalize that the project of contemporary Melanesian ethnography has been to show that a century-long history, as John Barker wrote about the Maisin, has "by no means Westernized" death (1985: 273). As recently as 2007, in fact, all the papers in a theme issue of *Le Journal de la Société des Océanistes,* which honored the centennial anniversary and "continued relevance" of Hertz's classic essay (Venbrux 2007: 6), briefly acknowledged globalization (e.g., Gnecchi-Ruscone 2007; Liep 2007; Revolon 2007). But modernity was not seen to demand a retheorization of mortuary ritual.

It is true that a few studies have foregrounded plural, if not plainly contradictory, discourses that answer Western religions, commodities, and the state.

Beginning in the 1960s, for example, Samoan immigrants in urban California circulated fine mats and conspicuous gifts of money during funerals, not only among the deceased's kin but also as donations to the church minister (Albon 1970). In the Kingdom of Tonga in the 1990s, moreover, beer bottles and cans, used as grave decorations, paralleled the form of a traditional chiefly tomb and also expressed concerns about local status in relationship to modernity (Burley 1995; Teilhet-Fisk 1990; Kaeppler 1993; see also McGrath 2003). These two cases begin to give us a glimpse of how Pacific Islanders, drawing from their own cosmologies, stake out their identities in voices and practices that answer both death and the historical moment.

A brief digression to postcolonial Africa, we believe, will bring some of the broader features of the relationship of mortuary ritual to Pacific modernities into sharper focus. There are no walking dead in the contemporary Pacific, no liminal spaces wherein the "'un-mooring' of social ties" has ruptured "the division between life and death" such that the dead freely intrude upon daily life (Lee and Vaughan 2008: 357). Ghosts do sometimes visit kin in the Pacific, mainly during dreams and in dreamlike cargo cults. But urban streets and rural paths do not "resonate with stories and rumors of returning dead" who have sex with spouses, dig for diamonds, and attend concerts, as in Kinshasa (De Boeck 2005: 18).

Even in the aftermath of collective trauma, such as nuclear testing in the early 1950s, the force and capacity of traditional death and mourning remained, if not intact, at least possible (see Carucci, this volume). Horrific road accidents in Papua New Guinea (PNG), graphically featured in local newspapers, have not given rise to beliefs in malevolent, "twice dead" corpses that cause further fatal crashes on the way to and from burials and funerals (Lee 2012). Nor are the sites of vehicular tragedies imbued with dangerous significance. In the Pacific, the dead continue to exist adjacent to, but do not supersede, the living. Death, in other words, remains a part of life—but has not become, as in parts of Africa, life itself.

Corpses in the Pacific are present and identified, not missing and unrecovered as in Zaire (White 2005). We are aware of no politically charged disinterments. By contrast, disputes in Southern Cameroon between local and immigrant groups, or between urban elites and rural villagers, may result in violent struggles over corpses and nighttime exhumations, partly since burial is a claim of "belonging," with legal implications for election polling (Geschiere 2005). No comparable violence occurs in Pacific states, even where burial signifies contested loyalties, as several chapters in this volume attest. And although funerals have become expensive in some Pacific communities, and quite large, death has not become commercialized. No Pacific businesses cater to, say, popular desires for custom-made coffins that often fantasize modern commodity desires, as in Ghana (see Griffiths 2000).

In many African states, the work of death and mourning is performed by specialized experts (e.g., de Witte 2003). For most Pacific Islanders, local kin still tend to and inter the corpse and arrange and stage the funeral (see, e.g., Wilson and Sinclair, this volume). Indeed, Port Moresby, the largest city in the entire postcolonial Pacific, hosts just two Western-style mortuary businesses. That the prime minister paid his personal respects when Dove Funeral Services opened in March 2012 indicates something about the overall novelty of the enterprise in the region. The business, according to a newspaper report, aims "to provide affordable ... service to the people of PNG so that they could give their relatives and loved ones a dignified send off" (*The National*, March 29, 2012).

As such, Dove Funeral Services promotes modern, decorous death, which only it can offer, and then only for payment, not gift exchange—all of which implicitly contrasts with "customary" rites. In another advertisement, this time for The Funeral Home, two hands appear to be releasing a white dove; and the caption reads, "caring people in your time of need." Here, the effort is made to appropriate death within the wider iconography of Christianity.[10] However, few Papua New Guineans or Pacific Islanders seem content to transform death in toto into Cartesian expressions of Christian, state-sponsored modalities of modern identity.

The target market of the funeral industry in the Pacific, such as it is, remains limited. With the exception of expatriate communities, funeral homes are used mainly by middle-class elites, such as government figures, who, unlike most rural and even urban dwellers, can afford the considerable expense.[11] At best, mortuary services are most commonly utilized to prepare a body for air transport back to the home community. And to afford the fee, people typically make claims on the collective assets of kin, thus fusing the modern memorialization of the individual with a broad network of social obligations. Even at its most modern, that is to say, death and burial in the Pacific engenders open-ended dialogue between the global and local.

In viewing mortuary rites in the contemporary Pacific as less subject to anomie than in parts of Africa, we do not mean to diminish colonial and postcolonial upheavals such as settler colonialism in Hawai'i and New Zealand/Aotearoa, political instability in Fiji, or "civil war" on Bougainville. Nor do we deny the presence of AIDS (see Butt and Eves 2008; Hammar 2010), episodic calamities like the 1994 explosion of twin volcanoes in PNG (Martin 2013), or the damage of rising sea levels to coastal communities (Lipset 2011; Rudiak-Gold 2013). But in the absence of genocide[12] and pandemics, as in Rwanda (Donovan 2002), our view is that Pacific mortuary rites have not become unrecognizable to the ancestors. Deaths and funerals throughout the Pacific evidence a measure of a persisting moral coherence—at least an ongoing plausibility—even as they reveal extensive transformation and revision. Or, as we prefer, anthropologists can best understand death and the funeral in the contemporary Pacific not in terms of sheer disruption or dogged continuity but as answers to contradictory moral forces, both local and global.

Another instance, this time terribly tragic, illustrates this quality of mortuary dialogue. In January 2016, a terrible road accident resulted in the death of five young women returning from a Seventh Day Adventist youth crusade in PNG. The accident, made known largely through newspapers and social media, such as the "Loop PNG" Facebook page, occurred near Wewak, the municipal town of the East Sepik Province, where the sole X-ray machine in the only hospital in the province was broken. While one girl's body was flown to her natal village, four were flown to Port Moresby, where their bodies were kept in one of the funeral homes mentioned above. They were then flown back to Wewak for a collective funeral, and will be interred in their home communities, scattered about the country. At the collective funeral in the modern church, the four bodies were encased in identical black coffins, and adorned with identical garlands and same-sized portraits. In other words, the young women were encompassed by the singular body of a globalized Christ and memorialized as equivalent souls. To assist with the expenses, elected officials donated money, and a "GoFundMe" appeal was launched. In their home communities, we are confident that kin will mourn them in both ancestral and modern, Christian voices.

Recently, one of our Melanesianist colleagues protested that cultural anthropology, particularly in studies of religious change, often amounts to little more than a "science of continuity" (Robbins 2007: 9). We disagree. Rather, we affirm the vital importance of our discipline at this moment in history, especially as practiced in the Pacific Islands, in identifying and defending local agency *through* encounters with global modernity. To do otherwise is to join the very hegemonic, universalizing institutions that would seek to mute local voices. Ever since Cook's arrival in Hawai'i, indigenous actors have responded to foreign interlocutors by asserting the cosmological autonomy of their beliefs and practices.

We are reticent to view Pacific communities as inferior, passive, defeated, or lost—even as we highlight discontinuities that Robbins claims our discipline largely neglects. Indeed, the Pacific Islanders who appear in the chapters to follow resoundingly answer global avatars, desires, and goods in discourses that are neither wholly continuous with the past nor wholly assimilated to Christianity, the cash economy, or the state. Death in the contemporary Pacific provokes multiple voices that express rival perspectives in support of, on the one hand, countercolonial or antiglobal, culturally conservative views of body, spirit, and community, and, on the other hand, modernist convictions about the person and society. Mourners and the dead, it might be said, are both subjects of, and subjects to, their own signifying discourses as well as objects of the universalizing sermons of Christianity and the values of capitalism. Death, as we overhear it, is thoroughly dialogized.

Where the Bodies Are Buried

Our theoretical compass is no less varied. That is to say, not one but several theoretical projects and empirical themes play out in this volume. Some authors deploy psychoanalytic frameworks, reference exchange theory or focus on the impacts of colonial history, capitalism, and development. While acknowledging biomedical and other universalist constructions, all chapters respond to the Hertzian paradigm that sees death in cosmological terms. In other words, death is seen to provoke debate about the autonomy of the ancestors and kin in the context of three modern dualisms: the separation of the body from the Christian soul, the separation of capitalist from local value, and the separation of the centralized state from the local community. At its most basic, our argument is that death compels voices that debate the reproduction of moral community in a historical moment that articulates with modernity in no single way.

Some locales in the volume have experienced a *longue durée* of missionary Christianity and petty capitalism yet still bury their dead in relative isolation from the state; other communities, dwelling in bicultural legal systems or transnational diasporas, devise funerals that involve multiple bureaucracies. Inflections of gender run throughout the volume, as men and women, sometimes separately, at other times together, stage vigils to deliberate causation, debate meaning from the passing, sing, play guitar, contest burial sites, and vie for status. Men and women, in other words, each express moral agency in what Clifford (1988: 228) dubs the "present-becoming-future." Several of our ethnographers, too, in the reflexive tradition of Rosaldo (1993) and Powdermaker (1966), make analytic use of personal grief to critically further their anthropological project. Death, as the other of reason, calls their authorial boundaries into question.

No fewer than seven of the nine chapters in the volume concern Papua New Guinea. The other two focus on Marshall Islanders and the Māori of New Zealand/Aotearoa (see Figure 0.1). But we mainly cluster the contributions according to how they are in dialogue with Pacific history.

In the five chapters making up the first section, local cosmologies assume a dominant voice in response to modernity. The tone of this assertion is not exactly triumphant. But neither is it subdued. Rather, the sentimental and narrative invocation of "tradition" or "custom" offers a sense of agency amid the upheavals of modernity.

This section begins with Laurence Carucci's epical account of death rites among Marshall Islanders, focusing on the colonial history and eventual exile of the people of Enewetak Atoll after US nuclear testing in the early 1950s. Repatriated in 1980, their dreams of a vibrant, emotionally satisfying, embodied return to the land of their ancestors came to naught. Some then resettled in Hawai'i in the early 1990s, where they began to insist upon a funerary relationship to a moral center through values that emerged in the course of that violent encounter.

Similarly, Che Wilson and Karen Sinclair, in their discussion of contemporary Māori death rites in New Zealand/Aotearoa, draw our attention to the complex role women play in overseeing the transition of the spirit to the afterlife. Although Māori today identify themselves as Catholics, women's voices and practices go on asserting the autonomy of Māori concepts of the moral person in the legally bicultural state.

Doug Dalton's chapter on the Rawa people of PNG also illustrates a degree of cultural resiliency amid modernity in Papua New Guinea. In their cemeteries, Rawa grave markers combine Rawa terms for death with Christianity. Yet some Rawa erect wooden shrines to the dead on lineage property rather than in the cemetery, thus staking a claim to land and, more broadly, challenging the modern and Christian dualism that divides the community from death.

David Lipset then analyzes dying and burial practices among the Murik Lakes people of PNG over seventy-five years. Despite changes, such as ritual abridgements and the waning of the Male Cult, a distinctively Murik concept of moral personhood, according to which the spirit is knotted to a "canoe-body" persists in the course of this period of time. The Murik erect crosses and recite prayers at cemetery gravesites. But, without apology to modernity, they still tie knots during mortuary rites, thus answering modern personhood with this cultural gesture of self-assurance.

In the last chapter in this section of the volume, Nick Bainton and Martha Macintyre compare the effects of recent mining revenues on death rites among the Lihir and Misima Islanders in PNG. When large-scale mining began pouring huge sums into a few rural communities in the Lihir Islands during the late 1990s, Lihirians began to practice ever more elaborate and expensive mortuary rites. The purpose of the funeral shifted away from celebrating the transition of the embodied person to the afterlife and started to focus on competitions for prestige through displays of wealth. On Misima, by contrast, the boom times of the local gold mine ended and left people with very little to show for them, other than massive ritual obligations and a society divided between haves and have-nots. In acrimonious dialogue, people argued in favor of abridging mortuary rites, or halting them altogether. Mining money, in other words, created an efflorescence of mortuary rites on Lihir, but only gave rise to rancor on Misima.

The second section of our volume is of a piece with the bitterness of Misima Islanders by offering glum appraisals of the fate of the dead amid Pacific modernities. In these four chapters, all of which focus on rural communities in PNG, mortuary rites do not culminate in a Hertzian ethos of triumph of moral community over the dead. Instead, we hear disconsolate expressions of personal and collective losses of power.

This section begins with the return of Nancy Lutkehaus to Manam, a volcanic island off the north coast of PNG, after long absence. In the years since her last visit, a huge eruption had forced the islanders into temporary, state-sponsored quarters on the mainland. In the meantime, however, a few people began to make their way back home, where they revive their old practice of homestead burial. With their island and future under threat, Manam Islanders valued physical closeness to the dead and their land. But their funerary petition for a unity of place and ancestors remained fraught and anxious.

A regretful mood pervades Alexis von Poser's account of mortuary rites among Kayan villagers, who live on the mainland opposite Manam Island. In the past, Kayan mortuary rites mirrored male initiation. Today, however, the elegant symmetries between these two ritual processes have all but vanished, most villagers having acceded to Catholicism, individualism, and linear temporality—that is, to modernity. Death no longer leads to rebirth but to signifiers of permanent loss: for example, to graves covered with cement. von Poser professes a bittersweet feeling about a fading culture, one he shared with a dwindling constituency of aging villagers.

In the penultimate chapter, Eric Silverman questions the extent to which contemporary mortuary rites among the Eastern Iatmul, who live along the middle Sepik River in PNG, reintegrate mourners back into moral community. Today, Eastern Iatmul mortuary rites do not seem to provide mourners with the "closure" they are expected to do. Grief persists, and this lack of resolution resonates with, and expresses, angst about their position in postcolonial modernity that is largely perceived as a grand failure. Mortuary rites remain informed by intricate Eastern Iatmul cosmology, to be sure. But at the same time they lay bare a sense of loss that is aggravated by modern concepts of personhood and global marginalization.

Lastly, Joshua Bell discusses mortuary rites among the I'ai people of the Purari Delta in PNG. Like the Manam, although for rather different reasons, the I'ai have also started to prefer homestead burials. The observation of mourning taboos and the very meaning of death now commemorate mistrust and misgivings within the community as well as powerlessness amid rural modernity. Death for the I'ai, no less than for Eastern Iatmul, has become an occasion for despondency, rather than triumphant closure.

Whether the tone is one of resolve or uncertainty, affirmation or anguish, continuity or rupture, or some combination therein, our argument is that death and mortuary practices constitute dialogue about the reproduction of moral community in the historical moment of locally constituted modernities. We have thereby revised the hoary theoretical question posed by the L'Année sociologique school, which was, how do people in communities go about repairing themselves from the moral damage done by what Malinowski once called the "supreme and final crisis of life" (1948: 29)? By situating the question in Pacific histories, each chapter demonstrates that persons and communities not only answer death in terms of local cosmologies and social structures but, in doing so, their multiple, rivalrous voices simultaneously answer the ongoing challenges of modernity.

Notes

1. For critiques of Hertz, see Miles (1965), Metcalf (1977, 1981), and Evans-Pritchard (1960).
2. Earlier, Malinowski explored Trobriand reincarnation (1916).
3. Similarly, the psychological work of mourning was the cathartic sublimation of sorrow and anxiety (see also Wellenkamp 1988; Brison 1998). Thus death, the great disruptor, was made moral.
4. For similarities between Freud and Hertz, see Lemonnier (2007).
5. Thus attention to the details of mortuary feasting on New Ireland, argues Bolyanatz (1994), much like Lieber (1991) for the Kapingamaringi of Micronesia, restores order and serves to defend against internal grief.
6. Of course, one could find confirmation of this sort of dialogicality in the cargo cult literature as well (see Schwartz 1962; Ogan 1972; and Lawrence 1964).
7. In Kaliai, West New Britain, the first stages of the funeral may be staged long before the honoree's death, "so that he can see before he dies how much we honour him" (Counts and Counts 2004: 894). For aging in the Pacific, see Counts and Counts (1985).
8. In the Massim, funerary ritual also enacts potent images of amorality within the matrilineage, such as witches and homicides (Thune 1989: 170), with the killer himself sometimes sponsoring the funeral (Montague 1989), and avuncular cannibalism (Young 1989: 198). For the role of cannibalism in an Amazonian funerary complex, see Conklin (1995) and McCallum (1999).
9. We note, with considerable ethical qualms, the ongoing interest of missionaries and indigenous catechists in Pacific funerals as entrée points "to recognition of the greater power of Christ over that of their former gods and spirits, including their ancestors" (Thorp 1997: 22).
10. Our source for the sign is http://www.panoramio.com/photo_explorer#view=photo&position=11213&with_photo_id=59480461&order=date_desc&user=2405290.
11. The Embassy of the United States in Port Moresby lists the fees in 2012 for The Funeral Home: embalming was the equivalent of US$2,800, standard casket $750, outfit for the corpse $750, viewing $250, funeral director's fee $500, administration fee $750, and so forth. http://portmoresby.usembassy.gov/dipositionpng_091112.html.
12. Having said this, we note the common use today of the term "genocide" in regard to the conflict in West Papua between indigenous Melanesians and paramilitary Indonesian forces. We neither endorse nor challenge this usage here.

References Cited

Aijmer, Göran. 2008. "The Temporality of Immortality in Lesu: The Historical Anthropology of a New Ireland Society." *History and Anthropology* 19: 251–79.
Albon, Joan. 1970. "The Samoan Funeral in Urban America." *Ethnology* 9: 209–27.
Bakhtin, Mikhail. 1984. *Problems of Doestoevsky's Poetics*. Edited and translated by Caryl Emerson. Minneapolis: University of Minnesota Press.
Barker, John. 1985. "Missionaries and Mourning: Continuity and Change in the Death Ceremonies of a Melanesian People." In *Anthropologists, Missionaries, and Cultural Change*, edited by DL Whiteman, 263–94. Studies in Third World Societies: 25. Williamsburg, VA: College of William and Mary.
Barraud, Cécile, Daniel de Coppet, André Iteanu, and Raymond Jamous. 1994. *Of Relations and the Dead: Four Societies Viewed from the Angle of Their Exchanges*. Oxford: Berg.
Battaglia, Debbora. 1990. *On the Bones of the Serpent: Person, Memory, and Mortality in Sabarl Island Society*. Chicago: University of Chicago Press.
Bloch, Maurice. 1971. *Placing the Dead: Tombs, Ancestral Villages and Kinship Organisation among the Merina of Madagascar*. London: Seminar.
———. 1982. "Death, Women and Power." In *Death and the Regeneration of Life*, edited by M. Bloch and J. Parry, 211–30. Cambridge: Cambridge University Press.
———. 1989. "The Ritual of the Royal Bath in Madagascar: The Dissolution of Death, Birth and Fertility into Authority." In *Ritual, History and Power: Selected Papers in Anthropology*, 187–211. London: Athlone.
Bloch, Maurice and Jonathan Parry. 1982. "Introduction: Death and the Regeneration of Life." In *Death and the Regeneration of Life*, edited by Bloch and Parry, 1–44. Cambridge: Cambridge University Press.
Bolyanatz, Alexander H. 1994. "Defending against Grief on New Ireland: The Place of Mortuary Feasting in Sursurunga Society." *Journal of Ritual Studies* 8: 115–33.
Brison, Karen J. 1998. "Giving Sorry New Words: Shifting Politics of Bereavement in a Papua New Guinea Village." *Ethos* 26: 363–86.
Burley, David V. 1995. "Contexts of Meaning: Beer Bottles and Cans in Contemporary Burial Practices in the Polynesian Kingdom of Tonga." *Historical Archaeology* 29: 75–83.
Butt, Leslie and Richard Eves, eds. 2008. *Making Sense of AIDS: Culture, Sexuality, and Power in Melanesia*. Honolulu: University of Hawaii Press.
Chowning, Ann. 1989. "Death and Kinship in Molima." In *Death Rituals and Life in the Societies of the Kula Ring*, edited by FH Damon and R. Wagner, 97–129. DeKalb: Northern Illinois University Press.
Clifford, James. 1988. "On Collecting Art and Culture." In *The Predicament of Culture: Twentieth-Century Ethnography, Literature, and Art*, 215–51. Cambridge: Harvard University Press.
Conklin, Beth A. 1995. "'Thus Are Our Bodies, Thus Was Our Custom': Mortuary Cannibalism in an Amazonian Society." *American Ethnologist* 22: 75–101.
Connor, Linda H. 1995. "The Action of the Body on Society: Washing a Corpse in Bali." *The Journal of the Royal Anthropological Institute* NS 1: 537–59.
Corlin, Claes. 1988. "The Journey through the Bardo: Notes on the Symbolism of Tibetan Mortuary Rites and the Tibetan Book of the Dead." In *On the Meaning of Death: Essays on Mortuary Rituals and Eschatological Beliefs*, edited by S. Cederroth, C. Corlin, and J. Lindstrom, 63–76. Uppsala: Almqvist & Wiksell International.

Counts, Dorothy Ayers and David R. Counts, eds. 1985. *Aging and Its Transformations: Moving Toward Death in Pacific Societies.* Lanham: University Press of America.
———. 2004. "The Good, the Bad, and the Unresolved Death in Kaliai." *Social Science & Medicine* 58: 887–97.
Damon, Frederick H. 1989. "Introduction." In *Death Rituals and Life in the Societies of the Kula Ring,* edited by FH Damon and R. Wagner. DeKalb: Northern Illinois University Press.
Danforth, Loring M. 1982. *The Death Rituals of Rural Greece.* Princeton: Princeton University Press.
De Boeck, Filip. 2005. "The Apocalyptic Interlude: Revealing Death in Kinshasa." *African Studies Review* 28: 11–31.
De Coppet, D. 1981. "The Life-Giving Death." In *Mortality and Immortality: The Anthropology and Archaeology of Death,* edited by SC Humphreys and H. King, 40–65. London: Academic Press.
De Witte, Marleen. 2003. "Money and Death: Funeral Business in Asante, Ghana." *Africa* 73: 531–59.
Donovan, Paula. 2002. "Rape and HIV/AIDS in Rwanda." *The Lancet* 360: (s17–s18).
Dureau, CM. 1991. "Death, Gender and Regeneration: A Critique of Maurice Bloch." *Canberra Anthropology* 14: 24–44.
Durkheim, Emile. 1951 [1897]. *Suicide: A Study in Sociology.* Translated by John A. Spaulding. New York: Free Press.
———. 1965 [1912]. *The Elementary Forms of Religious Life.* Translated by Joseph Ward Stain. New York: Free Press.
———. 1982 [1895]. *The Rules of Sociological Method.* Edited by Steven Lukes, translated by WD Halls. New York: Free Press.
Evans-Pritchard, EE. 1956. *Nuer Religion.* Oxford: Oxford University Press.
———. 1960. "Introduction." In *Death and the Right Hand,* translated by R. Needham and C. Needham, 9–29. Glencoe: Free Press.
Firth, Raymond. 1951. *Elements of Social Organization.* Boston: Beacon.
Fortes, Meyer. 1987 [1973]. "The Concept of the Person." Reprinted in *Religion, Morality and the Person: Essays on Tallensi Religion,* edited by Jack Goody, 247–86. Cambridge: Cambridge University Press.
Foster, Robert J. 1995. *Social Reproduction and History in Melanesia: Mortuary Ritual, Gift Exchange, and Custom in the Tanga Islands.* Cambridge: Cambridge University Press.
Frazer, Sir James George. 1900. *The Golden Bough: A Study in Magic and Religion.* 2nd ed. 3 vols. London: MacMillan.
———. 1933. *The Fear of the Dead in Primitive Religion.* London: MacMillan.
Freud, Sigmund. 1964 [1917]. "Mourning and Melancholia." In *The Standard Edition of the Complete Psychological Works of Sigmund Freud* (vol. XIV), edited by J. Strachey, translated by J. Strachey, 239–58. London: Hogarth.
Geertz, Clifford. 1959. "Ritual and Social Change: A Javanese Example." *American Anthropologist* 61: 991–1012.
Geschiere, Peter. 2005. "Funerals and Belonging: Different Patterns in South Cameroon." *African Studies Review* 2: 45–65.
Gewertz, Deborah B. and Frederick K. Errington. 1991. *Twisted Histories, Altered Contexts: Representing the Chambri in the World System.* Cambridge: Cambridge University Press.

Gluckman, Max. 1937. "Mortuary Customs and the Belief in Survival after Death among the South-Eastern Bantu." *Bantu Studies* 11: 117–36.
———. 1954. *Rituals of Rebellion in South-East Africa.* Manchester: Manchester University Press.
Gnecchi-Ruscone, Elisabetta. 2007. "Parallel Journeys in Korafe Women's Laments (Oro Province, Papua New Guinea)." *Le Journal de la Société des Océanistes* 124: 21–32.
Goldschmidt, Walter. 1973. "Guilt and Pollution in Sebei Mortuary Rituals." *Ethos* 1: 75–105.
Goody, Jack. 1959. "Death and Social Control among the LoDagaa." *Man* 59: 134–38.
———. 1962. *Death, Property and the Ancestors: A Study of the Mortuary Customs of the LoDagaa of West Africa.* Stanford: Stanford University Press.
Griffiths, Hannah. 2000. *Diverted Journeys: The Social Lives of Ghanaian Fantasy Coffins.* Edinburgh: Center of African Studies, Edinburgh University.
Hammar, Lawrence. 2010. *Sin, Sex, and Stigma: A Pacific Response to HIV and AIDS.* London: Sean Kingston.
Harris, Olivia. 1982. "The Dead and the Devils among the Bolivian Laymi." In *Death and the Regeneration of Life,* edited by M. Bloch and J. Parry, 45–73. Cambridge: Cambridge University Press.
Hayano, David M. 1973. "Sorcery Death, Proximity, and the Perception of Out-Groups: The Tauna Awa of New Guinea." *Ethnology* 12: 179–91.
Heilman, Samuel C. 2001. *When a Jew Dies: The Ethnography of a Bereaved Son.* Berkeley: University of California Press.
Helander, Berhard. 1988. "Death and the End of Society: Official Ideology and Ritual Communication in the Somali Funeral." In *On the Meaning of Death: Essays on Mortuary Rituals and Eschatological Beliefs,* edited by S. Cederroth, C. Corlin, and J. Lindstrom, 113–36. Uppsala: Almqvist & Wiksell International.
Hertz, Robert. 1960 [1907]. "A Contribution to the Study of the Collective Representation of Death." In *Death and the Right Hand,* translated by R. Needham and C. Needham, 29–88. Glencoe: Free Press.
Hogbin, Ian. 1970. *The Island of Menstruating Men: Religion in Wogeo, Now Guinea.* Scranton: Chandler.
Huber, Peter B. 1972. "Death and Society among the Anggor of New Guinea." *Omega* 3: 233–43.
Huntington, WR. 1973. "Death and the Social Order: Bara Funeral Customs (Madagascar)." *African Studies* 32: 65–84.
Jacobson-Widding, Anita. 1988. "Death Rituals as Inversions of Life Structures." In *On the Meaning of Death: Essays on Mortuary Rituals and Eschatological Beliefs,* edited by S. Cederroth, C. Corlin, and J. Lindstrom, 137–54. Uppsala: Almqvist & Wiksell International.
Jorgensen, Dan. 1985. "Femsep's Last Garden: A Telefol Response to Mortality." In *Aging and Its Transformations: Moving towards Death in Pacific Societies,* edited by DA Counts and DR Counts. Lanham: University Press of America.
Kaeppler, Adrienne L. 1993. "Poetics and Politics of Tongan Laments and Eulogies." *American Ethnologist* 20: 474–501.
Kan, Sergei. 1989. *Symbolic Immortality: The Tlingit Potlatch of the Nineteenth Century.* Washington, D.C.: Smithsonian Institution Press.
Lawrence, Peter. 1964. *Road Belong Cargo.* Manchester: University of Manchester Press.

Lee, Rebekah. 2012. "Death in Slow Motion: Funerals, Ritual Practice and Road Danger in South Africa." *African Studies* 71: 195–211.
Lee, Rebekah and Megan Vaughan. 2008. "Death and Dying in the History of Africa since 1800." *Journal of African History* 49: 341–59.
Lemonnier, Pierre. 2007. "Objets d'Ambiguïté. Funérailles Ankave (Papouasie Nouvelle-Guinée)." *Journal de la Société des Océanistes* 124: 33–43.
Lévi-Strauss, Claude. 1969 [1949]. *The Elementary Structures of Kinship*, translated by James Harle Bell, John Richard von Sturmer, and Rodney Needham. Boston: Beacon.
LeVine, Robert A. 1982. "Gusii Funerals: Meanings of Life and Death in an Africa Community." *Ethos* 10: 26–65.
Lévy-Bruhl, Lucien. 1975 [1922]. *How Natives Think*, translated by Lilian A. Clare. Princeton: Princeton University Press.
Lieber, Michael D. 1991. "Cutting Your Losses: Death and Grieving in a Polynesian Community." In *Coping with the Final Tragedy: Cultural Variation in Dying and Grieving*, edited by D. Counts and D. Counts, 169–89. Amityville: Baywood.
Liep, John. 2007. "Massim Mortuary Rituals Revisited." *Journal de la Société des Océanistes* 124: 89–96.
Lincoln, Bruce. 1989. "Mortuary Ritual and Prestige Economy: The Malagan for Bukbuk." *Cultural Critique* 198: 197–224.
Lindstrom, Jan. 1988. "The Monopolization of a Spirit: Livestock Prestations during an Iramba Funeral." In *On the Meaning of Death: Essays on Mortuary Rituals and Eschatological Beliefs*, edited by S. Cederroth, C. Corlin, and J. Lindstrom, 169–84. Uppsala: Almqvist & Wiksell International.
Lipset, David M. 2011. "The Tides: Masculinity and Climate Change in Coastal Papua New Guinea." *Journal of the Royal Anthropological Institute* 17 (1): 20–43.
Lipset, David M. and Eric K. Silverman. 2005. "The Moral and the Grotesque: Dialogics of the Body in Two Sepik River Societies (Eastern Iatmul and Murik)." *Journal of Ritual Studies* 19: 1–42.
Lohmann, Roger Ivar. 2005. "The Afterlife of Asabano Corpses: Relationships with the Deceased in Papua New Guinea." *Ethnology* 42: 189–206.
McCallum, Cecilia. 1999. "The Production of Death among the Cashinahua." *Cultural Anthropology* 14: 443–71.
Macintyre, Martha. 1983. *Changing Paths: An Historical Ethnography of the Traders of Tubetube*. Canberra: Australian National University.
Malinowski, Bronislaw. 1916. "Baloma: The Spirits of the Dead in the Trobriand Islands." *Journal of the Royal Anthropological Institute of Great Britain and Ireland* 46: 353–430.
———. 1929. *The Sexual Life of Savages in North-Western Melanesia: An Ethnographic Account of Courtship, Marriage and Family Life among the Natives of the Trobriand Islands*. London: Routledge & Kegan Paul.
———. 1948 [1925]. "Magic, Science and Religion." In *Magic, Science and Religion and Other Essays*, 1–71. New York: Free Press.
Martin, Keir. 2013. *The Death of the Big Men and the Rise of the Big Shots: Custom and Conflict in East New Britain*. New York: Berghahn.
Masco, Joseph P. 1995. "'It Is a Strict Law That Bids Us Dance': Cosmologies, Colonialism, Death and Ritual Authority in the Kwakwaka'wakw Potlatch, 1849–1922." *Comparative Studies in Society and History* 37: 41–75.

McGrath, Barbara. 2003. "A View from the Other Side: The Place of Spirits in the Tongan Social Field." *Culture, Medicine, and Psychiatry* 27: 29–48.
Metcalf, Peter. 1977. "The Berawan Afterlife: A Critique of Hertz." In *Studies in Borneo Societies*, edited by George Appell, 72–91. DeKalb: Northern Illinois University Press.
———. 1981. "Meaning and Materialism: The Ritual Economy of Death." *Man* NS 16: 563–78.
———. 1982. *A Borneo Journey into Death: Berawan Eschatology from Its Rituals*. Philadelphia: University of Pennsylvania Press.
Metcalf, Peter and Richard Huntington. 1991. *Celebrations of Death: The Anthropology of Mortuary Ritual*. Cambridge: Cambridge University Press.
Miles, Douglas. 1965. "Socio-Economic Aspects of Secondary Burial." *Oceania* 35: 161–74.
Mimica, Jadran. 2003. "The Death of a Strong, Great, Bad Man: An Ethnography of Soul Incorporation." *Oceania* 73: 260–86.
Montague, Susan P. 1989. "To Eat the Dead: Kaduwagan Mortuary Events." In *Death Rituals and Life in the Societies of the Kula Ring*, edited by FH Damon and R. Wagner, 23–45. DeKalb: Northern Illinois University Press.
Mosko, Mark. 1985. *Quadripartite Structures: Categories, Relations and Homologies in Bush Mekeo Culture*. Cambridge: Cambridge University Press.
Ogan, Eugene. 1972. *Business and Cargo: Socio-Economic Change among the Nasioi of Bougainville*. New Guinea Research Unit Bulletin No. 44. Canberra: Australian National University Press.
Ortner, Sherry B. and Harriet Whitehead. 1981. "Introduction: Accounting for Sexual Meanings." In *Sexual Meanings: The Cultural Construction of Gender and Sexuality*, edited by SB Ortner and H. Whitehead, 1–28. Cambridge: Cambridge University Press.
Parmentier, Richard J. 1988. "Transactional Symbolism in Belauan Mortuary Rites: A Diachronic Study." *Journal of the Polynesian Society* 97: 281–312.
Pearson, Michael Parker. 1982. "Mortuary Practices, Society and Ideology: An Ethnoarchaeological Study." In *Symbolic and Structural Archaeology*, edited by I. Hodder, 99–113. Cambridge: Cambridge University Press.
Powdermaker, Hortense. 1931. "Mortuary Rites in New Ireland (Bismarck Archipelago)." *Oceania* 2: 26–43.
———. 1966. *Stranger and Friend*. New York: Norton.
Radcliffe-Brown, AR. 1922. *The Andaman Islanders: A Study in Social Anthropology*. Cambridge: Cambridge University Press.
Reid, Janice. 1979. "A Time to Live, A Time to Grieve: Patterns and Processes of Mourning among the Yolngu of Australia." *Culture, Medicine, and Psychiatry* 3: 319–46.
Revolon, Sandra. 2007. "The Dead Are Looking at Us: Place and Role of the *Apira Ni Farunga* ("Ceremonial Bowls") in End-of-Mourning Ceremonies in Aorigi (Eastern Solomon Islands)." *Journal de la Société des Océanistes* 124: 59–66.
Robbins, Joel. 2007. "Continuity Thinking and the Problem of Christian Culture: Belief, Time, and the Anthropology of Christianity." *Current Anthropology* 48: 5–38.
Robinson, Gary. 1990. "Separation, Retaliation and Suicide: Mourning and the Conflicts of Young Tiwi Men." *Oceania* 60: 161–78.
Rosaldo, Renato. 1993. "Grief and the Headhunter's Rage." Reprinted in *Culture and Truth: The Remaking of Social Analysis*, 1–23. Boston: Beacon Press.
Roseman, Sharon R. 2002. "'Going over to the Other Side': The Sociality of Remembrance in Galician Death Narratives." *Ethos* 30: 433–64.

Rudiak-Gold, Peter. 2013. *Climate Change and Tradition in a Small Island State: The Rising Tide*. New York: Routledge.
Sahlins, Marshall. 1985. *Islands of History*. Chicago: University of Chicago Press.
Schram, Ryan. 2007. "Sit, Cook, Eat, Full Stop: Religion and the Rejection of Ritual in Auhelawa (Papua New Guinea)." *Oceania* 77: 172–90.
Schwartz, Theodore. 1962. "The Paliau Movement in the Admiralty Islands, 1946–54." *Anthropological Papers of the American Museum Natural History* 49: 207–422.
Sinclair, Karen P. 1990. "Tangi: Funeral Rituals and the Construction of Maori Identity." In *Cultural Identity and Ethnicity in the South Pacific*, edited by J. Linnekin and L. Poyer, 219–36. Honolulu: University of Hawai'i Press.
Stasch, Rupert. 2009. *Society of Others: Kinship and Mourning in a West Papua Place*. Berkeley: University of California Press.
Stocking, Jr., George W. 1984. "Dr. Durkheim and Dr. Brown: Comparative Sociology at Cambridge in 1910." In *Functionalism Historicized: Essays on British Social Anthropology*, edited by Stocking, 106–30. Madison: University of Wisconsin Press.
———. 1986. "Anthropology and the Science of the Irrational: Malinowski's Encounter with Freudian Psychoanalysis." In *Malinowski, Rivers, Benedict, and Others: Essays on Culture and Personality*, edited by Stocking, 13–49. Madison: University of Wisconsin Press.
Strathern, Andrew. 1981. "Death as Exchange: Two Melanesian Cases." In *Mortality and Immortality: The Anthropology and Archaeology of Death*, edited by SC Humphreys and H. King, 205–23. London: Academic Press.
———. 1982. "Witchcraft, Greed, Cannibalism and Death: Some Related Themes from the New Guinea Highlands." In *Death and the Regeneration of Life*, edited by M. Bloch and J. Parry, 111–33. Cambridge: Cambridge University Press.
Strathern, Marilyn. 1988. *The Gender of the Gift: Problems with Women and Problems with Society in Melanesia*. Berkeley: University of California Press.
Teilhet-Fisk, Jehanne. 1990. "Tongan Grave Art." In *Art and Identity in Oceania*, edited by A. Hanson and L. Hanson, 222–43. Honolulu: University of Hawaii Press.
Thorp, Russell. 1997. "Christian Life and the Living Dead." *Melanesian Journal of Theology* 13(2): 6–24.
Thune, Carl. 1989. "Death and Matrilineal Reincorporation on Normanby Island." In *Death Rituals and Life in the Societies of the Kula Ring*, edited by FH Damon and R. Wagner, 153–79. DeKalb: Northern Illinois University Press.
Tomlinson, Matt. 2007. "Publicity, Privacy, and 'Happy Deaths' in Fiji." *American Ethnologist* 34: 706–20.
van Gennep, Arnold. 1960 [1908]. *Rites of Passage*. Translated by Monika B. Vizedom and Gabrielle L. Caffee. Chicago: University of Chicago Press.
Venbrux, Eric. 2007. "Robert Hertz's Seminal Essay and Mortuary Rites in the Pacific Region." *Le Journal de la Société des Océanistes* 124: 5–10.
Volkman, Toby Alice. 1985. *Feasts of Honor: Ritual and Change in the Toraja Highlands*. Urbana: University of Illinois Press.
Wagner, Roy. 1989. "Conclusion: The Exchange Context of the Kula." In *Death Rituals and Life in the Societies of the Kula Ring*, edited by FH Damon and R. Wagner, 254–74. DeKalb: Northern Illinois University Press.
Wedgwood, Camilla H. 1927. "Death and Social Status in Melanesia." *The Journal of the Royal Anthropological Institute of Great Britain and Ireland* 57: 380–81.

Weiner, Annette B. 1976. *Women of Value, Men of Renown: New Perspectives in Trobriand Exchange*. Austin: University of Texas Press.

———. 1980. "Stability in Banana Leaves: Colonialism, Economics and Trobriand Women." In *Women and Colonization, Anthropological Perspectives*, edited by E. Leacock and M. Etienne, 270–93. New York: JF Bergin.

Weiner, James F. 2001. "To Be at Home with Others in an Empty Place: A Reply to Mimica." In *Tree Leaf Talk: A Heideggerian Anthropology*, 51–65. Oxford: Berg.

Wellenkamp, Jane. 1988. "Notions of Grief and Catharsis among the Toraja." *American Anthropologist* 15: 486–500.

White, Bob W. 2005. "The Political Undead: Is It Possible to Mourn for Mobutu's Zaire?" *African Studies Review* 48: 65–85.

Wilson, Godfrey. 1939. "Nyakyusa Conventions of Burial." *Bantu Studies* 13: 1–31.

Wilson, Monica. 1954. "Nyakyusa Ritual and Symbolism." *American Anthropologist* 56: 228–41.

Young, Michael W. 1989. "'Eating the Dead': Mortuary Transactions in Bwaidoka, Goodenough Island." In *Death Rituals and Life in the Societies of the Kula Ring*, edited by FH Damon and R. Wagner, 179–98. DeKalb: Northern Illinois University Press.

PART 1
Tenacious Voices

1
Fearing the Dead
The Mortuary Rites of Marshall Islanders amid the Tragedy of Pacific Modernity

LAURENCE MARSHALL CARUCCI

Since the time of Arnold van Gennep, if not before, mortuary practices have been viewed as a prototypical rite of passage (1960). van Gennep focused the attention of anthropologists and others on how rites detached people from one moral status, moved them to an ambiguous liminality and returned them anew to society (1960: 10–11). Detecting a common pattern "beneath a variety of forms" (1960: 27), he selectively attributed significance to some acts but not to others, that is, to those acts that accorded with his categories and tripartite schema. In doing so, van Gennep analyzed ritual in a way that differed from earlier theorists like Edward Burnett Tylor, William Robertson Smith, or James George Frazer. These eminent predecessors derived the theoretical significance of ritual from its relationship to a larger historical process. Ritual was an archaic moment in the evolution of rational society based in science. At a critical remove, the function of ritual for van Gennep was proximate rather than universal. Ritual allowed prestate actors, who were otherwise endangered by a Hobbesian ethos of *warre,* to safely cross a sociomoral no man's land lacking in rules and order and adopt a new identity. While van Gennep brilliantly turned the focus of analysis to ritual process and away from a unilinear teleology, the tripartite process he created was internal to its functioning. Outside its operational outcome, he thus removed ritual from history. Indeed, as in the L'Annee sociologique framework, his static conceptualization was necessary, since ritual practices could not change form without endangering their efficacy as causal components in sequences whose main purpose was to protect the status quo against violence from without and moral disorder from within.

As Silverman and Lipset point out in the Introduction to this volume, the ethnography of mortuary rites has made it clear to anthropologists that ritual practices possess this powerful double dynamic. Not only do they function with the transformative force of signifiers, to change actors and objects as morally and symbolically constituted entities, but they are reinvented to respond to shifting historical circumstances. In this chapter, I analyze this double dynamic, what Silverman and Lipset refer to as a "mortuary dialogue," in the outlying Marshall Islands atolls of Enewetak and Ujelang. I argue that these Marshallese people have changed burial practices and death celebrations over the past 150 years in relationship to their catastrophic encounter with colonialism. That is, in response to a history of missionization, capitalism, wars among foreign powers on local lands, nuclear testing, state-sponsored ecocide, resettlement, and transnational migration, they repeatedly devised new ritual forms that take long-standing Marshallese concepts of the moral person into account.

A brief overview of moral personhood in Marshallese society is therefore necessary to begin with. Marshallese society is divided into ranked, intermarrying matriclans from which chiefs, commoners, and intermediaries descend. At least since German colonial times (1885–1914), chiefly rank on Enewetak and Ujelang has come to be inherited through men. At the same time, people reside in bilateral extended families (*bwij*) that provide a counterbalancing force to clanship. The person is understood to be animated by a sacred, but morally problematic life-force and spirit-substance (*ao*) that remains understood as the definitive dimension of the person in Marshallese society—particularly should it become temporarily detached during crises of spirit-loss (*kālok* [literally "flight"]) or at death. The *ao*-spirit is inherited from the matriclan and thus differentially transmitted through women. Its power is unevenly distributed by age, gender, and rank. It is said to increase with age. The *ao*-spirits of the elderly are feared, for example, as far more dangerous than those of young children.

In addition, chiefs were once viewed to possess a supernatural "strength" commoners did not share. What is more, the human body was also viewed as composed of morally ranked parts, the head being of a higher rank than other body parts. Even today, it is disrespectful not to lower one's head when passing higher rank person, and it is forbidden to point feet at the body core or head of another. The differential moral rank of human bodies was also extended to geographic space inasmuch as ocean and land were ranked male and female as well as up and down. Being out of ranked space, the *ao*-spirit can become extremely dangerous to others after its host dies. But, for reasons discussed below, it can be partly placated and controlled by means of reinstalling into its proper space—by burial on homeland.

Burials at Sea

One story frequently told by Enewetak/Ujelang people is about Ben, a Peace Corps volunteer in the 1970s who fled to Kalo, the leeward-most islet on Ujelang, to live alone and escape from the rigors of village life. Kalo was uninhabited, but people saw it as occupied by the noncorporeal spirits (*timon*) that missionaries reckoned were demons. Local people took Ben to be daring, if not crazy (*bwebwe*), to stay there alone. Before finishing his stint as a Peace Corps volunteer, Ben told me that he had decamped to Kalo to escape a time of village-wide "cigarette craving" and peacefully enjoy a bottle filled with cigarette segments that he had secretly buried there (see Carucci 1987). In 1983, a man named Enok explained to me the foolishness of Ben's junkets from a cultural perspective:

> Enok: Remember that Peace Corps [worker], Ben who would go to Kalo and stay for weeks? This was amazing, because that islet is truly saturated with demon-spirits [*timonmon*]. But that fellow did not heed them, perhaps because as a "person of clothing" [i,e., a white man], he was almost a demon-spirit himself.
>
> LMC: Why is Kalo demon filled?
>
> Enok: Well, it is [located] at the westernmost extreme of [Ujelang] atoll and Ujelang is the closest atoll to Kapilōŋ [in the Caroline Islands]. Because of this, as the demon-spirits fly windward from Kapilōŋ, they first come ashore on Kalo. In ancient times, the westward side of Kalo was [also] the place to "set adrift" the people who had died [*kabeilok*]. The ancient ones did not know about "planting" [burying the dead], rather they only practiced sea burials.
>
> The good thing about sea burials [compared with land burial] was that if the dead person was cantankerous, and [his] spirit … was thinking about hurting [someone] … or making trouble, … the spirit [was prevented from doing so] because it had been sent away in the ocean so [it] would never reappear.

The dangers of Kalo islet, to which no Ujelang person would dare venture alone even today arise from the residual powers of ancient demon-spirits cast adrift there combined with foreign spirits from the Caroline Islands. Contemporary fears associated with the ability of the dead to damage or kill the living suggest uninterrupted anxiety about the afterlife, linking 1914 accounts to current-day stories (see Lipset, this volume). Enok, the narrator, documents this point for us. In his view, sea burials, which distance the living from the dead, remain preferable for their sort of moral efficacy.

Certainly, the practice appears to have been the norm in the early twentieth century. The German ethnographers August Kramer and Hans Nevermann, relying on their own data as well as materials from Erdland (1914) and Finsch (1893), write:

> Commoners were formerly wrapped in mats and taken out to sea in a boat. According to Steinbach, … bundled corpses were equipped with a small mast and sail. At sea they were thrown into the water unweighted, and the boat sailed back to the island. No one on board was allowed to look back at the corpse. The corpses of prisoners of war who were drowned in the lagoon were likewise taken out to sea and left to drift, but were not wrapped in mats.… Chiefs and the nobility … were also wrapped in mats and taken out to sea … on the third day after death. When the corpses of the chiefs were lowered into the sea, stones were wrapped in the mats at the head and foot so they could be submerged. (Kramer and Nevermann 1938: 56–57)

At least two points are made here. A distinction is drawn between ranked bodies, lower ranked bodies, and enemies. Wrapping the corpse and submerging it in the sea create moral boundaries between the first two categories, while enemies are disposed of without any ritual attention at all. Commoners, wrapped in mats, are sent off to the afterlife in a canoe (Lipset 2014), while ritual effort is made to sink chiefs, who are also wrapped in mats. The unspoken point would seem to be that the dead are differentially threatening. The spirits of deceased newborns only endangered other newborns and birthing mothers. In contrast, the corpses of high-ranked chiefs of the past are said to have created particularly high levels of risk to society at large. The risk from commoners (*kajur*) was much weaker.[1] People say that "setting adrift" also safeguarded commoners from the sacred force of chiefs.[2] Sinking chiefly corpses also protected chiefs' remains from magical manipulation by others (especially by rival chiefs and sorcerers).[3]

Sato Maie, a Marshallese man I interviewed in 1990, understood sea burials as the way the ancestors managed the boundary between the living and the dead. The boundary, which is located at the junction between the outer reef and the open sea, is the point where the safe zone of the local, the living, and the known come into contact with the foreign world of spirits and the relatively unknown. The area within the reef, the rim of coral islets, the internal lagoon, and particularly the lagoon side of the islets are all imagined as central, secure spaces that have womb-like associations. In local discourse, they are aligned with matriclans and women, through whom the *ao*-substance that clan members share is transmitted. The lagoons are a female space. However, the most downwind position in this space, the lowest-ranked part, is anomalous. At this juncture, the world of corporeal and noncorporeal spirit-beings is imagined to mix. Sato Maie told me about Epatōn islet on Kuwajleen atoll, where:

> there is a "long crevasse in the outside reef" which acts as a channel for canoes to come through the reef and get close to the islet. This channel is called a "place to climb down or disembark." … After do-

ing ... magical chants, it was decided that this [channel] was the best spot to release their dead into the sea. The currents around this part were such that corpses once thrown into the sea were never washed back up on the shore. They either drifted ... out ... or sharks took care of them. This spot is located on the northwestern-most point of [the islet]. (Carucci 1997c: 97)

Note the in/out and up/down referents used to characterize this location. Canoes come in through the reef here, but dead bodies "drift away" or are "thrown" into the sea through the same passage. Being the leeward-most point, the up/down designation situating the windward above the leeward is also applied to this passageway. Therefore, fishermen and seafarers had to make their way through the same route where corpses were cast out into the sea. In Sato's account, the danger of their return to come after the living is minimized, since physical remains are either eaten or carried off by currents.

Other threats remain beyond the reef. The most vulnerable people must be especially watchful in order to avoid the lethal force that noncorporeal spirits may exert. Caution must be taken by pregnant women, who are advised not to leave the boundaries of inhabited villages (e.g., safe "female" space), much less risk a trip to the leeward end of the atoll or a voyage out into the open ocean. The safety of such journeys is still debated today, when women who have high-risk pregnancies are asked to travel by boat to the government center for childbirth. Even air travel from Enewetak to Majuro is considered risky, and these risks are seriously weighed against the dangers of giving birth locally. The potential voyages of women with small infants, especially frail infants, are also viewed with hesitation on account of the dangers spirits pose outside of the village and, particularly, beyond the reef.

Land Burials

As much as sea burials eased peoples' fears of the dead, missionaries argued strongly in favor of land burials from 1857 to 1926 (Doane Letters nd).[4] If these men of God were among the pioneers of colonialism in the region, close on their heels came entrepreneurs interested in copra production. In tandem, they caused radical transformations of political as well as day-to-day life in the Marshalls (Carucci 1997a, 2003). Missionization and copra extraction demanded local labor and local cooperation, which were secured by chiefs, who turned from intermediaries between celestial gods and humans into intermediaries between Marshallese people and Euro-Americans.

As part of this change, not only did chiefs come to be considered the owners of the land, but the common people who had instantiated chiefs' strength and provided for their welfare became marginalized. Meantime, an increasing amount of productive capacity was being reallocated to working the land. Therefore, no matter how highly valued land had been in pre-European times, an entire "land-based" ideology, more rigidly hierarchized, was fashioned out of the colonial encounter. These changes refocused peoples' daily pursuits and energies. The shift to land burials was part of these comprehensive transformations.[5]

Clearing and working land may have been the primary way for clans to claim new plots, but with the introduction of copra, the primary claim to land was planting coconuts. This was quite unlike precontact life, particularly in the northern Marshall Islands. In the 1970s, the oldest Ujelang residents used to tell me that they were "people of the open ocean" who disliked working the land. Yet, agricultural pursuits eventually inscribed themselves upon daily routines. Nowadays, land parcels are typically delineated by the number of "lines" of planted coconut trees, and the trees themselves often mark property boundaries.

On Enewetak and Ujelang, an entire set of stories describes people's resistance to the coconut-planting regime. In stories set in preplantation days, coconut groves only appear in the central parts of most islets. Coconuts were not a preferred food and did not contribute much to local subsistence. In other words, coconuts simply grew; they were not systematically planted. With the shift to copra plantation labor, however, a change that particularly affected men's workdays, the land became a primary occupation.

By the second half of the twentieth century (if not earlier), investing labor in land came to be understood as a mode of self-fashioning as well as a claim to matriclan identity. In combination, this set of associations—working the land, consuming its products, and, ultimately, being buried on that land—came to be understood as a cohesive cycle that allowed people to see themselves and land as one. Land could be claimed and maintained through labor, labor that inscribed core elements of a person's being in the land.

Consuming fruits of the land also endowed living people with a physical embodiment of the place where one invested one's *ao*-spirit. The body became understood as a consubstantial result of its labor on the land. Ultimately, having one's body interred in the land completed the cycle that unified people and land as well as living members of extended families with their ancestors who had also worked that land. The land became far more than a symbol of family unity and belonging; it became iconically and metaphysically incorporated into each person by providing consumable products out of which living family members fashioned their identities.

Other elements of long-standing mortuary practices were readily incorporated into this vision of person/land. In particular, celebrations came to include an exchange of cooked food provided by the extended family of the deceased. Unlike other large food exchange events, however, what distinguished these feasts is the practice that after eating all or part of the meal, gifts are *not* given to the food providers. Since food is offered by the family to honor and commemorate its dead, the lack of reciprocity at this juncture is striking and perhaps is meant to fulfill a (hoped for) fantasy: an end to exchange with the deceased. Like sea burials, the purpose of a mortuary feast is to protect the living from the dead by creating a symbolic boundary that this absence of exchange signified (see Wilson and Sinclair, this volume).

Contemporary Burial and Mourning Practices

Kramer and Nevermann observed that in earlier days mats used to be distributed by the family of a deceased chief at the time of his burial: six mats were given to mourners by the closest relatives, while more distant relatives gave them three (1938: 57). They mention no food being distributed. Instead, food was placed near the grave or at the head of the chief's bed as an "offering to … spirits of the dead" (Kramer and Nevermann 1938: 61). Following Finsch, Erdland, and others, Kramer and Nevermann refer to these gravesites as *lup* or *uliej* and, indeed, these terms for "grave" and "cemetery," respectively, are still in use. Flowers and perfumes were often strewn around the grave (Kramer and Nevermann 1938: 57), and certainly today one sees this same practice, now supplemented by colorful artificial flowers and leis, fragments of broken colored glass, and other items of personal value to mourners.

The period of mourning (*eodaak*), they claimed, extended six days, although at times burial took place after three days. These same durations are still observed today, though contemporary demands may cut it short. In the case of a group of sailors lost at sea in 1981, mourning continued for six months, after which the community decided to hold a memorial service. In other instances, such as the deaths of respected community members living in Hawai'i (in 2006 and 2009), the length of the trip back to Enewetak determined the periods of mourning.

With the advent of land burial, cemeteries are now positioned in central, lagoon-side locations on properties that belong to the extended family. The positioning of a grave along the lagoon side of the island seems to contradict the former practice of sea burial, which sought maximal separation from the dead. While this is true, graveyard geography may be seen as another moment in their mortuary dialogues, in this case with missionary demands. Missionaries buried their own dead within the mission compound and insisted that local people do the same. Therefore, Marshallese began "planting" their dead on land but did so in the female-coded, lagoon-facing section of their own land parcels.

Missionaries taught that local spirits were false gods, that there was only one God, and that the *ao*-spirit of the person was immoral and forbidden. Therefore, Marshallese people had to rethink the power these spirits controlled in comparison to that of the Christian God: one person referred to contemporary spirits as being "policemen for God" who patrolled the community. The spirits, who were once seen as specific representatives of extended families and clans, became the moral center of a whole way of life, albeit one increasingly focused on land rather than the sea.

Graveyard use requires that kin of a recently deceased person (sometimes in line with his or her expressed desires) must claim membership in one of a number of overlapping extended family groups (see Lipset, this volume). Selecting a certain burial locale fixes a formerly animate body in space and, in so doing, identifies the person with a certain extended family for future generations. With thirteen overlapping families on Enewetak in 1980 and most people claiming membership in several of these large groups, choosing a burial site served to reduce the significance of status-related work performed on a daily basis. Certainly, astute (and often powerful) community members dedicate a great deal of time and energy in support of several family groups, thereby establishing the right to actively participate in their affairs. The burial site now asserts a primary alliance with one family, whereas multiple status claims are pursued during a person's life.

Cemeteries may be located just a short distance from village centers or in the bush. In either case, they are feared and people avoid them. Cemetery taboos are still observed that resemble those Kramer and Nevermann recorded nearly a century ago: "One should not make noise near a grave, one should not pick coconuts, breadfruit (or other foodstuffs) from near a graveyard, and one should not draw water (for drinking in particular) from near a cemetery" (1938: 60).[6] Following a death, however, people do repair to cemeteries to clean and rake; to refurbish old gravestones (nowadays often made of cement) with new masonry, paint, and decor; and, of course, to dig a grave for the deceased.

The location of graves in a family's cemetery also points to status rivalry and mortuary dialogue within it. That is, persons will try to fit high/low status with high/low status of space. Ordinarily, respected community members request to be buried on the most windward side of cemetery land or on the side closest to the exterior reef since these are more highly ranked plots than ones facing in other directions. In addition, however, mere proximity to a central point of collective significance, for example a pathway or road, may also demonstrate the prestige of the deceased to the living. Graves are positioned so the long axis of each coffin is placed from windward to leeward. Typically, a person's highest ranked body part (the head) is aligned with the higher ranked, or windward, end of the grave, much like the standard sleeping position in a house.[7]

During the "wake" (*eodaak*), the entire village is seen to be at risk. Spirits are then likely to wander around and create problems for people. Thus, graveyards are said to be "opened" by the living and then "closed" at the end of the funeral. "The cemetery is now closed" (*E kilik uliej eo kio*), one man declared to children who had become enthralled with playing in a typically off-limits space during a wake.[8]

Marshallese people build houses at a distance from cemeteries because of their perceived dangers. Yet in Majuro and particularly on Ebeye (Kuwajleen), overpopulation has meant that some people's houses abut cemeteries today. I have not conducted systematic research on this topic, but at least a few people who reside near cemeteries in these locales deny feeling risk while others, who believe such sites are "full of spirits," feel they have no choice but to live where they do. However, if keeping one's distance from a cemetery is typically seen as safer, not all people are motivated by fear of spirits. Indeed, when my adoptive older brother, Dabi, died on Enewetak, his wife, liMeyer, insisted that he be buried under the eave of her house in the style of a place like Tikopia (Firth 1963: 78). However much her father-in-law insisted that this was a bad idea since with Dabi's spirit around "there would never be any peace," she swore that doing so would not become a problem because his spirit would not be malicious and harmful.

Her assurance helps to draw our attention to the ambivalences aroused by death rather than just anxiety, ambivalences to which women seem more attuned than men. Fear inspired by noncorporeal spirits today, as well as in the era of *kabeilok* sea burials, are and undoubtedly were matched by feelings of extraordinary attachment. The first notification of a death on Ujelang and Enewetak atolls is carried by the wails of women mourners who are in attendance at the time of death or are notified immediately thereafter (see Cho and Sinclair, this volume; see also Silverman, this volume). For important community members and relatives, their keening will continue for hours or even days but, particularly, throughout the first night after the death. The women focus on the body, but their attentions are not restricted to it.[9] Almost as an afterthought, Kramer and Nevermann abruptly end their discussion of mourning with an astonishing datum. "Women," they tell us, "who deeply mourn [a] ... death, or even the unfaithfulness of their husbands, are said to begin to fly with their 'astral bodies'" (1938: 62).

Contemporary Marshallese are still said to "fly off" (*kālok*) to the deceased or loved ones from whom they have been separated. While women are more susceptible to such flight than men, men also experience flight, flight that is said to be provoked by "sadness" (*burōmuj*). But "sadness" is far too generic a gloss for what this term means. The *burō-* prefix refers to "the throat," the source of Marshallese attachment. Unfaithful husbands are more likely to be beaten with frying pans or clubs, but perhaps the notion of "astral flight" may be taken as a metaphor for the way in which death threatens the essence of the self, arousing as it would seem to do such an intense desire to be reunited with the loved one that the self must do no less than turn into a bird and "fly off" to do so.

Life and Death on Ujelang Atoll

Now we turn from Marshallese intimacy to global modernity. After World War II, the United States decided to export the risks of nuclear testing by making them someone else's garbage, medical problem, and environmental catastrophe. Bikini and Enewetak atolls were selected as testing sites, and the residents of these atolls had to be relocated. Following their removal, Enewetak people spent thirty-three years living on the small, environmentally impoverished atoll of Ujelang. In some respects, the suffering they endured there made the community more cohesive and resilient since, left largely to their own devices, they had to sustain themselves on a meager resource base. Yet, in other ways, the move required profound transformations as they were living on foreign land.[10] Initially, promises were made to Enewetak people that they would be allowed to return to home soon. However, after watching the apocalyptic 1952 "Mike" test on Enewetak from the deck of a vessel at a far remove, many people doubted that anything at all of their home atoll could have survived such a monumental explosion; they began to try to think of themselves as *diUjelang* (the people of Ujelang).

Life on Ujelang Atoll demanded innovation. As people died, they were "planted" in Ujelang soil, although of course they yearned to be buried on Enewetak. In some ways, Ujelang was refashioned on a Enewetak model, but in other ways, its design differed. The Americans (with the assistance of Marshallese workers) created a central village with two Enewetak chieftainships that occupied the windward and leeward halves of Ujelang. On Enewetak, however, each chieftainship had ruled separate islets (Enjebi and Enewetak) thirteen miles across the lagoon from the other. On Ujelang, some cemeteries were located in the windward and leeward "halves" of the central village, which roughly corresponded with the former Enewetak- and Enjebi-based chieftainships. But outside the village, individuals had been allocated one or more land parcels to plant coconuts and other food trees. On these lands, people also started to bury their dead. The latter cemeteries more closely resembled the ones they had left on Enewetak, though of course the deceased could not be interred alongside their ancestors there.

Over time, working the land, eating foods grown on it, and living there, people did begin to think of themselves as *diUjelang*. This is certainly how they spoke of themselves in the 1970s when I first lived among them. Jack Tobin, district anthropologist for the Marshall Islands in the 1950s and 1960s, mentions that Ujelang people were then referring to themselves as one of the lost tribes of Israel (Tobin 1967). During my first research on Ujelang in 1976, I also heard of this identification during church services. Apparently, "the people of Ujelang" saw themselves as a diaspora exiled from Enewetak, which they continued to see as their homeland.

When American officials offered them the opportunity to return home and receive some financial compensation for their suffering, people chose to return to Enewetak in the late 1970s. In negotiating the terms of their return with U.S. government representatives, one of their first requests was for a program that became known as "Temporary" (*Tempedede*). Its purpose was to allow the senior generation to go "home" immediately. As a hearty elder argued during a community discussion of the program:

> And if I die here on Ujelang, it will never be good. I will lie … next to … [a long-deceased grandchild], but my mother and father and all of … the ancient ones, they are planted there on the leeward end of Enewetak. And if things are … [in order] at the time I am gone, I will [get to] lie there next to them. If I die here on Ujelang, well, it is too late [nothing can be done], but it is … not right. … If we die here, perhaps the real Ujelang people from ancient times will be upset, and we will lie in an unsettled way [*abnono*]. So ask for this thing, *Tempedede*, and if the white people do not say "no," then I will die and [get to] lie down in a peaceful way.

In the event, this particular man did not pass away for another twenty years. But the two elders who did die during the *Tempedede* program were indeed interred on the chiefly Enewetak islet of Jeptan. Still, their two graves stand alone along the lagoon shore—in commemoration of their of deaths, to be sure, but also in commemoration of the thirty-three year exile of Enewetak people from their atoll home as well as the moment of *Tempedede* on Jeptan.

The two people Biola (through her husband) and Jimeon (through an ancestor) could claim the right to be buried on Jeptan. Jimeon's claim to be buried on Jeptan is acknowledged as much stronger than Biola's. Now, years after their funerals, Biola's spirit frequently disrupts Enewetak residents, which is attributed to her burial on Jeptan, where her grave is out of place. Again, we hear domestic mortuary dialogue about the reproduction of moral community that simultaneously answers Pacific modernity at its worst.

Dying Back Home

The U.S. government agreed to clean up five (of forty-eight) islets and then repatriate the community to Enewetak. Upon returning home in 1980, Ujelang/

Enewetak people were initially euphoric. However, the damage done to the atoll environment was so great that people soon questioned whether their longing to return had skewed their ability to judge what life would be like on New Enewetak. First, to build new homes for the returning residents, American contractors wanted to be told about land boundaries and property ownership. On an atoll where a 6,800-foot runway now occupied nearly 50 percent of the principal islet, it was virtually impossible for elders to do this with any certainty, much less accuracy. The lagoon had been dredged and the outer reef altered in search of soil to reinforce the airstrip. The natural markers that local people once used for orientation were simply gone.

People knew of one old cemetery that was located on the lagoon side of Bakien land, but huge arguments broke out about where Bakien was, or for that matter every other plot of land. Therefore, much as people longed to be buried near ancestors, it was anyone's guess exactly where their graves were. In some places, the former contour of the land had been covered over by work the Americans had done or had been dredged. Ultimately, cemeteries were built on private land plots, whose boundaries were widely acknowledged to be wrong (Figure 1).

For example, as Jimeon's younger brother Luta was dying, he refused to go on living in his own house because he had concluded that the house was not "really" on his land. Not wanting to die on the land of his ancestor's neigh-

Figure 1.1. Young men carry a casket to the extended family cemetery, Enewetak Atoll. Photo: Laurence M. Carucci, 2009.

bors, Luta moved in with a relative whose house stood, in his estimate, on his family's land. Nevertheless, when he died, his burial became disputed because of assertions that cemeteries had been mislocated. Luta was not buried next to his older brother, Jimeon. Although his substance had indeed returned to Enewetak soils, it was not to be comingled with his ancestors after all, despite his long-standing desire to come to rest on his own land.

After many years yearning to go home, ironically enough, nostalgia arose for Ujelang and a "true Marshallese" lifestyle. Indeed, the cleanup of nuclear waste had left Enewetak Atoll stripped of all topsoil and subsistence plants. Working the land and consuming its products were simply not possible in this damaged land. And, as in Luta's case, there was not even certainty that one would be able to be buried alongside one's ancestors.

While being back home was enough to stop people from yearning to be buried on Ujelang, the social and environmental disruptions on Enewetak were so great that residents could not achieve the kinds of cosmological resolutions of which they had dreamed while in exile. In short, the quality of life that had been left behind on Ujelang could not be sustained on New Enewetak, where bingo, cards, and drinking came to replace most subsistence activities. Soon enough, a new location beckoned where improved opportunities for schooling and health care and jobs were far more available than in the Marshall Islands. In 1991, a few young families were led to move to Hawai'i.

Dying in Hawai'i

When Enewetak people died there, new mortuary practices were once again improvised. When an infant girl died after they had been there two years, her death introduced them to how grief and burials in American society not only involved adhering to modern decorum and official regulations but also required engaging paid specialists. A young community leader, Joniten, recounted the story of the infant's death to me:

> When the [newborn] girl died, the hospital people were very upset because they did not like the women wailing.... So they asked us to "hurry and take the [body away] ... because the sounds are increasing the unease of ... other people ... in the hospital." And so, we called [to find a vehicle] ... but ...Timoti was working and he had taken the vehicle, and so there was no pathway until the time [he] finished work. [My relatives continued to] call around and [eventually reached me at] work.
>
> So ... I [hurried] to the hospital. But, when I got [there], the battle had already commenced. I had already stopped and bought ... a big

plastic ... [box-like container with] a lid.... The good thing was that there were some sheets in the car because the girls had just done the laundry.... So I backed the vehicle up next to the door and brought in the plastic box and two of the sheets. Well, the box was new and the sheets clean still, but it did not matter. They said we ... had no right to take [the girl]. We could not just "throw her" in some plastic box. I had already told them that it was ... new; I had just purchased it, but ... this made no difference to them. They asked:

"And what will you do with the box?"

"We will take the girl home and prepare her, rub her with oil and place her in new ... church clothes, and then after [the wake], we will bury her."

"Where? Where will you bury her?"

"We will make a ... cemetery, there behind the house." ... Well, maybe they thought I was lying. Perhaps they thought we were going to [mutilate] the [body] or eat her, like we were people of New Guinea, and so they would not give me the body of the girl.

Then the women really started wailing because there would be no place for the girl to lie down ... and ... her spirit would be restless [*inebata*]. And they were upset because ... sometimes [even] the spirits of infants can also be highly dangerous [*kaueitatta*]. Because of [their] noisy [keening], the hospital people [became] even more upset.

The row between hospital bureaucracy in Hawai'i and the Enewetak mourners over where the infant might be buried and the loudness of the women's grief illustrates an instance of yet another dimension of discord in mortuary dialogue between Pacific Islanders and modernity. As Joniten went on with his account of this dialogue, traditional Enewetak death-related anxieties surface:

So ... I asked them "What is the [right] approach?" And they said we would have to call "the people affiliated with the dead" [a funeral home]. We called them "the people of the dead" then, because we didn't know that in America ... [there was a specific] work group that just "made" the dead. But [at the hospital], they said they could not ... [recommend a particular group of] "death people" because the other [funeral homes] would get angry. Well, when the women heard [this] ..., they ... wail[ed even louder] and ... the hospital people became more upset. Ultimately, the hospital people gave us the names of three [funeral homes] that watched over and "made" the dead. And so I called one of [them], and they came and got the infant and prepared her for us. We did not [agree to] the [embalming] shots because nothing good will come from interrupting [the processes of] death, but still, all of this was very costly. The women were very upset because they could not prepare the girl, clean her and make her over [*kakomanmani*]. At the time [when the funeral home picked her up], they said that the women could come to their place and wail, ... but then they were not eager to let the women and the [other] mourners ... stare at the girl, because she had not [been given the embalming] shots.

Here perhaps we might say that the women are also crying for conceding their autonomous right and capacity to reproduce their moral community in the aftermath of the death. Needless to say, the Enewetak people find no reason to trust the intervention of the "death people," and they reject embalming "because nothing good will come from interrupting [the processes of] death," a qualm that of course recalls the Hertzian, processual view of death, wherein mourners become morally identified with the decomposing corpse until a secondary burial celebration. Needless to say, all of this is clearly part of this selfsame mortuary dialogue with Pacific modernity (see Introduction, this volume). Acknowledging humor, or perhaps irony, in his story, Joniten continued, now in a nostalgic voice:

Because we did not [take the embalming] shots, I had to hurry to find a place to bury the girl. And this ... also cost a lot, because we had not yet learned about Na'alehu [cemetery]. Yes, you could never simply live on this island; for everything, there is a cost. And because of this, there is a lot of hardship for those of us who live here. It is not like the days on Ujelang. As you know, there, when we were hungry you grabbed a sprouted coconut ... or if you craved fish, you went fishing and ate. And if you wanted to move your house, you ... moved to [an]other spot, and put down the house posts and rebuilt it. And if you died, all of your close relatives would [make] preparations and place you in the ground and all things would be in a state of peace [*ainemon*].

In short, the collision between capitalism and the requirements of the State of Hawai'i, on the one side, and Marshallese concepts of moral community, on the other, posed unanticipated challenges to the new immigrants, challenges that aroused a nostalgia not for the homeland of Enewetak but for the exile in Ujelang, where resources were abundant and life was autonomous.

The community subsequently discovered a small mortuary run by an aging Korean couple, who, being sympathetic to variations in cultural practices, were considerate of Marshallese approaches to death. In addition, they began to use a small rural cemetery at Na'alehu, where bodies in coffins had to be aligned in rows with heads toward the ocean or, in the adjoining row, toward the land. If the windward/leeward alignment was not as precise as on Ujelang or Enewetak, the cemetery seemed to offer a recognizable familiarity, not to mention a degree of autonomy. With fairly inexpensive cemetery plots, kinsmen are allowed to dig graves there. While the law is viewed as an imposition, the Enewetak diaspora in Hawai'i entertains no thought to contest or challenge it. Rather, they reproduce their moral community on the fringes of the state's disciplinary power.

Korean undertakers bring the body of the deceased to the cemetery; kinsmen carry the casket to the gravesite, lower it in place, and fill the grave (Figure 1.2).[11] A final day is dedicated to decorating the grave and cleaning the site before leaving it to weather until the next death within the community. Care is taken to label these graves with names and dates because in Hawai'i, graves are interspersed with those of strangers.[12] While youth are buried in Hawai'i,

Figure 1.2. With the extended family looking on, young men lower a casket into a grave at Na'alehu cemetery, Hawai'i. Photo: Laurence M. Carucci, 2014.

mature people who once lived on Enewetak or Ujelang were not because their powerful *ao*-spirits can imperil or benefit the moral community. It is considered important that spirits of senior people feel "at peace" in their graves. Relations of happiness and good health extend to the living when corporeal and noncorporeal worlds are said to be "in balance" (*e balan* see Figure 1.3). In the following three cases, the moral relationship between spirits and moral community is straightforward.

Joniten's relatively aged mother, Kreita, moved to Hawai'i to seek medical treatment for her diabetes-related kidney disease. She yearned to "see Enewetak one more time" prior to her death and stopped treatment for her disease. Knowing that dialysis was not available there, she still wished to visit family and homeland once more and to have her substance reunited with the land of her ancestors. By contrast, Enooji, a man who was terminally ill, also wanted to return to visit kin on Enewetak. However, he chose to live out his life with his children on the Big Island. Benjamin, the third case, also told me that he hoped to return to Enewetak when his time came. When he did die, despite the financial hardship transporting his corpse and several family members back to Enewetak created,[13] and even though the community wanted to avoid tinkering with the internal state of the corpse, the families of both Benjamin and Enooji did return them to Enewetak. Benjamin's son, Bilimon, expressed a fear that burying his father in Hawai'i:

> would never be O.K. [His unsettled spirit] would damage us. Because, even though [he] … was kind, [when] … he was angry, "ooow!" He could really do damage! It was his desire to go back to Enewetak,

Figure 1.3. A grieving husband/elder, standing behind headstone, is surrounded by extended family. Photo: Laurence M. Carucci, 2014.

so we children would never say no. It makes no difference that it is expensive, because there is no other path. Either take [him] back to Enewetak, or we [exclusive] would be gone!

Not all elders, however, do go home. Jentila, an elderly woman from a relatively poor family, was buried in Hawai'i. Her daughter explained to me that since:

this is our home now, she wanted to be buried next to her granddaughter. All ... [her daughters] now reside here, and she is happy to be here with us. She already brought pandanus and breadfruit and even one coconut from our house ... [on Enewetak].... We'll bring back other coconuts because ... my son's dog ... chewed up the coconut sprout, and ... it died. But we took a piece of the flower, a frangipani that was by the house (on Enewetak), and planted it next to her grave in Na'alehu [cemetery], so now her life there ... is with her here.

It is likely that this family chose not to return their mother to Enewetak on account of the substantial costs of flying the corpse back home. Nevertheless, they faced the same question that all Enewetak people living in Hawai'i must address: should they return their loved one to the land of her birth or have her spirit remain with the Hawai'i branch of the family? Since I was not in Hawai'i at the time of Jentila's death, I cannot be certain that she did not want to be buried on Enewetak. But what is significant in her daughter's account is the metonymic strategy appearing in it that other Enewetak in Hawai'i now use to bring the homeland to them. Through cuttings replanted on the Big Island and, in this particular case, through a frangipani tree, Jentila's gravesite was connected consubstantially with Enewetak. While the cuttings from Enewetak had to be smuggled into the Big Island, moral continuities were thus created between the new locale and the substance of the ancestors.

A final case. A momentous event occurred when Jemej, a highly respected community leader, died on Hawai'i in 2012. The expectation was that he would be sent back to Enewetak and be buried in a cemetery there, just to the windward side of his son's house (Figure 1.4). However, Jemej's daughters, having resided on the Big Island for several years, insisted on burying him in Na'alehu. A firestorm erupted about their decision that became so intense that even I was contacted in Montana by members of each side in hopes that my voice would help sway the community decision to either return Jemej to Enewetak for burial or to allow him to be buried in Hawai'i (see the chapters of Bell, Lutkehaus, and Silverman, this volume). The decision to bury Jemej in Hawai'i was a milestone in the commitment of Enewetak people to a transnational existence in which the boundaries of home could no longer be seen as the fringing reefs of Enewetak or Ujelang atolls.

Figure 1.4. Jemej gives a commemorative speech at Na'alehu cemetery, Hawai'i. His own grave site is now nearby. Photo: Laurence M. Carucci, 2010.

Conclusion—Marshallese Mortuary Rites and Pacific Modernity

For Marshall Islanders, one of the challenges of death has been to mediate the conflicted moral boundaries between corporeal and noncorporeal domains of personhood. Specifically, the problem has been understood to align bodies and sacred spirit-substances in a way that both defends the living from the dead and dignifies the dead. Sea burial in weighted mats was the precontact solution to the problem of risk and respect. Missionaries demanded that Marshall Islanders rethink relations with the spirit world and required that corpses be solidly moored in the shallow sands of local land. The shift to land burial resulted in innovations of ritual forms that did not fully satisfy local people's desire to keep the dead at a comfortable distance from the living. At the same time, a larger process was going on that involved reconceptualizing the value of land in day-to-day life. Planting coconuts in the land and "being planted" in the land became crucial components of personhood in the new cosmology. When the United States destroyed and recreated the Enewetak landscape and the Marshallese moved to Hawai'i, further strategies developed to reproduce moral community in new settings.

The sacred force that gives life and agency to the living continued to lend a characteristically Marshallese sensibility to mortuary practices. These practices, negotiated in dialogue among the living as well as between the living and the dead, continue to be refashioned in ways that account for the consubstantial relationship of spirits with the land, on the one hand, and with the requirements of a state-based society, on the other. To protect and sustain the moral community in Marshallese terms, efforts are made in mortuary rites to maintain a link between contemporary spirits and those of the ancestors. At the same time, these practices must be reinvented in dialogue with Pacific modernity.

Laurence Marshall Carucci, Letters and Science Distinguished Professor Emeritus of Anthropology at Montana State University, has done research with Marshall Islanders since 1976 on issues of social and cultural change among Enewetak people and the members of other communities who suffered through World War II and the subsequent era of U.S. nuclear testing in the northern Marshall Islands. His books include *Nuclear Nativity* (1997), *The Typhoon of War* (with Lin Poyer and Suzanne Falgout, 2000), and *Memories of War: Micronesians in the Pacific War* (with Suzanne Falgout and Lin Poyer, 2008).

Notes

1. The *ao* life-force, controlled by spirits and concentrated in high-ranked chiefs, can be used for positive ends as well as negative. Nevertheless, negative uses inspire fear, and fear that spirit forces may cause illness or death among the living, is highly disconcerting.
2. Such was the residual power of his body in a chief's hut, the dwelling was left to decay and no one entered it after his death (Kramer and Nevermann 1938: 61). Kramer and Nevermann's informants saw chiefly potency as so vast that a chief's death might be foretold by a comet crossing the night skies. I have described the symbolic association of chiefs and celestial lights elsewhere but, until recent chiefs tarnished their image (perhaps beyond repair), most Marshallese continued to believe in a direct connection between contemporary chiefs and chiefs of old, who appear as clusters of stars of Marshallese constellations (Carucci 1980, 1997b, 1997c).

3. Kramer and Nevermann also claimed that nobles and chiefs (but not commoners) were buried on land in premission times. Archaeological evidence of land burials is ambiguous in regard to chiefly commemoration. While supine burial was introduced by ABCFM missionaries (Kramer and Nevermann 1938: 56), it is not clear whether grave adornments, memorial stones, or building structures over noble burial sites, were pre-European phenomena, or were inspired by colonial practices.
4. As noted by Kramer and Nevermann (1938), the radical change has been the shift from sea burials to burials on land that began to take place during the latter half of the nineteenth century. Yet to say that the new practices were mission inspired fails to recognize the massive campaign of cultural reconstruction and rethinking that accompanied this shift.
5. Kramer and Nevermann (1938) offer no clue as to how Marshallese understood missionary-required land burials. My own research demonstrates that mortuary practices were not simply imported, whole cloth, at missionary command. Rather, land burial was reinvented and reinscribed in a Marshallese form, incorporating fragments of bygone practices as much as it derived elements from missionary forms.
6. These temporal prohibitions for the six days following a chief's death equally describe proper everyday cemetery demeanor in the current era.
7. Some people, however, follow an American-inspired biblical precedent with feet toward the windward (approximately east) to greet Jehovah upon his return. Burial arrangements were unsettled even in Kramer and Nevermann's day. Erdland indicated the head was pointed north. Finsch said the head pointed west, whereas Brandeis "learned that the head is placed pointing north or east." Grave depth also varied depending upon "the rank and sex of the deceased," the intent being to consider "the varying danger of the spirits of the dead" (Kramer and Nevermann 1938: 58).
8. Nowadays, when visiting graves some distance from home, people will enter the cemetery, deposit mementos, and even sit on the headstone of an endeared relative, such as a grandparent or mother's younger brother (normatively, an indulgent relationship).
9. For chiefs, Kramer and Nevermann state that mourning by relatives and subjects with shaved heads was kept up at the grave for six days. While they say nothing about wailing in the "mourning hut," they contend that making any type of noise near the grave was prohibited. According to Finsch, a fire was kept lit for weeks to frighten evil spirits (cited in Kramer and Nevermann 1938: 60–61).
10. A few people welcomed the move, seeing it as an opportunity. They were descended from Ujelang folks and married into the Enewetak community after German colonials took their atoll from them to use as a copra plantation. For them, the move represented a homecoming.
11. Later, men will return to the grave to frame and pour a cement headstone or build a crypt over it.
12. Back in the Marshall Islands, death records are kept in churches and, while some graves are labeled with names, community members walk by cemeteries every day and know the graves.
13. This was particularly true in the late Bush era, when restricted funding disrupted regular air service to the outer Marshall Islands. A multiday journey by boat brought the physical remains of these men back to their childhood home on Enewetak from Majuro.

References Cited

Bwebwenato in Majel, ND. *Bwebwenato in Majel*. Department of Education, collected and compiled by Billiet Edmond. Majuro, Aelon in Majol, 96960.

Carucci, Laurence Marshall. 1980. *The Renewal of Life: A Ritual Encounter in the Marshall Islands*. Ph.D. dissertation. The University of Chicago.

———. 1987. "*Kijen Emaan ilo Baat*: Smoking Circles in Marshallese Society." In *Drugs in Western Pacific Societies*, edited by Lamont Lindstrom, 51–74. Lanham, MD: University Press of America.

———. 1997a. *In Anxious Anticipation of the Uneven Fruits of Kwajalein Atoll: A survey of Locations and Resources of Value to the People of Kwajalein Atoll*. Huntsville, Alabama: USASSDC.

———. 1997b. "*Irooj Ro Ad*: Measures of Chiefly Ideology and Practice in the Marshall Islands." In *Chiefs Today: Traditional Pacific Leadership and the Postcolonial State*, edited by M. Lindstrom and G. White, 197–210. Stanford: Stanford University Press.

———. 1997c. *Nuclear Nativity: Rituals of Renewal and Empowerment in the Marshall Islands*. DeKalb: Northern Illinois University Press.

———. 2003. "Transformation of Person and Place on Enewetak and Ujelang Atoll." In *Globalization and Culture Change in the Pacific Islands*, edited by Victoria S. Lockwood, 417–33. Columbus: Prentice Hall.

———. 2011. "From Famine to Feast: The Give and Take of Food in a Global Subsistence Environment." *Pacific Studies* 34(1): 1–23.

Doane, ET. nd. Letters of E. T. Doane. In the Hawaiian Mission Children's Society Library. Honolulu, Hawai'i.

Erdland, PA. 1914. *Die Marshall-Insulaner: Leben und Sitte, Sinn und Religion eines Sudsee-Volkes*. Munster: Aschendorffsche Verlagbuchhandlung.

Finsch, Otto. 1893. *Ethnologische Erfahrungen und Belegstucke aus der Sudsee*. Translation is available in the Pacific Collection, Hamilton Library, 119–182. University of Hawai'i, Honolulu, Hawai'i.

Firth, Raymond. 1963 [1936]. *We, the Tikopia*. New York: Beacon Press.

Kramer, August and Hans Nevermann. 1938. *Ralik Ratak*. Translated by Elizabeth A. Murphy and Ruth E Runeborg. Available in Pacific Collection, Hamilton Library, University of Hawai'i, Honolulu. Standard translation in HRAF files from Ralik-Ratak (Marshall Inseln) by Augustin Kramer und Hans Nevermann, 11. Band der "Ergebnisse Der Sudsee-Expedition 1908–1910. Edited by Georg Thilenius. Berlin: Walter de Gruyter.

Lipset, David. 2014. "Living Canoes: Vehicles of Moral Imagination among the Murik of Papua New Guinea." In *Vehicles: Cars, Canoes and other Metaphors of Moral Imagination*, edited by David Lipset and Richard Handler, 21–47. New York: Berghahn.

Pollock, Nancy. 1970. *Breadfruit and Breadwinning on Namu Atoll, Marshall Islands*. Ph.D. dissertation. University of Hawai'i.

Tobin, Jack. 1967. *The Resettlement of the Enewetak People: A Study of a Displaced Community in the Marshall Islands*. Ph.D. dissertation. University of California, Berkeley.

van Gennep, Arnold. 1960 [1908]. *Rites of Passage*. Translated by Monika B. Vizedom and Gabrielle L. Caffee. Chicago: University of Chicago Press.

2

Into the World of Sorrow
Women and the Work of Death in Māori Mortuary Rites

CHE WILSON and KAREN SINCLAIR

For Māori people living in New Zealand/Aotearoa, work associated with mortuary rites (*tangihanga*, abbreviated *tangi*) is organized by age and gender. The outstanding role of women in this division of ritual labor, which is the topic of this chapter, has been well documented (Metge 1969; Salmond 1976; Sinclair 1990; Tauroa and Tauroa 1986; Ihimaera 1973).

It is women who host large numbers of guests who come to mourn. It is women who organize food and arrange sleeping accommodations in the sacred meeting house (*marae*) and elsewhere. It is women who clean linens and prepare lavatories and showers for everyone. Women's voices first call the body onto the *marae* and later offer chants of welcome and sorrow as visitors and mourners enter the sacred grounds. Most importantly, it is women who are the principal mourners (*pani*), and as such they oversee the transitions and transformations that are critical for the deceased and grieving kin during the *tangi*. Not all women are *pani*, but all *pani* are women. The many duties, practical and ritual, that fall to women preclude all but close relations and the elderly from assuming this singular role.

Over the course of the *tangi*, the *pani* women devote their time almost exclusively to the corpse (*tupapaku*). Eating and sleeping separately, they are isolated from all interactions until each of the three constituent parts of the deceased has been accorded proper ritual treatment—a ritual process (van Gennep 1969) that is meant to transform a once living member of the group into a deceased and commemorated ancestor. To be sure, men play significant and complementary roles: in speeches addressing and honoring the dead and paying respects to the family, their voices dominate the public mortuary dialogue on the *marae* where they alone are permitted to speak. Women may, and frequently do, accompany their speeches with chants and songs. Women are visible in this sacred space, but may not speak.

Men also prepare the earth oven (*hangi*) for the feast that occurs after the burial (*hakari*). Men work outside as they dig the *hangi* in the ground, while women are inside, working in the dining room and kitchen. In this sense, men traverse public spaces, while women, working in confined arenas or isolated as *pani,* are less visible and less accessible. Nevertheless, women maintain the sacred space of the *marae* and therefore sustain the ground on which the ritual takes place.

Māori people value *tangi* as the most significant and enduring of all contemporary rituals. They see them as emblematically and indisputably Māori. This is not to say that *tangi* have not changed over the more than two hundred years since Captain Cook arrived in 1769. Inevitably, they have been revised and modified in response to the settler state (Sissons 1998). In twenty-first-century New Zealand/Aotearoa, performances of *tangi* express ambiguities arising from tensions associated with biculturalism and modernity. Māori celebrate *tangi* as a distinct mode of mourning, which is public but at the same time esoteric.

The meaning of *tangi* remains unknown to all but those who participate in them regularly. Often, both Catholic clergy and Māori leaders co-officiate and accommodate one another. The relationship between Māori and *Pakeha* (non-Māori people) could not be plainer in such contexts. For political, social, and moral reasons, each side voices nothing less than the dignity and correctness of its treatment of the dead. Māori mourn, grieve, and bury their dead in distinctively Māori ways. More than the disposal of the deceased is at stake, however: mourners affirm the power and privilege of Māori identity within a multicultural state. Many *Pakeha* tolerate such occasions as a necessary evil in their commitment to live up to pluralist ideals.

Twenty-First-Century Whanganui

This chapter focuses on the Ngāti Rangi tribal confederation who live on a mountainous plateau in a region of the North Island and whose cultural distinctiveness is sometimes named for the Whanganui River, long an important resource. Ohakune, a small town where the research for it was conducted, is an important center for its Ngāti Rangi residents. Here at the base of Mt. Ruapehu, amid a thriving *marae,* Wilson was born and Sinclair has done fieldwork for forty-three years. What is called Whanganui custom (*kawa*) informs the organization of ritual, especially mortuary events, in the region. In addition, however, many Ngāti Rangi are Catholics, whose missionary work began in the nineteenth century and continues to be important into the present. People also adhere to a religious movement called *Maramatanga* (Light/Enlightenment), which began during the first decades of the twentieth century (see Elsmore 1999; Sinclair 2002).

Assisted by his kinswomen, the founder of the movement, Hori Enoka Mareikura, advocated Ngāti Rangi beliefs that spirits of the dead return as tutelaries to inform and assist the living. In 1935, a key event took place when Mareikura's granddaughter died. As her body lay in state during her *tangi* rite, the *pani* women who surrounded her body clearly heard her voice and then urged her grieving mother, who wanted nothing to do with what they were claiming to hear, to allow her to speak. The granddaughter's spirit subsequently became known as "the messenger" (*karere*) and has continued to maintain oracular contact with four generations of the *Maramatanga* Movement. That such a decisive moment in the history of the movement took place during a *tangi* not only illustrates its significance but also shows us the prominence of women as mourners. When a young woman returned from the dead, she was surrounded by women. Her grandfather, the prophet, had many talents, foremost of which were healing and sustaining traditions, but it was the women watching over her corpse who facilitated her return.

If Māori people living in this region hold multiple concepts of the afterlife, we may also note that Māori understanding of the physical environment of the North Island differs radically from that of *Pakeha*. Ngāti Rangi regard the mountain, Ruapehu, as an important, senior ancestor who is a source of life and sustenance. Visible as it is from almost all angles in Ohakune town and throughout the North Island, Ngāti Rangi see its presence as imposing but also in need of vigilant protection. At the same time, *Pakeha* ignore the moral dimension of the mountain. For them, Mt. Ruapehu is a recreational area and Ohakune town is nothing but a winter getaway with trendy restaurants, excellent skiing, and wonderful hiking trails. While young men and women from Ngāti Rangi are permitted to work, usually at menial jobs, on the mountain and abet the tourist takeover of the area by doing so, Māori elders and others refuse to use the mountain either for work or play. Other than to make pilgrimages associated with the *Maramatanga* Movement, they avoid the mountain altogether.

The absence of lucrative employment in such rural areas as Ohakune town has caused young people to seek work in New Zealand cities. The necessity to leave home, while shedding kinship attachments and obligations, has resulted in children who have been raised in different and alien places in New Zealand and further abroad. In such a diaspora, young people find themselves at a distance from kin groups and ritual events. The demands of work and the financial burdens of traveling, moreover, make attending *tangi* rites difficult. Jobs can be placed in jeopardy during prolonged absences, especially if employers are unsympathetic or unaware of the significance of *tangi* rites.

The twenty-first century also finds young Māori migrating to Australia, where they believe jobs are plentiful and well paying. Coming home from Australia, of course, creates an even greater challenge than does the journey from an urban center in New Zealand and may also put jobs in jeopardy. Inevitably, some young people simply decide, or have the decision forced upon them, not to return home at all.

In addition to the responses of youth to a capitalist economy, the costs of hosting a *tangi* have risen to prohibitive levels (Tahana 2012). As a result, mortuary rites around the country are at times held in homes rather than on *marae*, some of which are falling into disrepair. This shift and decline, this answer to modernity, is by no means uniform.[1] Despite the out-migration of the young as well as the burden of inflation, Ngāti Rangi people continue to assemble on their *marae* to observe *tangi*. And it is to their tenacious defense of Māori personhood that takes place during these rites that we now turn the discussion.

Preparations

Māori believe that the person possesses two spirits that are integrated into the body in life. The one is the *wairua* spirit, often glossed as a 'soul' which will join the ancestors; and the other is the *mauri* spirit, the vital life-giving essence that also departs when death occurs. After death, the body separates from these two spirits, and each must receive the proper ritual attention to insure its arrival at the appropriate destination. The *wairua* spirit is encouraged to leave the body during the *tangi*. However, for the members of the *Maramatanga*, some *wairua* do return. They are not seen as disruptive, but provide advice and prophecy for kin. Nevertheless, that the *wairua* is intended to be put to rest, and yet is still, at least at times, welcomed, suggests that there is some ambivalence toward death and toward those who have died. These beliefs are specific, but not limited to the *Maramatanga* and Ngati Rangi. The body must also be moved from the deathbed and prepared to lie in state. The corpse will finally be buried in a cemetery.

When a death takes place, the immediate family must make many pressing and thorny decisions about issues that may not be easily resolved. Where will the *tangi* take place? Which kin group will act as hosts? Which *marae* will be readied? And, not least, which cemetery shall serve as the final resting place? As Māori kinship and loyalties are defined and claimed by multiple cognatic subtribes (*hapu*), the location of visitation and burial can be contentious: several kin groups may compete both for the privilege of having the body lie in state on their *marae* and for the final site of interment. Most often, these issues do get settled. But, in rare cases, should a dispute fail to be resolved, the corpse may be disinterred, often secretly (see Carucci, this volume and Bell, this volume). Elders, who are especially known for genealogical expertise, frequently approve reburial. Such disputes show that the identity of the deceased is a question, not just for the immediate family but for the descent group as a whole. This contention also demonstrates that mortuary rituals may provide venues for intense dialogue.

Several hundred people may gather following a death. The *marae* must be readied. Sleeping arrangements, mattresses, and bedding have to be prepared, marquees and tents need to be ordered and assembled, adequate food and utensils must be on hand, and staff for the *marae* kitchen and the burial must be recruited. In the case of a large *tangi* at which important Māori and *Pakeha* dignitaries will gather, the New Zealand army may be called in to erect extra tents, install portable toilets and attend to the demands of an unusually large crowd of mourners. Usually, however, local women and men of all ages will work together cooking. The exception to this, as stated above, is preparing the final feast in the earth oven, which is the sole prerogative of men.

In the midst of all the hosts' preparations, the *wairua* spirit is urged on its way. Songs that are sung and prayers (*karakia*) that are said come from both the Catholic liturgy and the *Maramatanga* movement and combine in discreet but nevertheless public ways during the *tangi* to express distinct but overlapping meanings of *wairua* and "soul." As the *tangi* unfolds, in other words, opportunities abound for the expression of voices whose cultural and personal understandings of the ritual diverge but do so dialogically.

Pani and the "World of Sorrow"

Usually older women offer chants (*powhiri*) to greet guests who have come to pay their respects to the deceased and the family. After the women chant, visiting men may feel compelled to call out a final and public farewell to the deceased. Host women, standing in front of the meeting house, and their male guests, coming forward onto the *marae,* chant simultaneously. This combination of salutation and grief departs from welcome rites among other tribes throughout the country, in which women chant and guests then take seats on the *paepae* (a bench designated for visitors). Those speaking from and for the host community either take turns and speak sequentially, after which visitors reply, or hosts and guests may alternate, one at a time. But, whichever sequence is followed, the first male voice heard is that of a host orator who gives a welcoming speech (*whaikorero*) to the visiting mourners (Tauroa and Tauroa 1986; Salmond 1976). The men generally have come to an off-stage agreement beforehand, so that each side will make an equal number of speeches. Whether one side completes its speeches, which are then followed by others or oratories are delivered in an alternating pattern, is determined by the etiquette of the particular *marae* on which the speeches are delivered.

When Ngāti Rangi women welcome mourners, they sing a specific chant called *waiata tangi*, which is a kind of a dirge that arouses sentiments of grief. Nostalgic images in the lyrics, of setting suns and expected meetings with the deceased in the afterlife, provoke a somber and wistful mood (see Lipset, this volume).

More often than not, the women weep as the visitors make their way to the deceased, whose body has been laid out in a special tent pitched on the porch of the meetinghouse where it is surrounded by photographs of ancestors and floral bouquets that give off overwhelming scents. There, as newly arrived mourners weep, often profusely, grieving *pani* women, dressed in unrelenting black, their heads decorated with leafy wreaths, envelop the deceased's coffin. The force of the whole moment, drawing as it does upon so many senses at once, is very powerful.

Visitors continue to arrive up until the day of burial itself. However, arrival while the body is laid out is considered a more intimate, and more correct, time to pay respects. If work schedules do not permit sufficient time off, visitors will try to attend the *tangi* while the family is gathered but before burial has taken place. Failing that, although less than ideal, an appearance during the burial itself is considered acceptable. When kin arrive, a member of the mourner's family will arrange their formal entrance onto the *marae*. Reference will then be made to their relationships in both *powhiri* chants and *whaikorero* speeches. The formality and attention to etiquette, for visiting mourners and those grieving at home, sustain what has been threatened by loss. Indeed, this is the expressed reason why Māori value visiting the deceased and his or her family so highly and why attendance, if possible, before the burial shows the most respect.

In the Whanganui region, the *pani* women, many of whom are elderly, maintain a vigil over the body. They sleep with the deceased and with the immediate family and observe several taboos. One of the most important of these forbids eating with family or guests. The *pani* women are required to exit through a back flap of the tent and make their way to dine together in a private residence set aside for their exclusive use during the tangi rite. Commensality, otherwise a central Māori value and mark of moral personhood, is denied them because the space and time they occupy is defiled. In good Hertzian fashion, death is regarded as polluting and dangerous (see Introduction, this volume). The proximity of the *pani* to the corpse requires that they keep their distance from the living, although over the years pollution fears have diminished (see Lipset, this volume). In the nineteenth century, *pani* women were not allowed to handle food and had to be fed by others. Today they may feed themselves. Similarly, they were not permitted to bathe until the *tangi* rites were completed. This too is no longer the case. However, all who enter the tent, who have been contaminated by death, must wash their hands as they leave.

The Night before the Burial

The night before the burial has special significance for Ngati Rangi as well as for the members of the *Maramatanga*. While most Māori groups close the coffin before its removal to a church and its subsequent interment, Ngati Rangi secure the coffin at midnight.[2] Midnight closure of the coffin allows the closest kin final time with the deceased that is free of distractions.

As midnight approaches, *pani* women, family members, and extended kin working in the kitchen assemble. A context ensues that relies heavily on dialogical ambiguity. The priests who may be present offer prayers for the soul. Inevitably, Ngati Rangi orators will now allude to the *wairua* of the deceased. The priests may not understand precisely what is being conveyed, or perhaps they prefer to avoid overt conflict in a delicate and painful situation. Yet their presence suggests their sympathy with the basic tenets of the *Maramatanga* Movement. The somberness of the speeches, the presence of the *pani* women dressed in black and adorned in mourning wreaths, leave no doubt that a culminating phase of the ritual has come to pass. If the assembly has become very large, the scene may be shifted to a space that can accommodate everybody. If it is winter, heat and light will be provided.

Closing the casket is held to mark the departure of the *wairua* spirit of the deceased and effects a transformation of moral space. The *wairua* now joins other spirits in the afterlife and the "house of darkness" has begun its change into a "house of light." Members of the *Maramatanga* believe that the *wairua* spirit will continue to visit the living. But, they still regard the *tangi* as crucial to put the *wairua* spirit to rest with no outstanding conflicts in the community. Clearly, many clergy are aware of these expectations and perhaps they reconcile them with characteristic Catholic beliefs in saints.

Attention moves from corpse to mourners, who begin the journey from darkness to light, from sorrow to life in the moral community. The collective effervescence surrounding the corpse has ended; and the *wairua* should now join the ancestors. A once living member has been lost to society, but the group must be reconstructed. Expressions of gratitude are offered that reflect these transitions. Family and visitors thank the body for having provided the gift of life to the deceased. They also acknowledge the *wairua* spirit for joining the ancestors. The assembled mourners now officially recognize the *pani* women for facilitating this transition by safeguarding important ritual boundaries. Now, only they are left in the "world of sorrow" and they will not sleep until the burial is completed and a final feast is held.

Burial Day

The time remains "dark," but the overall mood lightens up considerably once the coffin is sealed. Several things must now take place. A lavish post-burial feast must be prepared. Abundant amounts of food will have to be set out on double-layered tables. A church service, while the mourners and *pani* women still surround the coffin, is held. Telegrams, emails, and letters from relations and friends will be read out. In preparation for the burial, genealogy is once again chanted by orators specifically trained in the knowledge of descent lines. They are accompanied by women who chant and keep the beat with flax *poi*. Many transitions have begun, but relationships are far from severed. Giving voice to complicated cognatic kinship ties, they once again proclaim that the deceased, now enclosed in a coffin, nevertheless remains connected to several descent groups that shared his or her identity while alive. In this manner, the continuity of kinship in the face of the death of the "social body" is reasserted, a continuity that interment does not rupture. In good van Gennepian fashion, the deceased's status as an emergent ancestor begins to become evident. Indeed, once the burial is completed, a photo, painting, or some other visual image of the deceased will be placed in the meeting house, a space reserved solely for the deceased members of the descent group.

Gravediggers, recruited from strong, young kinsmen of the deceased, are dispatched to the cemetery, where they remain until the burial work is complete and the mourners have left. For large *tangi*, when many busloads come and leave the graveyard, this can mean that gravediggers do not return until well after dark, whatever the season. Having dug the grave, the youth must cover the coffin with dirt and ritually stamp it down with their feet.

The burial involves youth whose inadequate knowledge of tradition otherwise prevents them from speaking or playing a role on the *marae*. This important and physically onerous ritual duty now emphasizes their inclusion in the mourning process. They are not dismissed as nothing more than muscle-bound young people mindlessly helping their elders. On the contrary, their role as gravediggers is considered to be an important precursor to their future involvement in all aspects of *marae* ritual.

A Catholic Mass, held in the funeral tent on the *marae*, is the final event before burial. Because tents may not be large enough, it may broadcast across the entire *marae* by a sound system. Congregants and clergy may interpret the Mass differently, a dialogical process which we have been tracking in this chapter. For example, members of the *Maramatanga* understand the *wairua* to be a tutelary spirit who can appear in dreams, and move back and forth between the living and the ancestors. Most Catholic priests, by contrast, equate the *wairua* with the soul, the presumptive essence required for immortal union with the divine in eternal life, but one that is not necessarily connected with living persons and ongoing events in daily life. The Mass is nevertheless conducted in a comfortable tone; neither side feels the need to correct the other.

Many families in the Whanganui region own private cemeteries. Wreaths and floral arrangements from the tent are taken there. If there are busloads of people to be shuttled back and forth from the *marae* to the cemetary, the graveside service will be kept brief. The closest kin and friends of the deceased will put flowers or some personal valuable in the grave or on top of the coffin.

The gravediggers remain present, but off-stage. They go to work as soon as the mourners and visitors return to the *marae*. Once the burial is completed and the ground has been stamped down, ritual services for the body are considered finished. Having been interred, the living person is now "dead."

Visitors and relations leave the cemetery to return to the *marae*, where the *hakari* feast awaits them. This is a van Gennepian rite of re-incorporation (see Introduction, this volume) during which mourners, both *pani* women and kinsmen, otherwise separated for days from others, now rejoin the guests and the newly reconstituted moral community, as local singers and dancers entertain everyone. The hosts, however, while joining in the pleasure of the celebrations, do not eat with the mourners and the guests. Further ritual work, and status transitions, remain to be done.

Status Readjustments and Cleansing the House

Women offer *powhiri* chants to call everyone to the feast. There are visible and overt signs that visitors, former mourners, and kinsmen have now returned to the "world of light and life" and have left the world of "death and sorrow." What are these signs? The tent, housing the corpse, has been dismantled. The *pani* women, having washed and changed clothes, make their first public appearance since the death was announced. This is not only a return to "a world of light" but a ritual reversal. The women, who have only eaten food prepared for them by the cooks, now feed the cooks, who are the last to eat. Thus, the *pani* women, who now nurture those who have nurtured them, exemplify that moral exchange continues to be a major value of the *tangi*. Relations between mourners and workers, hosts and guests, living and dead, have all been built on ideals of mutual sympathy and reciprocity, ideals, in other words, of moral community.

After guests leave, those who remain, close and intimate kin, congregate that night in the meetinghouse on the *marae*. There, the costs of the *tangi* are reconciled with the *koha* gifts, which are monetary, or locally available food from different regions, contributions made to the host's *marae* to facilitate hosting a major ritual. *Koha* money is placed (in a discreet envelop assembled beforehand) in front of the edifice chosen by the donors. e.g. money placed in front of the dining room is used to defray the costs of feeding the people during the *tangi* and for the *hakari* after. This final accounting, particularly of the *koha* gifts, is important because when the host family attends the next *tangi*, they will be expected to give more *koha* than their *marae* has now received.

In general, a few, sympathetic Catholic priests may attend this meeting. They recite prayers for the family and open up the occasion to a more wide-ranging discussion during which both men and women may stand and address the group. Unlike the public quality of speeches made during the *tangi*, a personal mood now prevails. Tensions are aired and examined; to the extent possible, these are expected to be reduced by the experience of shared grief and good will. The long days of intense public scrutiny will ideally yield to a renewal of moral community and kinship relations.

If the deceased was a man, the future of his widow will be decided by his family at this time. So long as her husband has been buried among his kin on their land, her affines will declare her free to remarry. They have no further claims on her and do not expect her to fulfill any other obligations to them. They lift her widow's veil, to signify her release from their jural control. The situation differs when a woman dies. Should she have been buried on her husband's land, elders in the husband's kin group will advise against remarriage, for as they maintain, her permanent interment on his land has withheld her from her kin group and its land. These issues, involving kinship, marriage, and jural claims are, if not sacred, out of the ordinary. Discussion of the future status of the widow or the widower explores very basic claims upon their *post mortem* relationship to society at large.

One effect of the death in the community remains unsettled. The deceased's house must be made "safe" once again. As we have indicated, death is viewed as both dangerous and impure (see Salmond, 1976; Ortner 1981; and Hanson and Hanson 1983). Symptoms of pollution are evident in restrictions imposed on the *pani* women. A blessing, performed by a specialist, is now offered to reverse the moral status—or cleanse—the house of the deceased and thereby make it once again habitable by the immediate family of the deceased. Through prayers and chants known only to a select few, the house is transformed and brought back into the "world of light."

A few remaining taboos do continue for approximately one year after burial. During this time, the closest kin of the deceased continue to bear the burden of death. Women wear black. People recognize and greet them as "survivors." They remain apart until a headstone is erected and unveiled—at which point the ritual process that began at death finally ends. The erection of a headstone is seen as analogous to a Hertzian secondary burial (see the Introduction, this volume). The deceased has become an ancestor, its *wairua* spirit may or may not return, and his or her kin return to their place in the moral community (cf. Silverman, this volume).

Conclusion—Partial Understandings and Partial Victories

Needless to say, Māori have buried their dead for hundreds of years (Davidson 1984). Obviously, there are political advantages to suggest that Māori mortuary rituals have sustained the culture across the contingencies of time. However, all aspects of the ritual have changed, particularly since the arrival of missionary

Christianity, the teachings of the nineteenth-century prophets, and the movement of Māori, first to urban areas in the post-World War II era and more recently, to Australia. But, despite these pressures, *tangi* remain a misunderstood, if variously interpreted, institution, a point of misapprehension, but also one of dialogue, between Māori and *Pakeha*, between youth and elders and between the clergy and the Māori laity. Māori view the changing circumstances as opportunities for creativity, while those who view *tangi* as an obstruction to progress, not to mention, an inauthentic cultural form, argue that it ought to be given up (cf. Sissons 2010). Such voices are generally those of government or *Pakeha* officials, who react unfavorably to assertions of Māori sovereignty.

In this chapter, we have argued that specific Ngāti Rangi customs, their prophetic tradition, and their Catholicism have shaped the relationship of *tangi* rites to contemporary society. Māori mortuary ritual, that is to say, cannot be understood ahistorically. It is a human construct that results from voices in dialogue, a dialogue in which Māori social and political voices persist if not in unalloyed form, at least in a significantly contemporary expression.

Since Captain Cook and the Europeans arrived in the eighteenth century, the ritual work of moving the living to the afterlife has been important in Māori life. Contemporary Ngāti Rangi ritual leaders now master new tasks and assume new responsibilities. But the transformation from the living to the dead still resides with women. Why is the ritual work of women so critical? Do not men, who speak to the dead, bid them on their way, and prepare the major feast for guests, make an equally valuable contribution to the mortuary process? The answer, we argue, is that they do not.

Mythology that speaks of goddesses of dawn and dusk render womanhood as an ambivalent, ambiguous duality. Women are positioned on the margins and their power derives from their liminal position. *Pani* women, who safeguard the physical and cultural boundaries between life and death, have been likened to mythic changelings or quislings as a result. Yet it is precisely their interstitial position that makes women guardians of the dead and equips them to cope with the movement between the distinct realms. That older women guard the corpse as the *mauri* spirits quit the body is fitting. Women serve as guardians of socio-moral margins and borders; they alone may move between the worlds of light and sorrow (see also Ortner 1974).

In addition, twenty-first-century globalization, cable TV and migration are ushering in new possibilities of modernity that challenge both cultural conviction and Māori autonomy. As New Zealand/Aotearoa has defined itself as bicultural, and as the mortuary rites of prominent individuals are viewed on television news (e.g., the *tangi* of the Māori Queen, Dame Te Atairangi Kaahu), members of the *Pakeha* audience are left, whether warranted or not, feeling informed. As the feminist philosopher, Uma Narayan has argued, it "is not acceptable to make 'foreign phenomenon' seem comfortingly intelligible while preserving their foreignness" (1997: 104). And yet *tangi*, now so widely accessible, are subject to just this kind of homogenizing gaze, one that simultaneously expresses difference and alienness.

Partial understandings yield partial victories for both *Pakeha* and Māori: *Pakeha* can champion the significance of *tangi*, whatever their (mis)understanding of the ritual may be, and remain firm in their view that New Zealand/Aotearoa is a moral, bicultural, bilingual society. On the other hand, Māori can assert, despite enduring centuries of colonialism and transition, that they have maintained the proper, indeed the only, way to put the dead to rest.

Che Wilson attended Victoria University of Wellington, where he is a member of the Institute of Directors. He serves on the Māori Kings Council as well as on the boards of several trusts and philanthropies. He is coauthor of *Te Ara Tapu*, a book about the Māori Collective at the Whanganui Regional Museum. Most recently, he has served as the chief executive of his tribe, the Ngāti Rangi, and as the lead negotiator for the Ngai Tahu tribe with the New Zealand/Aotearoa government.

Karen Sinclair is Professor Emerita of Anthropology at Eastern Michigan University, where she was a faculty member from 1974 to 2011. She has worked with Ngāti Rangi since 1972, testifying before the Waitangi Tribunal in 2009. She has published many articles on colonialism, religion, and gender. She has also published *Prophetic Histories,* which appeared in the United States under the title *Māori Times, Māori Places.*

Notes

1. As the *marae* was and still is a stage for hospitality, cohesion, and transition (of the mourners and the deceased), the movement of *tangi* into houses may reduce their scale and their significance. Urbanization has led to the creation of new ritual forms in New Zealand cities (see Rosenblatt 2011), and the same will in all likelihood occur in Australia. *Tangi*, in some form, can be expected to be held as families gather in their Australian houses.
2. The closing of the coffin at midnight is, so far as we know, a ritual observed solely by Ngati Rangi. It has certainly been observed for the years that we have been attending *tangi*.

References Cited

Bloch, Marc and Jonathan Parry eds. 1982. *Death and the Regeneration of Life.* Cambridge: Cambridge University Press.

Collins, Stephen. 2011. "18 Per cent of Māori Now Live Overseas." *New Zealand Herald.* November 29.

Davidson, Janet. 1984. *The Prehistory of New Zealand*. Auckland: Longman Paul Limited.
Elsmore, Bronwyn. 2004 [1999]. *Mana from Heaven*. New Zealand: Reed Publishing.
Hanson, Alan and Louise Hanson. 1982. *Counterpoint in Māori Culture*. London: Routledge.
Hertz, Robert. 1960. "A Contribution to the Study of the Collective Representation of Death." In *Death and the Right Hand*, edited by Rodney Needham, 27–86. Glencoe: Free Press.
Heuer, Berys. 1969. "Māori Women in Traditional Family and Tribal Life." *Journal of the Polynesian Society* 78: 448–94.
Howard, Alan. 1990. "Cultural paradigms, History, and the Search for Identity in Oceania." In *Cultural Identity and Ethnicity in the Pacific*, edited by Jocelyn Linnekin and Lin Poyer, 259–80. Honolulu: University of Hawaii Press.
Ihimaera, Witi. 1973. *Tangi*. Auckland: Heinemann.
Metcalf, Peter and Richard Huntington. 1991. *Celebrations of Death: The Anthropology of Mortuary Ritual*. Cambridge: Cambridge University Press.
Metge, Joan. 1969. *The Maoris of New Zealand*. London: Routledge & Kegan Paul.
Narayan, Uma. 1997. *Dislocating Cultures*. London: Routledge.
New Zealand Census. "2006–2013 Census Data." Statistics New Zealand.
O'Regan, Stephen. 1994. "Māori Control of the Māori Heritage." In *The Politics of the Past*, edited by Peter Gathercole and David Lowenthal, 95–106. New York: Routledge.
Ortner, Sherry. 1974. "Is Female to Male as Nature to Culture?" In *Woman, Culture, and Society*, edited by M.Z. Rosaldo and L. Lamphere, 68–87. Stanford: Stanford University Press.
———. 1981. "Gender and Sexuality in Hierarchical Societies: the case of Polynesian and Some Comparative Implications." In *Sexual Meanings: The Cultural Construction of Gender and Sexuality*, edited by Sherry Ortner and Harriet Whitehead, 359–411. Cambridge: Cambridge University Press.
Povinelli, Elizabeth. 2002. *The Cunning of Recognition: Indigenous Alterities and the Making of Australian Multiculturalism*. Durham: Duke University Press.
Rosenblatt, Daniel. 2011. "Indigenizing the City and the Future of the Māori Culture." *American Ethnologist* 38: 411–29.
Salmond, Anne. 1976. *Hui*. Auckland: Penguin.
Sinclair, Karen. 1990. "Tangi: Funeral Rituals and the Construction of Māori Identity." In *Cultural Identity and Ethnicity in the Pacific*, edited by Jocelyn Linnekin and Lin Poyer, 229–36. Honolulu: University of Hawaii Press.
———. 2002. *Prophetic Histories*. Wellington: Bridget Williams Publishing.
Sissons, Jeffrey. 1998. "The Traditionalisation of the Māori Meeting House." *Oceania*: 69, 36–46.
———. 2000. "The Post-assimilationist Thought of Sir Apirana Ngata: Towards a Genealogy of New Zealand Biculturalism." *The New Zealand Journal of History* 34: 47–59.
———. 2005. *First Peoples*. London: Reaktion Books.
———. 2010. "Building a House Society: The Reorganization of Māori Communities around Meeting Houses." *Journal of the Royal Anthropological Institute* 16: 372–86.
Tahana, Yvonne. 2012. "Demise of Tangi: A Threat to Culture." *New Zealand Herald*. June 9.
Tauroa, Hiwi and Pat Tauroa. 1986. *Te Marae: A Guide to Customs and Protocol*. Auckland: Reed, Methuen.
Van Gennep, Arnold. 1969 [1908]. *Rites of Passage*. Translated by Monika B. Vizedom and Gabrielle L. Caffee. Chicago: University of Chicago Press.

3
Death and Experience in Rawa Mortuary Rites, Papua New Guinea

DOUG DALTON

Introduction

In this chapter, I employ an inductive, experience-near approach to the study of death in Rawa society in Papua New Guinea in order to turn Hertz' (1960) celebrated thesis on its head. I show that Rawa mortuary rites, rather than being a means to restore a threatened moral order by making deceased relatives into sociologically relevant ancestors, are themselves part of a common and constant element of village life that involves the experience of the physical disintegration of the body. This experience entails and constitutes the foundation of social life, as it fosters an understanding of the embodied, existential neediness of human beings. This neediness is the basis of reciprocal exchange, giving, and the symbolic "elicitation" of embodied capacities to entice people to give gifts, marry, and pass on their lives to others, which Wagner (1981, 1986a, 1986b) and Strathern (1988) find are fundamental to Melanesian cultures.

In Hertz's L'Année sociologique view, the dead threaten the social order, and their ritual initiation into the afterlife as ancestors is its guarantee. But instead of being made into ancestors, the disposition of deceased Rawa spirits is variable and uncertain, and mortuary rites, rather, become part of a dialogue in which existential neediness, social pathology, and reciprocal altruism find their full expression and moral community is continually refashioned. Rather than death being the disruption of a reified social ideal, the moral community is constituted through the reciprocal take and give that is predicated on embodied neediness, the most poignant instantiation of which is found at death. Rawa society can be said to be predicated on death instead of being imperiled by it.

This chapter begins with a narrative of a death and ensuing mortuary rites among the Rawa people who live in the southern Finisterre mountains in Papua New Guinea.[1] The narrative is meant to introduce several significant themes in these rites, such as experiencing the corporeality of death, individual and social historical conflict, notions of "watching" and "death," and Rawa and Christian concepts of spirits and personhood, which show much variety and uncertainty. I then discuss significant changes in Rawa mortuary practices from prehistoric to modern times, when contemporary Rawa villagers integrate indigenous notions of and values associated with the person into Christian burial practices that both recollect pre-Christian notions of death and dying and assert local power in the context of their dialogue with globalizing forces.

After Lutheran missionaries had villagers remove the remains of deceased relatives from their houses and bury people in a graveyard, thus effecting the Western separation of death and life and "denial of death" that underlies Hertz' understanding, village residents nevertheless symbolized their embodied understanding of moral community wherein life is predicated on death by putting inverted bowls on the crosses that marked individual gravesites. More recent innovations show a further dialogic engagement with Western modernity (Silverman and Lipset, Introduction). The analysis suggests that the L'Année sociologique sociology of death should be rethought in relation to local, experience-near understandings across historical circumstances (see Carucci, this volume and Wilson and Sinclair, this volume) and that the efficacy of death rites and their separation from or opposition to moral life should be questioned.

A Death in the Southern Finisterres

Since the creation of nucleated villages in the 1930s, Rawa houses have been built along extensions of footpaths connecting villages that are typically about an hour's walk from one another, sometimes somewhat more. Most houses have two rooms: one in front, which is somewhat more public, and another in back, where any wealth or possessions a family might want to keep out of view are stored in a suitcase or two. Guests do not usually enter the latter space. Social life is nothing if not flexible, however. And both rooms may be used for large gatherings, when events warrant it. Indeed, anyone may enter a house unannounced so long as someone is home. However, it is a good idea to make some noise on the way to the door to avoid surprising the inhabitants. Doors are often left open so that dwellers know what is going on outside and their presence at home is known.

One morning, I entered Jared's home to listen to some stories, as I often did. On this particular occasion, I found his daughter-in-law in the back room nursing a baby and looking after her husband's dying grandfather, Jared's father.[2] He had walked there from the family's bush house recently—in order to die. This move was in some respects a political act because his kin "line" had not fared well during the colonial era, regional wars and process of village consolidation that took place in the early 1930s; dying in the village would assert his aggrieved presence in a moral community by which he felt marginalized. In other words, it was meant as a comment on the position of his family in the local political setting that was being debated in the mortuary dialogue his death would provoke.

This was my first meeting with him and his grandson's wife, who rarely stayed in the village. He managed to raise himself off of the thin cloth "bed" laid upon the bamboo floor of the house and offer me food. I declined and conversed briefly with him and his "daughter" about his illness, which was very nonspecific, mostly to express concern and sorrow and exchange niceties before he went back to sleep. A little while later, as I spoke with his "daughter," he sat up again, uncovered himself, pushed aside the woven bamboo flooring that had been cut and loosened for him, moved his bowels, and lay down again. His daughter leaned over, raised the floor slightly, looked below at the shit he had deposited on the ground, and offered but one word, "blood" (*situ*).

Jared's father had not been a happy man. As with many others, his kinsmen's lives were disrupted in the early 1900s with the appearance of warriors from over the crest of the Finisterre mountains to the north. They in turn had been displaced by punitive raids of German and Australian colonial authorities in cooperation with traditional enemies from the Maclay or Rai Coast. When villages were established, with encouragement from the Australian mandate administration and early missionaries, he and his family lost local prominence and power to the Rai Coast warriors. His kin scattered among several villages, in some cases marrying first "cousins," rather than more distantly related classificatory "cousins," that is, marrying much more closely than usual indicated a relative isolation from modern life.

In those days, men used to make a potent beverage from the methylated spirits that were used to light kerosene lanterns and stoves. They would drink, talk, laugh, and fight. Jared's father used to get violent and threatened people with sorcery that, it was thought by some, he had tried to practice. It is possible that drinking this alcohol gave him ulcers because some of the men who did so told me it was very hard on the stomach. This could be why he was experiencing ulcerations in his bowels as his body was shutting down. Perhaps it was more directly the cause of his death, in addition to his general despondency.

A few days later, he died. A great number of relatives came, along with many others, who wished to participate in his mortuary rite. There was intense interest in his passing, not so much because he was a prominent man in the village but because he might have been and on account of the rumors and suspicions of sorcery associated with his life. While I sat on the grass outside Jared's house, some men who came to attend the event from a distance reviled him as a "man no-good" (*oni piyomi*). Female kin arrived, entered the house, and viewed the body. They sent up a loud, piercing, magnified wail interspersed with barely discernable phrases, some of which were vaguely accusatory (e.g., "How did you die?"). Then, they settled down and wept gently, until shifting back to more pleasant conversation with nearby relatives.

Rawa mortuary rites feature the display of violent emotions. The people themselves describe and designate funerals with the verb "to watch" (Tokpisin *was*; Rawa *meyero*), the implied object of their spectatorship being the body or corpse of the deceased. In this phase of the rite, an assembly sits in the house of the deceased with the body all night. The Rawa verb *meyero*, "to watch," denotes an intense kind of viewing, a kind of meditative state of careful, mindful attention, more than is suggested by the more common and simple act of "looking" or "seeing" (*kenoro*). *Meyoro* is what one does hidden behind a screen built to shoot birds or other game.

In mortuary rites, the viewers are watching to discern signs of life from the corpse, to make out something of the disposition of the spirit, and possibly to identify a signal that could be used to divine sorcery. Since the Rawa villagers converted to Christianity and created villages, "watching" the corpse is far less likely to end in a violent raid to kill the sorcerer suspected of causing the death, as was common a generation ago: such raids indeed are unheard of anymore, for they were ended during the period in the early 1930s, when the villagers adopted Christianity. But debates and speeches, or mortuary dialogue, about sorcery and threats, mystical or otherwise, remain part of many funerals.

After a night spent watching the body, a communal meal is often held the following morning. No one eats during the night, although plenty of tobacco and betel nuts are consumed. One of the guests might buy food from a trade store and ensure that it gets cooked and that everyone there is fed: this meal helps relieve any misgivings and concerns among the guests attending what becomes a kind of a "wake." Speeches may now be made but often there are few or none. Christian evangelists dampen sorcery suspicious with "talk about God": the idea of an all-powerful God who decides peoples' fates and takes "the soul" to the afterlife holds sway in public discourse and is effective in combating any discussion of sorcery. Their voices were notably absent during the mortuary wake for Jared's father.

Even people who were dissatisfied with my presence in the village publically said how admirable it was that I had spent so much time helping people do the "work" (*ko*) of "watching" corpses of deceased villagers.[3] People help "watching" the corpse to lend support to the family but also not to be accused of being sorcerers or being themselves in any way guilty of causing the death. In the time of "the ancestors," that is, in the early decades of the 1900s, to "watch" the body meant to look for a bit of necrotic effluent in relation to a particular person present or named or to see if the body might unexpectedly move or otherwise indicate who took its life.

I sat in the back room of Jared's large house with a great many others—mostly men. They spent the night playing cards, talking, and joking with one another. Rawa funerals are not as somber as their Western counterparts: laughter and casual conversation are not uncommon, but perhaps the loudness and tenor of this particular funeral exceeded the norm. In the front room of the house, close kin were rather more staid and perhaps became somewhat bothered by the relative lack of solemnity shown by the men in the back of the house.

Jared sat on one side of his father's corpse holding and rubbing his father's arm and chest, and his wife—Jared's mother—sat on the other. I had a clear view of them though the doorway connecting the two rooms. At one point in the wee hours of the morning, I glanced at the body and clearly saw Jared's father's corpse open his eyes, look around the room, including through the doorway at me, and close them again (see Lipset, this volume). I was certainly surprised if not somewhat shocked by what I saw. I can only suppose that he was not yet dead, although everyone thought that he was, and that the process of death is less definitive and certain than generally supposed.

I wondered if anyone else had noticed it and thought perhaps that Rawa people might have a different idea about defining death than do Westerners. Linguistically, like many Melanesians, Rawa speakers do not distinguish clearly between lying immobile from illness, sleeping, dreaming, and dying. The Rawa verb *kumoro* includes both prostration from illness and death. In order to indicate that someone has died, one has to add something like the declarative *kini tewo*, "completely gone."[4] And, as with so many people EB Tylor (1889) once dubbed "animists," Rawa speakers suppose that some sort of dreaming-body awareness leaves its corporeal self while sleeping and has experiences in an alternate reality.

When a person is completely dead and a funeral ceremony and burial is all said and done, she or he may also be described as *oni-pi*, which means something like "man finished" or "completed," as when one completes counting a numerical set ending with the number "twenty." The Rawa counting system consists of a recursive analogy with the body enumerating the digits of the hands and feet; when one reaches the number twenty, however, one simply says *onipika*, which can be translated as literally "man-dead-one."

When Western doctors and relatives of a dying person observe a patient to assess her or his state of "life," they look to see if the body evidences any sort of responsiveness to or recognition of itself.[5] In a similar manner, but for different ends, when Rawa people "watch" a dead body, they look for signs or "pictures" (*kapokapoyi*) indicating the possible identity of a sorcerer or for any physical movement that might indicate something about the disposition of the spirit and simply to see if the corpse might just get up again. Defining the moment of death in the West is predicated upon an assumption that a relatively clear line between life and death exists. This makes little sense to the Rawa people I knew (see Introduction, this volume).

I decided to ask as discretely as possible after the funeral was over about Rawa notions of death. In the course of my inquiry, I let it be known that the corpse of Jared's father had looked at me. The story spread around the village quickly and after a few days my adoptive "mother" finally told me at a public gathering that the "spirit had followed me" (Tok Pisin *dewel behainim yu*). This is what a spirit would typically do to the sorcerer responsible for its death, but was I not a pretty benign character? What was more, I had little relation to the deceased and was a particularly good friend of Jared, so the observation remained a curiosity, one that did leave open the possibility that I was deceptive and was perhaps up to something in the supernatural realm. The implication was that the spirit of Jared's father had attached itself to me in some way, which might be positive or negative but nevertheless smacked of magical manipulation (see Bell, this volume).

Jared later admitted to me that he also felt his father's body flush in the middle of the night around the same time that I saw him open his eyes. In his mind, his father's animation indicated that something semimystical and nefarious was going on. The fact that we both saw or felt life in his father's corpse seemed to put us on the same side of interpreting his father's death. I took Jared to understand that his father's vitality was related to the residual antagonism of village leadership against him: they had secured their positions in competition with his father and his "line" of kin and he supposed that we both recognized it. The revival of the corpse may also have been partly in response to the relative rowdiness of the men I was sitting with in the back room.

Of all the deaths I joined in "watching," this was the one in which I was most directly and closely involved (or, one might say, implicated). The death of Jared's father illustrates several points. One is that funeral rites do not necessarily resolve things or put them to rest and may do as much to instigate conflict as resolve it, as Counts and Counts (2004) show in a Kaliai example (see also Kaufman and Morgan 2005: 329–30; see Silverman, this volume).

As Silverman and Lipset argue in the Introduction, anthropological theories of mortuary rites have tended to stress how they redress and repair the moral crisis that death creates.[6] But for Rawa speakers, the line between life and death is not so easily drawn, and mortuary rites, though they no longer degrade into vengeance raids, often provoke dialogue that expresses and amplifies local-level antagonism. Yet, as always happens in postpacification Christian-influenced Rawa mortuary rites, Jared's father was buried in a collective graveyard outside the village that separated him from his family, a location that supposedly induced him to find repose. In pre-Christian times, the corpse would have been placed under a mat of banana leaves in a hole dug under the floor of the house so it could continue to be inspected. Dried bones would eventually be collected and hung on the wall in a net bag, where they would become the subject of all sorts of offerings, divination procedures, and observances (see von Poser, this volume).

Rawa Experiences of Death

Like Jared's father, Rawa people typically die at home surrounded by close relatives and they encounter the process of death directly and frequently. Children grow up seeing dying and death in their homes and for adults, it is part of family life. They thus confront the gross physical disintegration of the person. Regardless of the changes in Rawa mortuary practices attendant upon Christian conversion and modernity, the experience of dying remains central in local understandings of death. Many Rawa emphasized this to me.

I myself have seen three people die. One of them was Jared's father. Another was my father-in-law, after his family had his life support removed when it became clear that he could not possibly recover from lung cancer. The third person was my grandmother, who passed away in a nursing home. These are rare and atypical experiences for most Americans and Europeans: in industrial-capitalist cultures with complex divisions of labor, people are usually too busy to spend much time with dying relatives; the management of death and dying is the province of a variety of healthcare professionals. With Rawa villagers, the experience of physical disintegration and end-of-life care is commonplace and, as I have suggested, "watching" a corpse to see the life pass from it is practically the core element of their mortuary rites.

A Rawa friend once told me that some people go peacefully while others sit up and grasp aimlessly with their arms in a violent and animated display at the moment of death. He was not sure of the significance of this contrast but, as a good Christian, he felt it had something to do with the moral-religious status of the person who died. I have never seen anyone die in the violent way he described. It may be that this kind of death is the result of emphysema, which is relatively common in Papua New Guinea due to widespread tobacco smoking and the inhalation of smoke from the open fires in households. I take my Rawa friend's observation to indicate how common it is for Rawa villagers to watch people die and, as was several times emphasized to me, how frightening the experience can be.

After one old woman died, her sons and a number of other young men told me very emphatically that taking care of terminally ill people is just like taking care of a baby. "The two ends of life are the same!" The dying must be spoon-fed softened food just as infants are and have to be wiped clean just like infants. I did not think much about these remarks at the time because it seemed perfectly obvious to me and not very culturally specific, but they were so ardent and reiterated it so many times that it stuck in my mind. I came to think that their insistence on this point reflected the horror of experiencing their mother's physical disintegration.

Another villager died in the national capital, Port Moresby. Even though great efforts were made to bring back his body and hold a mortuary rite as soon as possible, the corpse had already begun to putrefy and bloat by the time it reached the village (see Bell, this volume). I did not attend the funeral because I did not know the man or his brother very well. Afterward, several young men related to me how nearly impossible it was to stay in the same room with it and concluded that this disturbing kind of physical disintegration must be a sign of sorcery.

Another man I knew quite well apparently died of chronic filariasis, a tropical parasitic disease often transmitted by mosquito bites. In its chronic form it usually manifests in elephantiasis, the thickening and swelling of the skin, often, as in his case, of the genitals. His relatives attended him at home and his entire community, which had split off from the village where I resided, also interpreted his repulsive physical disintegration as a sure sign of sorcery; after he died, they rampaged through the village and destroyed the water supply pipes I had helped them obtain. Other people diagnosed the swelling of his genitalia as a sign of his sexual promiscuity: he had married two wives and was known to have had adulterous affairs.

Since Frazer (1933), anthropologists have postulated a universal fear or horror of death. There has been some debate regarding how much non-Western people fear death in comparison to Western European peoples, among whom, as Huntington and Metcalf (1979) point out, death and life have apparently been nearly entirely separated from one another and death has been made, in Ariès' (1981) term, "invisible" (cf. Becker 1973). Bloch and Parry (1982) indicate that the horror and pollution of death is emphasized in what Woodburn (1982) calls "delayed-return" societies and approvingly quote Hertz' statement that the "emotion aroused by death varies extremely in intensity according to the social status of the deceased, and may even in certain cases be lacking" (Bloch and Parry 1982: 14; Hertz 1960: 76; see Palgi and Abramovitch 1984: 390–92).[7]

This is certainly true of Rawa, who are a "delayed-return" culture. Less prominent and very young people generally have smaller and more sedate mortuary rites than do elders active in leadership and politics. Rawa infants who die have very small mortuary observances indeed. In addition, however, I also noticed that the strength of emotional expression is also directly related to the grotesqueness of the physical disintegration of the dying individual. Hertz' (1960) sociological thesis that mourning rites triumph over death by transforming deceased individuals into morally significant ancestors is certainly compelling (Venbrux 2007: 6–7). But what many Rawa people told me about the experience of death suggests that there is more to mourning than an elementary reflection of society. Their point, and their experience, I believe, is an existential one: the gross physicality of the corpse is related to their understanding of human personhood as irreducibly needy, which is critical for the reciprocal sharing and giving that is so much a part of living, as I explain below.

It is possible that Frazer's view that death evokes instinctive horror was a projection of Western attitudes, and anthropologists' emphasis on the sociological functioning of funeral rites has made us too inclined to ignore the ugliness of death. Fabian (1972, 1983) points out that anthropology has long been guilty of overemphasizing cultural difference and that, particularly with regard to dying, its studies have been of "how other's die," that is, at a safe distance from one's own experience and culture. Ariès similarly describes the twentieth-century European attitude toward death as "the death of the other" (1981: 407), which developed as death became so individuated that the traumatic experience of the few survivors within the nuclear family became the focus rather than the—what came to be sentimentalized, even romanticized—experience of the dying person. Western anthropologists have perhaps neglected the ways in which the existential spectacle of dying has been experienced, acknowledged, and sometimes commemorated in culture.

As Silverman and Lipset noted in their Introduction, Hertz associated the repulsive, gross decomposition of the body with the unsettled, homeless situation of the soul who is starting to make its way to the afterlife (1960: 32–37). He viewed death rites in a manner similar to van Gennep (1960) as the transformation from the living to the afterlife through a process of rebirth whereby dead relatives are turned into ancestors. This model applies well in an ideal sociological world, and Rawa-speaking people have a way of imagining such a transition. But in their view it is far from certain that the soul will indeed follow such a moral course, particularly in modern historical times. Among Rawa, uncertainty about the disposition of a dead relative is related to their concepts of the person.

Rawa Concepts of the Person

When my adoptive Rawa "mother" told me that the spirit of Jared's father had "followed" me, using the Tokpisin term for spirit, *dewel*, she was referring specifically, at least, to the "picture" or "shadow" soul. Rawa speakers recognize three human "souls" or "spirits." One of them translates as "shadow," "reflection," "dream," "picture," and "spirit" (*kapokapoyi*). When someone dies and gives a sign to her or his dead relatives or others, Rawa people speak of it as a "picture." Such a "picture" does not have to come from the deceased; however, it may be used to diagnose unhappiness between in-laws, as when bride-wealth does not add up correctly because a part of it has apparently gone missing, or loud unaccountable noises issue when a man breaks the taboo against calling the names of his wife's parents in their absence.

Well-disposed ancestors should send their relatives "pictures" to warn them against enemies and sorcerers and to help them find wayward pigs and lost objects. We might speak of *kapokapoyi*-spirit as an "image" or "spirit-double" because it includes shadows, reflections, and photos, all of which are figures given by corporeal embodiment. Dreams are similarly understood as projected images of the body, the insubstantial dreaming body, which departs the sleeping body to meet other such spirit entities in an alternate reality. When someone is sleeping deeply and dreaming it is often said that she or he "sleep dead finished" (Tokpisin: *slip indai pinis*; Rawa *wetero kapero*).

Rawa speakers also identify a second spirit, the "breath"-spirit (*yuka*), in the human body. This spirit enables a degree of autonomous physical existence; it animates an infant when it draws its first breath and departs a dying person with her or his last gasp. It may be good or bad, giving a person an affable or hostile disposition. Between the breath-spirit and the image-spirit, one might say, inside the body that the breath animates and that radiates images, Rawa people imagine that there is a fire, like the sun (*sa* or *okisa*). The term for this entity does not translate as "soul" or "spirit" but rather as "star" or "firefly," that is, as more common beings that are manifestations of this inner power.[8]

Before Christianity, it was apparently assumed that when a person died, if she or he had been initiated in an obscure, sacred rite that included having the nasal septum pierced, the spirit of the deceased would "go up" and become a star in the sky. A very great and magnanimous leader may still sometimes be thought to become a prominent star in the heavens after he or she dies (see Carucci, this volume). Fireflies were also thought to be benign ancestor-spirits visiting relatives. The stars are associated with the sun (*mata*), and the "eye of the sun" is the major emanation of the Rawa creator-spirit. If one had not undergone this initiation, however, one only became part of the jungle and garden landscape, perhaps becoming something like a "bush-spirit" after death.

In any case, an ancestor is generally thought to merge with the jungle and garden lands, whether or not she or he has "gone up." One old woman told her children before she died that when she passed away she would like to be buried along a particular path on the edge of the village so that she (or her spirit) could look after the comings and goings in this particular spot. In other words, it can be said that when a person dies, her or his consciousness, which might produce "pictures," merges with the dream spirit world in the landscape. Whereas the generosity of dead relatives whose spirits have become stars is without question, the ancestor-spirits who inhabit the landscape require more attentiveness by descendants, for their moral dispositions are uncertain.[9]

Taken together, these three spirits—"image," "breath," and "fire"—seem to suggest that Rawa personhood and embodiment is understood as a process in which air and food are burned to create mystical forces that are visible as apparitions and doubles. The disposition of the "soul" or "spirit" of the deceased is consequently far from simple. It is not at all clear what kind of an ancestor the person will become in the afterlife. Indeed, she or he might end up in some remote, unresolved, morally ambiguous state. This seems to have become all the more possible in modernity with its extraordinary pathos and antagonisms. Death is and was regarded as a cataclysmic event in which the moral loss of the person is difficult to recoup.

This is why Rawa people made great efforts to cultivate and maintain connections with deceased relatives by, in pre-Christian times, carefully and elaborately treating the remains of dead relatives and, more recently, by visiting the village graveyard to petition ancestors for succor and aid. Furthermore, even after the disintegration of the body, the bones remain for a long time, as do the "pictures" sent by the spirits of the deceased. The moral boundary between life and death, in other words, is not clearly drawn: the living and dead kin go on living together in the garden and jungle landscape as well as in "picture" and dream imageries. Indeed, before the coming of Christianity, people went to great lengths in the care they took of the corpse, for just this reason.

Sometime in the early 1930s, following the lead of a number of young men, including the village head where I did research, Rawa people reacted against the rampant violence, treachery, and sorcery that had ensued from their displacement by German colonists. They recruited a native Lutheran missionary into their midst and adopted a new religion. Among much else the missionaries had people change were their mortuary practices.

Changing Mortuary Practices

Before Christian missionaries arrived in the area, the north coast was awash with immigrants who were already influencing Rawa death and mourning practices. These earlier shifts arose from the prehistory of relationships between indigenous New Guinea cultures and the maritime Austronesian peoples who the German ethnologist Carl A. Schmitz distinguished in his comparative study of the Huon Peninsula (1960). In particular, his earliest pre-Austronesian, or "culture A," mixed with and was being replaced by a later pre-Austronesian "culture B" that was coming down from the northern slopes of the mountains.

I knew many people from this second group and obtained accounts from them of common practices in the area. But I also heard stories about earlier arrivals. According to Schmitz, these earlier peoples were known for platform burials and for making ancestor shrines with skulls. In addition, corpses were exposed on trees. These trees had a definite meaning, and each patrilineage had a tree of its own near its village. The souls of the dead were believed to live in this tree, and it was in this tree that the creation of mankind first occurred. Corpses and souls went back to the place where they had come from (Schmitz 1960: 411).

Some men I knew occasionally made fun of their ancestors for worshiping trees, and Jared, whose family hailed from lower down the mountains, shared origin stories from Schmitz's "culture A." The village head, however, reported seeing something associated with the earlier arrivals that Schmitz did not. Apparently, they suspended the corpse over the fire pit inside the house in a manner very similar to that depicted by Schieffelin among the Kaluli (2005). As the corpse dried and rotted, the putrescence dripped upon the food cooked over the fire, which was eaten in a kind of endocannibalism. I was unaware of Schmitz' ethnography while doing fieldwork and did not pursue sorting through his prehistory, assuming that earlier mortuary practices were very much like the ones I investigated among villagers' immediate ancestors.[10]

I mentioned that following German colonial expeditions around 1914, fighting ensued in the southern mountains. During this period of warfare, I was given to understand that corpses were bound against a post in a sitting position in the house and elaborately decorated with shell ornaments. As today, people "watched" the body for signs of life and, as visitors came from elsewhere to view the body, the family "watched" for signs of guilt and sorcery. The body was then allowed to rot in a grave dug in the floor of the house covered with banana leaves. Bones were eventually collected and hung in a net bag on the wall. They were then fed pork and beseeched for help in detecting enemies and sorcerers as well as finding wayward pigs and lost objects.

When the Lutheran missionaries were invited to create communities in the 1930s, they instituted a collective village graveyard. The Australian government later condemned the practice of keeping remains and watching rotting corpses as gross and unsanitary. Although people have been known to visit their ancestors' graves to appeal for magical favors, often to afflict others with whom they are angry, the separate graveyard was meant to indicate that the souls of the dead are taken by God and no longer subject to such earthly manipulation. This idea is reiterated frequently at contemporary funerals to preclude sorcery accusations and undo the violence of older generations.

Today, corpses are dressed in new clothing and placed in wooden coffins, which the villagers build out of bush materials. Following readings and a sermon from a village evangelist, the coffin is nailed shut and carried to the graveyard, where it is deposited in a deep hole. Everyone participates in the burial by throwing dirt onto the coffin, again to assert that the soul is joining God on a permanent basis and will no longer impact the living. A wooden cross is erected at the head of the grave and, on top of the cross is nailed, upside down, a ceramic bowl (Figure 3.1).

The juxtaposition of the bowl on the cross is interesting from the viewpoint of mortuary dialogue, although Rawa villagers said little about it. The only thing they were able to tell me about it was that the bowl was the same one from which the deceased ate during her or his life. Two points might be made about this bowl: One is that it emphasizes a dimension of reciprocity that both the culture and anthropological analysis downplays, that is, taking and eating. The other is that it would seem to apprehend the physical neediness of the person. This latter significance is particularly poignant in the context of the replacement of ancestor magic with a transcendental Christian God.

The appearance of inverted bowls on top of a cross in a Christian graveyard is dialogically remarkable insomuch as together they combine an image of irreducible neediness in a local, supernatural world and a transcendental Godhead. Though the two ideas may be nailed together in the graveyard, the Rawa and Western traditions differ. The Rawa experience of the immanent powers of the ancestors in nature and death as decomposition, I suggest, continues alongside Western transcendental notions that seek to silence them (see Wilson and Sinclair, this volume).

Revolon (2007) discusses bowls used in secondary burial festivals celebrated by Aorigi people in the Eastern Solomons, together with food placed inside them. The bowls represent the temporary living presence of the deceased as part of a process of "the transformation of subjects into objects" (Venbrux

Figure 3.1. Village graveyard with ceramic bowls on wooden crosses. Photo: Doug Dalton, 1983.

2007: 9), or ancestors in the afterlife. The symbolism of Rawa bowls works differently, for the bowls are inverted and emptied out. Moreover, they are not new but are rather a kind of a relic of the person who is no longer eating.

In the Rawa view, people are needy and, being needy, they are vulnerable to everything from love magic to the "pull" of trade store goods. It is neediness, particularly with regard to food, which leads men to practice suppressing hunger when food is in short supply and to seek after the privilege of being hosts and feast givers.[11] However it is impossible not to want (cf. Weiner 1992; Godelier 1999). Although adults, especially men, practice self-denial to make themselves powerful, they remain irreducibly needy, like everyone else. The embodied dependency of persons culminates in the experience of attending a dying loved one, whose terminated moral essence is memorialized by an overturned bowl, a bowl that sits upside down upon a cross in the village graveyard.

It is not difficult to see these bowls as a quintessential expression in Rawa mortuary dialogue with modernity, or more specifically with Christianity. Another innovation has recently developed that would seem to be part of this selfsame dialogue. Ancestor shrines, consisting of a carved post or, in the case of the village head, a concrete tombstone, are now erected in the ground near the residence of the deceased's relatives in the village (Figure 3.2).

I was able to observe a handful of shrines erected in 1999 for prominent men that were remarkable for several reasons. First, graves had been taken back to residences from the cemetery (see Lutkehaus, this volume; Bell, this volume). And second, erecting a wooden shrine in the soil recalls tree burial from the archaic, pre-Austronesian era. These shrines must also be seen in the context of modern Papua New Guinea. With the creation of an independent nation-state and coming of commercial enterprises, Papua New Guinea has emerged as a weak, rentier state on the periphery of the world system. It supplies minerals, energy, and coffee to the world and previously unimaginable concentrations of capital to its postcolonial elites. On the periphery of a periphery, Rawa people endeavor to participate in this modernity with their voices, most notably through population increases but also in attempts to attract development.

For Rawa, power above all consists of expanding kinship as far as possible through procreation, that is, in the reproduction of moral community. Kin afford people support for any productive and political purpose. In the modern world of increasing concentrations of power, one Rawa response has been children. People were ecstatic when I was able to show them the extent of their lineages in a series of kin diagrams. Between 1982 and 1999, the population of the village where I did fieldwork doubled from 500 to more than 1,000 people and split into three communities. Kin also have claims to land, where the productive capacities of the earth to which they have ties reside. When the creation of a nucleated village built around the Christian Church in the early

Figure 3.2. Ancestor shrine within village. Photo: Doug Dalton, 1999.

1930s brought a period of violent, territorially expansive, and destructive warfare to an end, the political fates of different kin groups varied and the jostling for power in villages increased the importance of ties the different lineages have to land.

Both population growth and the innovation of establishing ancestor shrines in association to specific areas of land are Rawa answers to increasing concentrations of power in modernity that maintain connections with ancestors (see Bell, this volume). The government (I believe at the behest of the World Bank) encouraged Rawa people to list and register clans, which did not previously exist, and delineate clan lands. I observed that with population increase, large areas of jungle reserved for hunting, garden lands, and resources near the village were beginning to show signs of overuse.

People were beginning to use bamboo instead of wood from trees to build garden fences because trees near the village had become scarcer. The claim to land asserted by ancestor shrines is understandable as an answer to modernity while, at the same time, it might also be seen as a subversive response to the Christian goal of dividing death from life. Instead of clearly asserting this contradictory position, however, the shrines may simply be said to add an element of moral complexity to the ongoing dialogue about the disposition of the "soul" after death.

A Methodological Conclusion—On Rawa Mortuary Rites, History, and Modernity

In good Hertzian fashion, perhaps I have shown how Rawa-speaking people transform the dead into moral ancestors through mortuary rites. Yet the chapter has also conveyed the point that maintaining ties with ancestor-spirits is uncertain and varies with historical circumstances, having gained much in significance and complexity in modern times. For Rawa people, Hertz' thesis must be predicated upon their understanding that persons are mortal, finite, needy beings and that death and mortuary rites are far from anomalies or separate from social life but instead constitute it. I am therefore led to distinguish between two kinds of "denial of death," one Western Christian and anthropological approach involves definitively separating death from life; and the other, Rawa one, entails viewing death as an ongoing part of physical and social life.

Rather than postulating a reified notion of "society" that mortuary rites serve, Rawa people premise their ongoing fabrication of human society on the comprehension of embodied neediness that their experience of death and mortuary rites demonstrates to them. One might say that, instead of making death subservient to moral life, thus predicating collective existence upon the transformed deaths of its members, they make social life subservient to death, predicating everyday moral life upon their understanding of neediness and dependency, which death makes most apparent.

As Wagner (1981, 1986a, 1986b) and Strathern (1988) argue more generally, in Melanesian cultures, like Rawa, people invent culture through the symbolic "elicitation" of embodied physical and emotional capacities that entice people to give gifts, get married, and so forth. Among Rawa people, this kind of symbolic elicitation is predicated on the assumption that persons are not independent and autonomous but needy, which they clearly experience in and around funeral wakes. What is remarkable about Rawa mortuary rites is that, in the context of the momentous social and religious change and the consequent shifts in mortuary practices and circumstances, in their prehistory but also in Christian ideologies and global power concentrations, this experience-near understanding of the physical disintegration pursuant at death not only has persisted but taken on increased significance.

Continuities in Rawa death rites do not result from some analytical prejudice to find culturally informed agency, although my training has made me aware and appreciative of cultural difference (cf. Barker 1985; Robbins 2007). It rather derives from an inductive methodology that emphasizes the historically and culturally situated experiences that people employ to understand who they are. Above all, this approach led me to avoid the intellectual conundrum of opposing "continuity" to "change" on which reified, overintellectualized notions of "religion" and "culture" founder.

To appreciate the Rawa context, I have referred to political histories, war, and demographic variables, among many other factors, in addition to religious and cultural concepts of the person as parts of the experiential context in which Rawa invent culture. My conclusion is that the relation between experience, culture, and history needs to be rethought. I suggest taking a cue from Weber's (1958) famous study of the role of religion in Western social economic history and adopt an open-ended, historical view of culture wherein values persist yet change as they move through complex historical trajectories.

In their Introduction to this volume, Silverman and Lipset argue that the L'Année sociologique school elevated the moral force of society and ritual in general, and death rites in particular. Durkheimian sociology and anthropology, they proposed, can be seen as falling into the same idealist trap according to which persons in society may find exemplary moral solutions in reified social institutions. While Durkheim may be correct that the cultures people create and inhabit are "social facts" that enable collective existence, cultures have proven to be far less stable than he had hoped or imagined. Yet as Durkheim supposed, Rawa are no less prone to sanctify their cultural mirages than anyone else. The village head where I worked, who did much to bring Christianity to the area, used to mock Rawa magicians and laugh about how they were prone to self-flattery in the illusion that they controlled much more in the world than they actually did.

Many of their illusions were dashed with the coming of Western colonial institutions. At the same time, however, their practices were solidly grounded in the experience and understanding of the neediness of human beings rather than in a Durkheimian ideal or mirage of "society." In the modern world, Rawa people are increasingly subject to institutions, powers, and metaphysical illusions that originate elsewhere, and their experience-near cultural understandings of personhood in life and death are challenged as never before. So too are some key analytical assumptions in anthropology. It is in this historical context that the Rawa existential understanding of the person has come to take on unusual significance, not only in their mortuary dialogues with modernity but in analytical dialogues with our theoretical ancestors as well.

Doug Dalton is professor of anthropology at Longwood University in Farmville, Virginia. He has done research in Papua New Guinea, has published numerous articles, and teaches a number of core courses in anthropology.

Notes

1. This case is an entirely realistic composite of several instances. It should not be compared with any particular set of events that took place during my fieldwork.
2. Names, relations, and indirect identifiers have been changed to protect the anonymity of individual Rawa persons.
3. I counted about one person each month who died in the village of about five hundred where I resided, and I attended the great majority of their funerals over about a fifteen-month period.
4. This word is constructed thus: *kini*, negative, "nothing" or "not," and *te*, "to go" plus *wo*, the completed past marker.
5. In Western medical discourse, the question of how to define death is also an important one. The biomedical community adopted the definition of "brain death" in 1968 and set off a series of controversies regarding the relation between brain death and the physical existence of a body kept alive on respirators, the bioethics of transplantation technologies, the nature of consciousness, and other ambiguities of states between life and death (see Kaufman and Morgan 2005: 329–30). In the highly publicized 2005 US case of Terry Schiavo, the issue of discontinuing life support came down to whether or not she was in a "persistent vegetative state" or "minimally conscious state" of awareness, and the distinction was clearly drawn between brain death and biological death (Annas 2005, 2007; Kaufman 2000; Noah 2004).
6. See also Bamford (2007: 124–49).
7. In postforaging, postneolithic cultures, in other words, where there is considerable investment made in future social and economic returns through, for example, bridewealth exchange that involves the delayed return of marriage partners and collective ownership of garden territory, the fate of the individual is wrapped up in a relatively

autonomous corporate group to such a degree that individual emotions regarding death are magnified. In such cultures, the death of politically prominent persons is presumably more emotionally significant because it has a greater bearing on the fate and well-being of the mourners.

8. It is conceivable that, with one additional secret concept known, perhaps to women, this Rawa idea of "spirit" entails a theory of reincarnation, but the information I was able to gather fall just short of such a theory. See Obeyesekere (2002) and Mills and Slobodin (1994) for discussions and examples of how widespread the idea of reincarnation is in cultures across the globe.

9. In addition to this somewhat inconsistent picture, Rawa people recognize a variety of fiery half-men spirits who are sometimes encountered in the jungle at night. They are thought to be the souls of unhappy men. One type of sorcery also entailed the sorcerer essentially shedding his outward embodiment to reveal an inner fiery core that could destroy his enemies. What happened to such a sorcerer when he did this is not clear, but his actions were not seen as the sort of generous activities that would lead to a man's spirit becoming a star.

10. However Schmitz reports that the original "culture A" lacked the elaborate system of shell valuables the later culture had, which is confirmed by Rawa mythology. The earlier layer of pre-Austronesian culture therefore lacked the significant decoration of the corpse that was used to pay the members of a successful vengeance raid against a supposed sorcerer. The picture that emerges of the mortuary practices of the earliest culture is of relatively small isolated hamlets practicing sister exchange and forgoing bride-wealth. This is still relatively common in that part of the mountains. The earliest hamlet communities maintained ties with ancestors primarily in relation to the landscape through endocannibalism, tree worship, and skull shrines, and lacked the terrible violence of later culture. The later pre-Austronesian culture of the old men I knew and their fathers and grandfathers included elaborate shell valuables and bride-wealth exchanges, which instituted and also ameliorated conflict between in-laws.

11. Women are less concerned with such self-denial because they give with their bodies through childbirth and suckling, although they, too, more so in later years, practice ascetic self-denial. Such austere practices regarding food and sex are also required of practicing magicians as well as to safeguard personal health. Anyone who wishes to be generous must learn to practice the art of suppressing hunger, and I have known children to do it, often out of necessity, when food is short or otherwise not readily available.

References Cited

Annas, George J. 2005. "'I Want to Live': Medicine Betrayed by Ideology in the Political Debate over Terri Schiavo." *Stetson Law Review* 35: 49–80.

———. 2007. "Foreword: Imagining a New Era of Neuroimaging, Neuroethics, and Neurolaw." *American Journal of Law & Medicine* 33: 163–70.

Ariès, Philippe. 1981. *The Hour of Our Death*. New York: Oxford University Press.

Bamford, Sandra C. 2007. *Biology Unmoored: Melanesian Reflections on Life and Biotechnology*. Berkeley: University of California Press.

Barker, John. 1985. "Missionaries and Mourning: Continuity and Change in the Death Ceremonies of a Melanesian People." In *Missionaries, Anthropologists, and Cultural Change*, edited by Darrell L. Whitemen, 263–94. Williamsburg: College of William and Mary.
Becker, Ernest. 1973. *The Denial of Death*. New York: Simon & Schuster.
Bloch, Maurice and Jonathan P. Parry. 1982. *Death and the Regeneration of Life*. Cambridge: Cambridge University Press.
Burridge, Kenelm. 1995. *Mambu: A Melanesian Millennium*. Princeton: Princeton University Press.
Counts, Dorothy and David Counts. 2004. "The Good, the Bad and the Unresolved Death in Kaliai." *Social Science & Medicine* 58: 887–97.
Durkheim, Émile. 1965 [1915]. *The Elementary Forms of the Religious Life*. Translated by JW Swain. New York: Free Press.
Fabian, Johannes. 1972. "How Others Die—Reflections on the Anthropology of Death." *Social Research* 39: 171–201.
———. 1983. *Time and the Other: How Anthropology Makes Its Object*. New York: Columbia University Press.
Frazer, James George. 1933. *The Fear of the Dead in Primitive Religion: Lectures Delivered on the William Wyse Foundation at Trinity College, Cambridge*. London: Macmillan.
Gell, Alfred. 1993. *Wrapping in Images: Tattooing in Polynesia*. Oxford: Clarendon Press.
Godelier, Maurice. 1999. *The Enigma of the Gift*. Cambridge: Polity Press.
Heidegger, Martin. 1962. *Being and Time*. New York: Harper & Row.
Hertz, Robert. 1960 [1907]. "A Contribution to the Study of the Collective Representation of Death." In *Death and the Right Hand*, translated and edited by Rodney Needham and Claudia Needham, 27–86. New York: Free Press.
Huntington, Richard and Peter Metcalf. 1979. *Celebrations of Death: The Anthropology of Mortuary Ritual*. Cambridge: Cambridge University Press.
Kaufman, Sharon R. 2000. "In the Shadow of 'Death with Dignity': Medicine and Cultural Quandaries of the Vegetative State." *American Anthropologist* 102: 69–83.
Kaufman, Sharon R. and Lynn M. Morgan. 2005. "The Anthropology of the Beginnings and Ends of Life." *Annual Review of Anthropology* 34: 317–41.
Lee, Rebekah and Megan Vaughan. 2008. "Death and Dying in the History of Africa Since 1800." *Journal of African History* 49: 341–59.
Mills, Antonia and Richard Slobodin. 1994. *Amerindian Rebirth: Reincarnation Belief among North American Indians and Inuit*. Toronto: University of Toronto Press.
Noah, Barbara A. 2004. "Politicizing the End of Life: Lessons from the Schiavo Controversy." *University of Miami Law Review* 59: 107–34.
Obeyesekere, Gananath. 2002. *Imagining Karma: Ethical Transformation in Amerindian, Buddhist, and Greek Rebirth*. Berkeley: University of California Press.
Palgi, Phyllis and Henry Abramovitch. 1984. "Death: A Cross-Cultural Perspective." *Annual Review of Anthropology* 13: 385–417.
Revolon, Sandra. 2007. "The Dead Are Looking at Us: Place and Role of the *Apira Ni Farunga* ("Ceremonial Bowls") in the End-of-Mourning Ceremonies in Aorigi (Eastern Solomon Islands)." *Journal de la Société des Océanistes* 124: 59–66.
Robbins, Joel. 2007. "Continuity Thinking and the Problem of Christian Culture." *Current Anthropology* 48: 5–38.

Schieffelin, Edward L. 2005. *The Sorrow of the Lonely and the Burning of the Dancers.* New York: Palgrave McMillan.
Schmitz, Carl A. 1960. *Historische Probleme in Nordost-Neuguinea.* Wiesbaden: Franz Steiner.
Stibich, Mark. 2008. "Understanding Sleep." Retrieved 2013 http://longevity.about.com/od/sleep/a/sleep_facts.htm.
Strathern, Marilyn. 1988. *The Gender of the Gift: Problems with Women and Problems with Society in Melanesia.* Berkeley: University of California Press.
Tylor, Edward B. 1889. *Primitive Culture: Researches into the Development of Mythology, Philosophy, Religion, Language, Art, and Custom.* New York: Holt.
Van Gennep, Arnold. 1960 [1908]. *The Rites of Passage.* Translated by Monika B. Vizedom and Gabrielle L. Caffee. Chicago: University of Chicago Press.
Venbrux, Eric. 2007. "Robert Hertz's Seminal Essay and Mortuary Rites in the Pacific Region." *Journal de la Société des Océanistes* 124: 5–10.
Wagner, Roy. 1981. *The Invention of Culture.* Chicago: University of Chicago Press.
———. 1986a. *Asiwinarong : Ethos, Image, and Social Power among the Usen Barok of New Ireland.* Princeton: Princeton University Press.
———. 1986b. *Symbols That Stand for Themselves.* Chicago: University of Chicago Press.
Weber, Max. 1958 [1904–1905]. *The Protestant Ethic and the Spirit of Capitalism.* Translated by Talcott Parsons. New York: Scribner.
Weiner, Annette. 1992. *Inalienable Possessions: The Paradox of Keeping-While-Giving.* Berkeley: University of California Press.
Woodburn, James. 1982. "Social Dimensions of Death in Four African Hunting and Gathering Societies." In *Death & the Regeneration of Life,* edited by Maurice Bloch and Jonathan Parry, 187–210. Cambridge: Cambridge University Press.

4

The Knotted Person
Death, the Bad Breast, and Melanesian Modernity among the Murik, Papua New Guinea

DAVID LIPSET

In this chapter, I analyze deaths that occured over a seventy-five-year period among the Murik Lakes people, the fisherfolk and regional traders who live at the mouth of the Sepik River in Papua New Guinea (PNG). It begins by introducing Melanie Klein's psychoanalytic view of death (1975) in relationship to Bakhtinian dialogism (see Introduction, this volume). Next, I survey the broader institutional context of modernity in PNG. After outlining moral personhood among the Murik, subsequent sections focus on deaths that took place, and mortuary practices that were going on, in 1936, 1982, and 2010.

I argue that these deaths and practices express Murik voices in an equivocal dialogue with modernity. On the one hand, the deaths portray a gender-specific, but regionally commonplace, vicissitude—namely, the waning of ritual masculinity. On the other, they suggest that characteristically Murik notions of personhood, consisting of culturally constructed relations between body and spirit, were abiding. In conclusion, I discuss how the overall balance of contemporary Murik mortuary dialogue is part of the ambiguities of the position of the society in the context of colonial and postcolonial PNG.

The Kleinian Breast and Postcolonial Dialogics

According to Melanie Klein, death and mourning recall a moral vision of the maternal body from preverbal infancy. At an early stage of development, babies associate the gratification and frustration of desire with what Klein calls "part-objects" (1975: 264). This is not the mother, but only separate pieces of her body, her breasts, hands, and face, in particular. On the positive side, infants take pleasure from the "good breast," which they idealize as the source of value and safety. On the negative side, when hungry and frustrated, infants may become overwhelmed with hatred of the "bad breast."

Violent fantasies arise in imagery attached to feeling states in which they assault the breasts, emptying them out, ripping them up, or attacking them with poisonous urine and explosive feces (Klein 1975: 262). This nightmare may arouse fears that the bad breast will retaliate in kind and chop up, poison, or otherwise destroy the infant, fears that may leave him breathless, choking, weak, or ill. Klein called the desire to possess the good breast and the oral-destructive, anal-sadistic attack fantasy against the bad breast, as well as the breast's symmetrical revenge, the paranoid-schizoid position (1946: 99–110).

Subsequently, infants enter the "depressive position" (Klein 1975: 345) when they begin to recognize that these two morally contrary breasts are not unrelated but rather belong to one and the same object, namely, the mother. This realization results from identifying—by incorporating or internalizing—"her" into their bodies. Infants associate the integrity of the mother, Klein argues, with a fantasy of "eating" her. As such, they continue to suffer from feelings of persecution by the bad breast, on the one hand, and must overcome anxiety about loss of the good breast, on the other, anxiety from imagined guilt that they killed "her" out of greed and destructive rage.

The infant may be overcome with helplessness and "pine" nostalgically for the lost object (Klein 1975: 348). Or, it may attempt to bring her back to a state of integration. Through acts that serve, gratify, and restore the beauty of the good mother, the child may try to make restitution for imaginary injuries done to the beloved object with whom it has become fully identified. The moral fantasy of putting her damaged body back together Klein calls the process of "reparation" (1975: 312). And this process, she declares, is the central project, not only in this phase of childhood but also in mourning.

These two orientations, the paranoid-schizoid and the depressive positions, preconceive mourning for deceased loved ones (read, kin) in adulthood. Actually, Klein puts it the other way around: "The child," she avers, "goes through states of mind comparable to the mourning of the adult" (1975: 344). Death may arouse anger: the oral-destructive fantasy against the bad breast, as well as the fear that "she" will retaliate in kind. Defense mechanisms ward off having to admit guilt for causing the death of the loved one. The cause of the loss—the subject—may be projected outward into the external world, where it can be disowned.

Feelings of persecution and distrust, fears of being robbed, and a pervasive sense of danger may then come to characterize the social world. Scapegoats, culprits, and other external targets, such as sorcerers and witches in Melanesian contexts, protect the subject from punishing itself by dispersing its sense of culpability. In addition to projection, manic fantasies of omnipotence and triumph that dispose of bad, dangerous objects or defend and revive loved ones may arise. The lost object may also be idealized as wise, tutelary ancestors or devalued as demons. Denial of death is also possible. The dead may go on living as uncanny ghosts. Lastly, mortuary obligations may be fulfilled, demonstrating the subject's innocense and respect for the deceased while returning mourners to the community. Being a metaphor for the loss of the one irreplacable object that signifies love and security, death arouses complicated moral ambivalences about the maternal breasts, good and bad.

Needless to say, Kleinian theory adopts an atemporal, acultural view of the subject. Relationships and fantasies that have been internalized or introjected during infancy recur regardless of place or historical forces. Death may indeed revive the two infantile positions, but in my view it does so in dialogue with multiple concepts of the enculturated subject. To be sure, the nation-state, capitalism, and rationalized religions authorize powerful voices that engage the subject. However, what is distinctive of postcolonial nation-states is how distinctively egalitarian and dynamic these voices are. Indeed, if the ambivalences of the Kleinian subject are static and acultural, I would say that an outstanding quality of the postcolonial subject is an unusual temporality that is neither static nor dynamic. It has *no telos* other than an ambigiuous authority that offers no last word (Mbembe 1992).

What circumstances or preconditions gave rise to this kind of society and subject, whose "essence ... lies precisely in the fact that ... [its plural] voices remain independent" (Bakhtin 1984: 21) thus to combine with, while not becoming subordinate to, a single, official voice? According to Bakhtin, this kind of a context arises where it comes "upon an untouched multitude of diverse worlds and social groups which had not been weakened in their individual isolation, as in the West, by the gradual encroachment of capitalism" (1984: 20). The constituent societies in such a setting then collide with each other and with modernity in a "particularly full and vivid" way (1984: 20).

Modernity in Papua New Guinea

Not to underestimate economic exploitation, colonial racism, and violence, but PNG was and goes on being just such a setting. Comprised of an unweakened multitude of societies, it is not a new state that emerged from, or is experiencing, large-scale bloodshed. In comparison to European colonization elsewhere in the world, it was rather buffered from, rather than buffeted by, colonial history (1884-1975), brief, uneven, and understaffed as it was. Development, and market integration, remains inconsistent today. During the first decades of postcolonial sovereignty, PNG has become a rentier state more concerned with facilitating extraction industries than providing services for its citizenry.

The introduction and enforcement of colonial law—public hygiene regulations, in particular, cemetaries, and the provision of healthcare—was sporadic in the best of times (Frankel and Lewis 1989). While PNG has the highest incidence of HIV in the Pacific region, spread of the disease has been localized to urban areas, such as the capital, and rural enclaves, including transportation routes and mining and logging sites. Of course, European missionaries sought to condemn sorcery and local healing methods doctrinally and through the differential provision of rudimentary medical sevices. The result is a pragmatic view of both Melanesian and Western concepts of illness and death (Lewis 1976). All in all, modernity in PNG has a distinctively Melanesian/Western quality.

Death epitomizes it. Death is held to infect the subject with mystical impurities and leave him feeling angry but also persecuted by and vulnerable to ancestors, ghosts, and sorcerers (Stephen 1999). Meanwhile, advocates of Christianity and the state accuse the mourning subject of holding satanic and/or backward, irrational values. The former, in turn, criticize voices of modernity, for selfishness, for disrepecting the dead, and for seeking to obstruct the reproduction of custom by any means. Amid this dialogue, ritual masculinity, whose right to take up arms was the object of colonial nullification from first contact, is called into question. Death is never natural: it is a failure in men's collective capacity to protect the community from mystical peril.

The "Knotted Person" in Murik Culture

Murik villages stand just west of the Sepik River on the coast separating a large system of mangrove lagoons, the Murik Lakes, from the Pacific Ocean. In addition, a growing diaspora lives in Wewak, the provincial capital 40 miles up the coast to the west. Murik mourners, both urban and rural, are citizens of PNG, PNG having received independence from Australia, under the leadership of no less a personage than their own native son Sir Michael Somare (see his 1975 autobiography). Possessing postcolonial entitlements to statutory rights, they have all absorbed the state's universalisms in varying degrees. In 2010, nearly everyone had gone, or was going, to school. Some degree of literacy and numeracy was almost universal. Everyone had received innoculations, triage, and hospital care, in the course of their lives. Despite the lack of development of the Murik small-scale fishery, everyone also had both informal and formal relationships with markets, currency, bank accounts, and, of course, commodities, small and large. Lastly, each and every mourner had either worshiped in a Catholic or a Seventh-Day Adventist (SDA) church at some point, though they might or might not go on doing so.

In brief, the influence of modernity among the Murik is pervasive. This is not to say that everyone is *convinced* that the world is made up of self-determining egos who act in a material environment ruled by a monotheistic deity in combination with the universalities of biology, the market, education, and the state. But it is to say that in 2010 this viewpoint, or ideology, is an irrevocable part of Murik culture. In modernity, of course, death is both organically and temporally differentiated from life. The moment of death is "punctual," as Bloch once put it (1982: 14; see Dalton, this volume). Death occurs at a precise time, when breathing stops and the heart no longer beats—which moment the state certifies. The soul or the subject then exits the body, either to enter into an atemporal eternity as a spirit-being in heaven or to pass into a spatial and temporal alterity, that is to say, nothingness. No rural or peri-urban Murik, however modern might their orientation be, subscribed to the latter view in the early twenty-first century. Their Melanesian modernity, so I suggest, simultaneously espouses universal and vernacular values.

In the early twenty-first century, the Murik sought health care, erected crosses over graves, and went on understanding persons as canoes. In other words, they still construed the person as a spirit-passenger (*nabran*) in a canoe-body, the distinguishing quality of this relationship being movement, and the principal signifier of its moral unity being the act of lashing or binding. More literally, lashing was a metonym for lashing a canoe to its outrigger or mooring it to shore (Figure 4.1). I am referring to the act of tying a knot (cf. Kuchler 2003).

The *nabran*-spirit is not directly perceptible but may only be seen as an other, as a shadow, or as a reflection in water (*sansam*). In a broad sense, the

Figure 4.1. Two senior men bind an outrigger boom to a hull. Photo: David Lipset, 1981.

nabran-spirit is a life-force without which the person dies. But what is culturally elaborated is not its soul-stuff, or putative vitality. Rather like Murik persons themselves, the *nabran*-spirit is an object of desire sought after by other spirits, or it is weakened by magic and impurities. It must be secured or bound to the body through the nurture, care, and love of kin—by tying mystical knots.

The Murik habitus is relatively rare, although not unheard of, in Melanesia. Villages occupy narrow beaches that barely divide the Pacific Ocean from the Murik Lakes. The people practice aquatic foraging, run a small-scale fishery in dugout canoes and small fiberglass boats, and conduct intertribal trade (Figure 4.2).[1] Although the Murik speak a Sepik language, the Austronesian influence on the culture, with its flotilla of boat metaphors for persons and society, is unmistakable (Lipset 2014). Their canoe-based worldview has given rise to an unusual apprehension of the body (cf. Ingold 2000: 57).

In Murik cosmology, the *nabran*-spirit is understood to be "transported" as a passenger through space, the body being a canoe (*gai'iin*) and the canoe being a body, with a face, belly button, and spirit. Additionally, the canoe met-

Figure 4.2. Murik canoes docked at a rural market. Photo: David Lipset, 2012.

aphor is extended within the body: the ribcage is called a "canoe" for the torso, while a mother's womb is also said to be a "canoe" for the fetus. Moreover, when babies are born, a knot may be tied in front of the infant's face to secure its *nabran*-spirit to its new canoe-body and prevent it from drifting back to the spirit-world it just left (Barlow 1985: 142). The existence of the moral person in society, in short, is partly seen to depend on sustaining a relationship between *nabran*-spirit and canoe-body by binding one to the other. When a *nabran*-spirit leaves its canoe-body permanently, death (*pre*) is said to occur, and the newly disembodied spirit must travel to its ancestor-spirit community (*pot kaban*). Just as living travelers prefer to wash prior to departure, soon after death a corpse will also be washed and dressed up to get ready to go to the ancestor-spirit community. Just as an initiate is introduced to the lineage for the first time dressed in sacred lineage regalia and toting the lineage basket (*sumon sunn*), the new *nabran*-spirit is "given" a lineage basket whose spirit-image (*sansam*) he or she may take, like a kind of numinous passport, to show ancestors and be admitted into their community upon arrival.

In part, new *nabran*-spirits are treated solicitously because a Kleinian revival, the melodrama of love, murder, guilt, and persecutory fears, begins to play out during and after a death. Ghosts and people are thought to possess like vanities. Both become jealous at being excluded from use-rights to moor at the family dock (*mogev*), which is to say they become angry at being separated from kin for whom they long. They become the "bad breast." *Nabran*-spirits serve as tutelaries to the living, whom they may punish when surviving kin, such as an elderly widow, is neglected. Illness may then befall, not the inconsiderate person, but objects of his or her desire, namely, children. *Nabran*-spirits, that is to say, are attributed disciplinary qualities in the afterlife: should a child cry in its sleep, when he or she awakens, a mother or grandmother may inquire: "Who was scolding you?"

Familiar yet foreboding, dead yet alive, *nabran*-spirits appear as involuntary repetitions, reflections, and shadows who duplicate human life. As apparitions, they travel among the living as spirit-beings in between the known and comfortable, which is the maternal, and that which is feared, which are the dead. *Nabran*, as I have said, means spirit. But the word also means "spider" and mothers will play upon this homonym (Abraham 1927). They may tickle toddlers and young children seated on their laps. Faintly running fingers up and down their arms, a mother may then squeal: "*Nabran! Nabran!*" And the association of this odd but intimate sensation of something uncertain crawling about the skin in the context of the maternal—the *heimlich*—is subsequently reported by adults who may perceive or sense a ghost touching them or standing close by.

In 1982, a woman allowed that she felt her deceased husband in bed one night as she climbed inside her mosquito net and stepped on his arm. The unexpected presence of his spectral repetition, in the form of his *nabran*-spirit, she assumed, meant that something was about to happen, likely a death. That which is uncanny, Freud agreed, ought to have remained hidden but has come to light (1955: 225). *Nabran*-spirits reveal, yet deny, death. They threaten and protect society and the subject against the loss of the irreplaceable object.

The desire of new *nabran*-spirits to kill their kin is also aroused when the latter become despondent over loss. To "pine" (Klein 1975: 348) for someone who has died may thus be fatal. Twilight in Murik is thought to be an especially melancholy and hazardous time of day. Pastel cirrus clouds bespattered by the last rays of sunset are called "sun sprites" (*akun menumb*). These sprites may evoke nostalgic reveries in the subject. To call out the name of a deceased spouse, parent, sibling, or child may then draw their *nabran*-spirit near. Meanwhile, shadows (which are *nabran*-spirits) lengthen and disappear into the darkness. Frightening, the uncanny is strange yet familiar.

Since dreaming is understood to take place among spirits, waking up is precarious and, like dusk, the dawn is considered an unhealthy moment. Having just returned to its canoe-body, the *nabran*-spirit's position is weakened by impure death sprites (*mwak*), the residues of which have been contracted during its dream travels. The lashings of its canoe-body, in the Murik idiom, are loose. To smoke or chew betel nuts first thing in the morning may make one dizzy and faint helplessly, which means that one's spirit is insecurely tied to its canoe-body. Eating anything at all is dangerous upon first awakening because, as I say, one's *nabran*-spirit can be lured by food.

"It" remains among, or partly among, the dead, for whom sharing tobacco and food are no less strategic enticements than they are for the living. In addition to tying knots, immersion in the ocean is thought to be particularly salubrious and effective. The spirit-passenger's position in his or her canoe-body is thus cleansed, or tightened up, from the uncanny dangers of the night by a morning bath. If the uncanny depicts that which should not be, the living-dead, then immersion in the sea restores what is culturally normative, the good breast.

In an essay on Austronesian-speaking, insular Southeast Asia, Manguin drew the conclusion that above all else the boat was "a metaphor for an organized social unit" in this region (1986: 190–91). Here in seaboard Melanesia, we also find the Murik person "traveling" in several collective canoe-bodies, of which three—ornament-bearing, cognatic lineages; male and female spirit-cults; and a public masking society—are ritually significant for his or her personhood in society.

Murik lineages are made up of age-stratified sibling groups, called lines or ropes (*nog*), each of which is led by their firstborn "canoe prow child." These groups and their affines are also called "platforms" (*maig*), the platform being a metonym for an outrigger canoe (see Chapter 7). The person is ritually recruited during rites of passage by the senior leaders of one or several of these lineages, who present kin with an outfit of ornamental regalia that signifies their moral identity. In turn, lineages are protected by two secret, initiatory spirit-cults, a warrior society of men and a love magic society of women. The Male Cult is housed in a canoe-like building from which the opposite sex is banned. It recruits boys through matilrateral relations. The Female Cult, housed from time to time in a large domestic house, recruits girls through patrilateral relations. These two societies are divided into competitive moieties in which rival partners serve as canoe-bodies for their named, war-spirits (*brag*), on the one side, and for named, love spiritesses (*Sambam meruk*) and war-spirits on the other. The Male Cult is also supported by the Gaingiin Society. This is a public masking organization that consists of seven initiatory age grades, each of which manufactures and wears its own spirit-masks who have different privileges, such as tabooing the harvest of coconuts. The cane framework on which its masks and leafy bunting are attached is also called a "canoe-body."

Now membership in the two cults affords rights and duties that extend outside of their halls. Every person in Murik society participates in hereditary exchange and feasting partnerships, called the "Wealth Path" (*mwara yakabor*). The *mwara* kin provide ritual services during life cycle events, such as birth and death, when the relationship of the *nabran*-spirit to his or her canoe-body is vulnerable. It is they who tie a knot in front of the face of a newborn or tie a knot around the foreheads of mourners to protect them from soul loss during the initial phase of grief.

In daily life, senior lineage leaders, parents, and others urge children to "stand up." That is, they are encouraged to engage in moral acts that lead to social reproduction. The *mwara* kin, when not offering ritual support, take part in oral-sadistic and phallic-aggressive joking relations in the guise of warrior ancestor-spirits (*brag*), whom they impersonate. They mock each other and laugh at the "underside of ... life. At the center of their ... comedy is obscenity, the seamier side of sexual love, alienated from reproduction, from the progression of generations, from family and lineage" (Bakhtin 1981: 128). Their joking may become phallic, but *mwara* kin are contradictory kin on whom the person depends to stay afloat, but who he or she also tries to insult, embarrass, and defeat. *Mwara* kin provide the ritual means by which moral community is reproduced after it has been desecrated by death.

Not a binary combination of body and soul, the Murik person is a vehicle that ferries multiple spirits. He or she is viewed as a canoe-body that transports a *nabran*-spirit as well as several warrior or love spirits and has ties to ancestor-spirits by means of lineage insignia. Men, in addition, hold rights to spirit-masks in the Gaingiin Society. These spirits are bound together into what I call the "knotted person." In the following cases, this concept of identity appears in a state of becoming Melanesian/modern. When facing death, the mortuary dialogues of the knotted person express Kleinian ambivalences by shedding tears, offering prayers, and giving new and old funerary goods and through expressions of anxiety about ghosts, sorcerers, and culprits. In modern contexts, that is to say, mourners continue to become dissociated upon losing a loved one. They continue to express guilt over and projected fears about the lost breast, good and bad, as well as through strenuous ritual efforts to make reparation and, not least, by tying knots.

1936

The first cases occured during the time of the Australian administration. To discuss them, I rely on two sources: the Society of the Divine Word priest Joseph Schmidt, who lived among the Murik for thirty years (1911–1940), and Louis Pierre Ledoux, a young adventurer of independent means who, at the suggestion of Margaret Mead, spent six months in 1936 in the Murik Lakes upon graduating from Harvard College.

Father Schmidt provided daily triage of cuts and bruises. Ledoux, who did so too, mentions a smallpox epidemic that had occurred in living memory. But their data do not suggest that the general run of village health was bad. I do not know what the average lifespan was in 1936, but both the Westphalian priest and the young American refer to a whole range of generations, including elders of both sexes.

Most measures taken to treat critical illness seem to have been intended to stave off spirit-loss. A terminally ill person would not be left alone. Kin would fill up the house, leaving others to gather out in front. Leafy branches might be hung above the doorway to block, so Schmidt understood, the entry or exit of spirits. The soles of feet might also be burned with hot coconut shells, the idea being that this injury would hinder their spirit from leaving the body, rather like hulls are singed to make wood watertight. Kin might also "chase" ancestor-spirits with bunches of bespelled leaves or use them to sweep them away, as if tidying up.

Should a critically ill person decline to eat, Ledoux was told, kin began to fear the worst, food being a claim upon the moral identity of the recipient, which, if refused, meant that the nurture of "the other" had already been accepted. When someone began slipping out of consciousness, both Schmidt and Ledoux overheard screams of kin terms meant to call them "back" from the spirit-world, the human voice apparently being the last line of defense against losing a loved one. Attendants yelled loudly enough that everybody in earshot could hear.[2] If the "patients" did happen to revive, they would be questioned about what they had seen or done "there." Did they eat with their parents? If so, as I say, little else could be done.

In 1936, Ledoux himself was involved in waking up a middle-aged, Catholic man called Moiega "who had [been thought to have] died and [had been] removed to his brother's house [where] kin were expected to gather. Slit-drum beats signaled the death. Moiega's lineage ornaments were brought [to him]. … He was dressed in a new loincloth. A long prayer was recited and a young boy prayed the rosary. Noticing that Moiega was still breathing … [Ledoux] administered smelling salts and roused the 'dead man,' who was so weak that he died for good the following day" (Ledoux 1936; see Dalton, this volume). Death was not understood as a biological transition or punctual event at this time. It was not coincident with the cessation of breathing but was reacted to in terms of imagery of the good breast, that is, through acts of care, nurture, sociality, and domesticity. Dying was "treated" by dialogue in vigils and shouting as well as by the offer of food, sweeping up, and the singeing of feet.

Death also provoked expressions of affect, otherwise unheard in daily life. Mourners, of either sex, would wail and weep at first blush and then cry melodically. Ledoux saw a husband plead with his wife to come back and not leave him. He lay down on top of her corpse and literally caressed her breast. Schmidt also witnessed a woman "throw herself on … her husband, embrace him and lay … in his arms" (1926: 56). Shortly thereafter, the moment gave way to burial preparations. After being washed, corpses were painted and decorated in lineage ornaments.

Schmidt saw the forehead of one man smeared with yellowish chalk down to his nose into which red flowers were inserted. Ledoux watched a nose being measured so a nassa shell and bead ornament might be fashioned in its likeness. Another woman had marks of a crocodile drawn on her eyelids and forehead. The crocodile-spirit was expected to come, he was told, and carry her *nabran*-spirit on its back "as if he [the crocodile-spirit] were a canoe" to the neighboring village where she was born (Ledoux 1936). The priest also reported Murik use of canoe imagery, like a kind of totemic, Stygian ferry to the afterlife (Schmidt 1926).

When a person died, one of the zoomorphic canoe-bodies associated with an ancestor that he or she had otherwise not eaten while alive, might "bring," or escort, the new spirit to the afterlife, unless, that is, the dietary taboo, that is, the good breast, had been violated, in which case the new spirit could be condemned to wander around lost because "its ancestor" had been killed and cannibalized. Other parishioners, Schmidt allowed, differed about this point. They did not see the relationship between the canoe-body and the new spirit it took to the afterlife as consubstantial. Instead, they distinguished the canoe-body from the ancestor. Eating its zoomorphic canoe-body merely deprived the spirit of its vehicle, or its "pathway" (*yakabor*), as the Murik refer to canoes, to come and get the new spirit. The good breast should not be consumed, attacked, or otherwise violated.

However one might or might not reach the afterlife, new spirits provoked persecutory fears in the 1930s. They made trouble after having died, appearing as mischievous and somewhat intimidating presences, stealing food, spilling water, and making children cry in their sleep. Darkness became dangerous because of them. Ledoux mocked some adult men who asked for a flashlight to light their way home from his house a night after a death. Women who had not visited the deceased as she lay dying and men who were her lovers but had refused to marry her felt threatened by her new spirit. Schmidt (1926) mentioned an instance of a new spirit who was said to have attacked and drowned such a man out fishing alone. Death induced representations of guilt among survivors, guilt for having been selfish, guilt for being unloving, guilt for mistreating children. Death aroused anxiety: the new spirit became a devouring, aggressive breast that scared children, stole food, and punished withheld desire.

Under the rules of the colonial administration, homestead burial was neither permitted nor practiced in 1936. Cemetaries were located on the edges of villages. Graves had to be shallow so as not to hit water. Walls were lined with canoe boards and the floor was covered with tree bark. Corpses, whose faces were left exposed, were positioned facing toward uterine kin, the hope being to ease their way home. Ornaments were removed, but a shell ring might be placed on the arm or pressed into hands to be given to a spirit encountered along the way so it might escort the new spirit to the community of its ancestors. If the deceased had not eaten during his final days, fish and sago were put into the grave so he or she might have a snack en route. When filled up, graves were usually fenced in and covered by a small, roofed shelter, complete with a shelf stocked with water, tobacco, and betel nuts (Figure 4.3).

Figure 4.3. Sheltered grave. Photo: David Lipset, 2012.

Sometimes, a bark torch was lit at night so the new spirit need not walk in the dark. If a man had killed enemies, a pole was erected at his grave that was decorated with red malay apples and pig mandibles.

When Moiega, whom Ledoux had revived, did die, his body was placed in a canoe-prow coffin and a vigil began in his house. Outside, men gathered around an open, thatched structure of benches made of old canoe sides[3] and sang the canoe songs Moiega liked.

> [Next day] Moiega was placed on a decorated bier and carried to the cemetery by male kin. On the way, "the bier" bumped into people, "talked" to them, and "ran" wildly about. "It ran" back into Moiega's own house at one point before "directing" the pallbearers to the church where it was set down. Men kneeled and a long prayer was said (Ledoux 1936; see von Poser, this volume).

Anxieties motivated by death were nothing if not palpable. They gave rise to collective formations and expressions of mortuary dialogue, on the one hand to vigils and prayer, and to mysterious, dissociative states, on the other, in which "the ghost's desire" to remain among the living "overwhelm" the intentions of its pallbearers.

The bier was then taken to the graveyard, where it was placed in a grave and covered with a thin bark shroud. Knots were tied over Moiega's head. The grave was shallow and his head was left exposed. A cross was made and planted next to it. A few more knots were tied over the body by men. One man put a coin into the grave at the last moment.

In 1936, mourners and caregivers were treated solicitously. Contact with the dead was polluting, the corpse being a site at which death sprites (*pre menumb*) congregate and infect people in its proximity. Knots were tied to protect "the breath" of the mourners, men in particular, from being "buried" with the corpse (Figure 4.4).

The corpse is unclean and contagiously so. "Pollution dangers," so Mary Douglas taught us, "strike when form has been attacked" (1966: 104). What form was attacked? From the point of view of kinship, a husband, wife, brother, daughter, and so on has been lost. From a cosmological point of view, a spirit-passenger has lost its canoe-body. Notable consequences threaten men's agency, in particular their breath but also their eyesight. In this sense, death pollution is not associated with Oedipus, the blinded criminal whose self-punishment was "a mitigated form of ... castration" (Freud 1955: 231), but with the Murik belief that sexual contact with menstruating women causes shortness of breath and damages eyesight in ageing men. Recall the Kleinian conceit: the revenge of the bad breast is said to cause loss of breath, uncertainty, and illness.

Later that day, a few men uncovered Moiega's body to check for sorcery markings, such as distention of the tongue and discolorations of the teeth or

Figure 4.4. Men tie knots over a corpse in an open canoe-coffin. Photo: Louis Pierre Ledoux, 1936.

the chest. The body was reburied. But near twilight, some men went back to the cemetery to catch Moiega's ghost.[4] They inserted a bamboo tube into the ground by Moiega's head. "This is your canoe," they told the ghost and coaxed it to "get in" the tube with a leaf of tobacco. They took the tube back to Moiega's house. There, "the ghost" caused the hand of his widow to shake and led her about the room, making signs about who had killed him (Ledoux 1936).

Moiega's death aroused ambivalences among kin. Men, occasioned to enter trancelike states, experienced fears of invasive malevolence that they deny as originating from their rage or sadistic pleasure. They dissemble and project it outward through divinatory rites that accuse the other. Murik houses are and were filled with loads of imported goods, for example, wooden plates, clay pots, canarium almonds, as well as store-bought objects. Moiega's ghost would have pointed to these by way of indicating where his murderer had come from. Men put themselves in harm's way as they search for the killer so as to assert agency and potency. But, at the same time, men fail to domesticate death, which now converts neighbors into adversaries.

> The next day, a small group of men from the neighboring village of Big Murik charged into Kaup [village]. Wearing loincloths, and armed with real spears, they were decorated in red ochre and other war regalia. The people ... hid. The men were hunting for a pig, but found none. Someone

planted a tall banana tree with a cassowary feather wig near the Men's House. The warriors charged this 'enemy' and 'killed' him. They went home bearing a fat pig, given them by Moiega's family (Ledoux 1936).

Having battled sorcery threats, endured pollution, and suffered the indignity of this attack, interment in 1936 left Murik men and the community of the deceased in a state of defeat, if not collective depression—a result that was largely oblivious of modernity. A similar conclusion, by and large, might be reached fifty years later. Death continued to evoke the Kleinian breast in signifiers, old and new.

1982

The second set of cases, to which I now turn, draw from fieldwork I conducted during 1981–1993.[5] This research took place during the initial period of postcolonial sovereignty when PNG was first administered by nationals, most notably, as I say, by Sir Michael Somare, a Murik native son. Leadership of both the Catholic and SDA missions had also been taken over by the Murik themselves. Healthcare was provided by local Aid Post Orderlies. Only prenatal care remained in the expatriate hands of a Catholic nun from Germany. People used over-the-counter drugs to treat minor ailments. Folks with serious health problems were taken to the hospital in the provincial capital, which was then a full day's voyage via motorized outrigger canoe. The population, for the most part, remained healthy. There were no cases of HIV/AIDs, but there were a few cases of leprosy, tuberculosis, and epilepsy. Malaria, dengue fever, and skin problems (tropical ulcers and the like) were the most commonplace illnesses. In the following instance, death appears in a form that would be sensible to the Murik of 1936.

Around midmorning on 9 January, word went around Darapap village that a senior woman called Saimek had "died." Mortuary dialogue began in the Male Cult House, where men discussed which lineage ornaments ought to be brought to her and by whom. Meanwhile, a man pounded out a slit-drum beat (*brag debun*) that signaled kin living in neighboring villages of the death. Given the time of day, many women were away fishing. A largely male group of Saimek's kin and affines thus gathered in her son's house; the latter draped themselves over her body and wept. Chanting terms of relationship, they asked, why did Saimek go and abandon them? Why did she not want to stay? *Mwara* sisters, from the Female Cult, tied strings around the foreheads of their brothers. A senior man entered the room carrying a lineage basket. Crying nervously, he was about to call its name, when the old woman awoke and sat bolt upright (see Dalton, this volume).

In 1982, that is to say, the body did not index its own mortality. No pulse was taken. Nor had breathing been checked. Death remained viewed as an asocial state, along with sleep, rather than an irreversible, somatic transformation. Observe, also, that Saimek's "death" prompted cross-sex *mwara* kin to tie strings about the heads of mourners. This was said to reduce their pain and protect their souls from escaping through the fontanelle, which might split open from the pain of crying. The knotted person was still cared for like a canoe-body in need of repair (see Figure 4.1).

Two slit-drum beats were sounded in the Male Cult House. The first was the drumbeat of her war-spirit, which was meant to signal Saimek's death to matrikin. The second heralded that her lineage *sumon* had been put on public display. This act instituted an interval of "quiet" in the community, when all work and conflict were banned until the senior sibling group of the lineage sat down, had a meal together, and returned their insignia to its basket. In part, the taboo was meant to keep people away from the new spirit who was desperately lurking about its canoe-body, filling that space with desire, despair, and anger.

In response to Saimek's "death," signifiers were set in motion: lineage insignia, slit-drum beats, taboo time, and knots. Here, I take a cue from Bloch (1982), who argued that there is a close relationship between mortuary rites and the legitimization of sociopolitical order. However, instead of positing a functional relationship as he did, I want to suggest that these signifiers attempt to replace what has been revealed as inadequate, the magical agency of collective masculinity. Death betrays men's claims to defend or protect the community from the bad breast, its enemies, numinous and sentient, internal or external. Men react, I suggest, by attempting to bind the "leaks" in their power and potency that death has revealed.

This is not to claim, of course, that nothing changed. Corpse painting had ended. Graves were not provisioned with food. There was no disinterment. Death pollution had become less threatening. Knots were no longer tied above the head of the deceased. But the image of a husband, walking to bury his wife in 1982, with a bandana tied around his head (Figure 4.5), illustrates that neither the knotted person, nor his anxieties, nor the threats death posed to masculinity had changed beyond recognition. Neither the concept of a *nabran*-spirit lashed to his or her canoe-body nor its dispersal in metonmynic embodiments and consequent vulnerability to projections of the bad breast had been displaced by a modern, biosocial person.

All of this appeared again when another elderly woman, called Moru, died on 8 March 1982. On that day, her body was laid out on an open bier in her daughter's house. As Weem, the middle-aged daughter, clutched the edge of her mother's bier and wept melodically, Moru's *mwara* nieces appeared. Sporting rafia skirts decorated in shell and dogs' teeth ornaments, they pranced about the room, gleefully demanding that she get up and join them. "This is the moment of greatest antagonism from the joking partners.... They shout angrily and strike at the bier with hatchets normally used to chop firewood"

Figure 4.5. A grieving husband on his way to the cemetery with knotted headband, Darapap. Photo: David Lipset, 1982.

(Barlow 1992: 75). The new spirit of the deceased was still viewed as unready or disinclined to give up its relations with loved ones. The manic performance of the Female Cult was meant to defend the living from Moru's ghost and compel her to leave them alone, healthy and alive. Dressed in precapitalist wealth, they triumphed over their longtime rival by showing up her inability to join their antics. Onlookers responded to the performance with shrieks of nervous laughter.

Four grandsons hefted Moru's bier onto their shoulders and took it out the door and down the houseladder (Figure 4.6). Instead of heading straight for the cemetary, they carried the bier toward other houses where the dead woman's kin lived. Her ghost, people said, was directing them to do so. Eventually, one of Moru's sons exhorted his mother's ghost to let go.

Despite the interventions of the Female Cult, the death still spun people into possession states they disowned. A train of villagers proceded to the cemetary located about thirty meters beyond the last house. Weem, the grieving daughter, was escorted by *mwara* brothers while her uterine brothers were accompanied by *mwara* sisters. Dressed in a new skirt and top, Moru's body was placed in a sawed-off canoe hull and lowered into the ground, perhaps a few feet deep. Her *mwara* nieces put money on her chest. As a prayer was said, the daughter cried. A few young men covered her with dirt, erected a cross over her head, planted a couple of croton plants, and edged the grave with shells. People drifted home.

Figure 4.6. Moru's body, her daughter clinging to her bier, is carried from the Death House. Photo: David Lipset, 1982.

The main features of the burial—the performance of the Female Cult, the pallbearers ego-alien experience of Moru's *nabran*-spirit, the *mwara* kin escorting the mourners, Moru's new store-bought clothes, the cemetary, the canoe-coffin, the money her *mwara* kin placed on her chest, the prayer offered by the SDA pastor, the cross marking her grave, and the return directly home without tying knots or washing—succinctly and richly expressed voices of death in 1982. Here was a mortuary dialogue about the conditional position of the knotted person in Melanesian modernity. And, as I say, it had implications for ritual masculinity.

Two days later, there were rumors that an "attack" was being readied by a neighboring village in retaliation for a prior raid that the Darapap Male Cult staged years earlier. "Warriors" were expected to charge the village, armed with the right to plunder any property they might wish to claim. In response, villagers tied knots in coconut fronds around things of particular value, such as paddles, canoes, and outboard motors (Figure 4.7). After the "raid" ended, the warriors would expect a meal. Women began to cook. In the event, however, no invasion took place.

If death revived Kleinian ambivalences in 1982, arousing fears of external aggression, intrusion, and theft, that is, persecution by the bad breast, how were they allayed? By tying knots, the metonymic act of canoe maintenance. And how were moral relations to be repaired? By acts of oral-satisfaction, signifying

Figure 4.7. Knotted property marker tied onto the shaft of a canoe paddle prior to the "attack." Photo: David Lipset, 1982.

the good breast. The depressive position takes a specifically masculine register in Murik and more generally in rural Melanesia: death threatens not just the person and the community but the Male Cult.

By the same token, change had already redefined burial practices by 1936. The afterlife of the knotted person was no longer defined in terms of the ancestors and the magical agency of the Male Cult. The colonial state had imposed cemetary regulations. Prayerful poses were assumed, and prayers were recited. Graves, dug with shovels, were marked with crosses. Funerary goods included coins. By 1982, the knotted person had become more deeply engaged in dialogue, now not with the colonial Australian modernity but with a postcolonial Melanesian and a global one. The body was dressed in Western clothes and not painted. Most graves were not provisioned for the voyage to the afterlife. Bodies were not partially buried. Faces were no longer left exposed. Disinterment divination practices had been abandoned. Death pollution fears had diminished.

Meanwhile, however, important elements of the knotted person persisted. *Nabran*-spirits continued to possess pallbearers. Bodies were still buried in sawed-off canoe hulls. Knots were still tied to "moor" the spirit in the body when the subject was grief stricken and to secure property from "attacks" by neighboring "enemies." In the aftermath of death, the mortuary dialogue between Kleinian ambivalences and Melanesian modernity had become more equivocal than in 1936.

2010

In the last case, Rhiana, a middle-aged mother of six, was murdered by her husband, Michael, on the grounds of the Malaysian timber company where he was employed.[6] Allegedly, Michael had beaten her for years because she refused to consent to his desire to take a second wife. Now it was said that he struck her repeatedly across the head and shoulders with a thick board. Other than that, I am unaware of what specifically happened that provoked the husband's fatal attack. Rhiana was brought to a district hospital and pronounced dead there, after which her body was transported to the morgue in Wewak, the provincial capital. In this instance, in other words, there was a human, rather than a spectral, culprit.

I was in Wewak town in August 2010 and met Joe Kabong, Rhiana's disconsolate, but busy, father, who was engaged in yet another kind of mortuary dialogue: he was filing charges against his son-in-law. Kabong wanted a postmortem examination of his daughter's body done in order to establish an official cause of death, thus to gather evidence against Michael, who was eventually arrested and jailed. As part of a legal proceeding, a kinsman told me that

Rhiana's corpse had become a "public body," which now "belonged," in some kind of legal-proprietary sense, to "the state."

The family had no access to it and would only have twenty-four hours to remove it from the morgue after the postmortem was completed. Kabong was rushing about town to prepare his daughter's funeral in the village and to conclude obligations to urban *mwara* kin, whom he was obliged to acknowledge for having staged a mourning vigil when the news of the death first broke. Kabong approached a Malaysian manager of the timber company with demands for monetary compensation since the daughter died on its property. He was also calling in debts from trading partners, debts both of money and produce. Meanwhile, he had dispatched a kinsman to buy a coffin. Eventually, a relative was located who gave him a cut-rate price for a simple plank coffin.

About two weeks later, the funeral party made its way in two fiberglass boats to Darapap village, where Kabong lived with his second wife. En route, stops were made in Kaup, the husband's village, as well as in Karau, Darapap's sister community, where one of Rhiana's brothers and other lineage members from Kayan had gathered (see von Poser, this volume). Out of refrigeration for two days when it reached Darapap, the body was brought to the Death House (*Pre Iran*) upon arrival, the house of Kabong's neighbor. The father's house was much too small to accomodate the many mourners expected, and although the adjacent building belonged to a leading family in the SDA Mission, being kin, its owners were willing to allow elements of the funerary proceedings, such as the visitation by the Female Cult, that their Christianity strictly repudiated.

The Death House was decorated by nothing less than a canopy of knots (Figure 4.8). Strips of clothing, some tied to each other, were tied on strings that crisscrossed the ceiling, like a kind of bunting. Beneath this canopy, a throng of women immediately fell upon Rhiana's coffin and began to weep and wail. Rhiana's *mwara* kin draped the coffin with a cotton sheet and then repaired to the corners of the house, where they watched passively. The house, now full of people, became the temporary sanctum of the Female Cult. Men, for their part, gathered in the Male Cult House only a few meters away. Later that day, three senior men brought insignia baskets representing the lineages into which Rhiana had been initiated and hung them up from the rafters above her coffin so she could take them, or rather their spirit-images, to the afterlife and be recognized by her ancestors.

In his nearbye house, Joe Kabong and his two wives, Paulina and Du, began to ready large pig feasts for each of the two secret societies following Rhiana's burial. The Female Cult stayed up all night talking and singing to keep Rhiana's *nabran*-spirit company. In the Male Cult House, where the death was discussed, one young man recounted going with his wife to visit Rhiana several months earlier. "I will soon die," he recalled her predicting, without admitting that her husband was regularly beating her. "How did she know she was going to die? She kept crying. She told us, 'You will leave and I will die!'" Rhiana was a good woman, generous to a fault, everyone seemed to agree, shaking their heads. Youth were angry and threatened that should her husband appear to grieve, he wouldn't get out of the village alive.

The following morning, the Female Cult, now in white face, dressed in raffia skirts, and sporting shell ornaments over their blouses, walked in a great line under the arch that the SDA Mission had erected in front of the Death House. Upon entering the building, they put clothes and money on the coffin, gifts to their fallen comrade that she could wear and use en route to the afterlife. Rhiana's initiation outfit, a rafia skirt, shell bandoliers, and a painted palm spathe cap, was also placed on the coffin. Then, they called out to Rhiana to get up and join them. As a few women danced suggestively about the coffin, others proceded to jump over her coffin one by one, calling out the names of their warrior spirits as they did (Figure 4.8). After their celebrations subsided, Rhiana's sisters and mothers were given a last opportunity to approach the open casket before it was nailed shut. One sister fell into a trance and began to punch women standing by her until she was restrained by *mwara* kin, who lay her down on the floor. Rhiana's angry ghost, it was said, had possessed her body, being irate at having been shown up by the Female Cult.

That afternoon, after Rhiana's sister had been helped away from a final embrace with the corpse, the coffin was closed. Six young men, her *mwara* brothers all, then shouldered it out of the house and down a footpath toward

Figure 4.8. Members of the Female Cult take turns jumping over Rhiana's coffin beneath a canopy of knotted strips of fabric. Photo: David Lipset, 2010.

the cemetary. Along the way, as her uterine brother approached the coffin in tears, they turned off in a direction toward the beach and away from the graveyard. Rhiana's father, who had positioned himself at the intersection of the two footpaths, put his hand on the coffin as if to stop it (Figure 4.9).

"My daughter," he said, "do not worry. I will bring your husband to court. He will not go free. He will get time for what he has done to you." The pallbearers turned back toward the cemetery. A long parade of mourners, who included perhaps a dozen visitors from the family in Karau and Kayan, trailed behind. At the cemetary, a shallow grave had been prepared. Three thick green coconut stems had been placed across its width. Seawater had begun to seep into the floor. One of Rhiana's *mwara* brothers scooped it out with a yellow plastic bucket as best he could. The coffin, still covered with a cotton sheet, was lowered into it. Leaning against the trunk of a coconut tree, one of Rhiana's sisters cried into a towel. A village deacon in the SDA Mission offered a brief prayer: Rhiana would be soon resurrected, he said, along with the rest of the dead, when Christ returned. Kin dropped flowers onto the coffin (Figure 4.10).

While the Death House was turned into a thoroughly knotted space, knots were not tied before young men shoveled the wet sand into the grave. As Rhiana's father watched the youth finish filling the grave, he leaned over to

Figure 4.9. Rhiana's brother cried (l.) while her father consoled her *nabran*-spirit. Photo: David Lipset, 2010.

Figure 4.10. A prayer is said at Rhiana's grave. Photo: David Lipset, 2010.

me standing next to him. Should any dirt dug out of a grave fail to get shoveled back into it, he said, what remained was an omen that another death might soon follow. Some *mwara* kin began the conventional horseplay and insulting mockery of their joking relationship. Everyone else drifted off, rather quietly. I went to the beach for a swim but found none of the pallbearers there. They had gone back to their homes or card games.

In 2010, with Rhiana's death and her subsequent classification as a "public body"—that is, as the state's legal property before it was returned to her kin and their cosmologies, Murik and Christian—a new position entered the mortuary dialogue between the knotted subject and Melanesian modernity not heard of before. However, the general balance of sentiment, imagery, and views in it still remained recognizably Murik. Death continued to provoke a display of vernacular expressions of care and support as well as denials of guilt, that is, the reparation of the good breast.

To be sure, these signifiers, and here I refer to the supportive role of Rhiana's *mwara* kin and the pseudoantagonism of the Female Cult in particular, were supplemented by nationalized Christianity as well as the postcolonial state. At the same time, Rhiana's death itself at the hands of her enraged husband, the belligerent trance state into which her sister fell, the suspicious dicussion in the Men's House I cited, and the ego-alien indirection of the coffin on its way to the cemetary all imply one thing. The bad breast, which is threatening and angry, had vividly split off from its counterpart in externalized terms that also remained decidedly Murik. In all, the meanings of Rhiana's corpse both were and were not part of an introjected, local other: her "public body" became local where it aroused the breasts, both good and bad, but in ways that were subdued and toned down compared to 1936.

By contrast to the conspicuous role played by the Female Cult, the Male Cult had little to say. Other than providing an event space for the men's vigil, I heard no slit-drum percussion emanating from it either to declare a taboo time of death or to end it. Moreover, while the Female Cult maintained their vigil through the night before the burial, the men did not. No attempts were made to secure mystical knowledge from the corpse about its demise. In this instance, the Male Cult had been displaced by medical practices conducted in the name of the legal system of the state, the postmortem.

Why Do the Enemies Remain Local?

I have compared Murik death and funerary practices in 1936, 1982, and 2010. The problem I think they raise is to account for the relationship of a local concept of personhood to a succession of modernities. That is to say, the shape of the Murik person in the context of death has changed over the period of time in question. How do we see its new shape? How can we explain what has been preserved and lost in it as well as what has been added to it? Rather than see identity change in terms of cargo cult millenialism or conversion, that is, as involving a wholecloth rejection of the past (Smith 1982; cf. Robbins 2007), answering such a question in shades of gray is meant to advocate a nuanced approach to the circumstances that have given rise to a historically particular concept of Murik personhood amid Melanesian modernity. What are these circumstances?

Although there is no clear-cut relationship between demography and attitudes about death, mortality rates in Murik seem relatively stable in the twenty-first century. Indeed, village population spiked in the 1990s. The spread of HIV/AIDs throughout PNG has had little effect in villages, and or on their conventional life-cycles or attitudes about death. This is not to overlook urban-rural migration cycles which attract male youth in particular. But thus far, epidemic diseases have not devastated the cultural landscape of death in Murik.

Between the 1930s and 1980s, Western health care, pharmaceuticals, and biological concept of illness were never widely or thoroughly available. Indeed, hospitals used to send terminal patients "home to die" rather than have them die under medical cares and thus be seen as unable cure them. People were then confirmed in their sorcery-based, local explanations of death. Nor did Christianity, despite its long history on the Murik coast, transform peoples' thinking (cf. Schram 2007). But while funerary practices in particular were subjected to rules that banned body painting, homestead burial, disinterment, keeping bone relics of kin, and so on, missionaries never demanded that Catholic or SDA converts stop attending the funerals of non-Christian kin.

Death may have played a central part in conversations between missionaries and the Murik in connection with the resurrection, for example, but the sacrifice of the Christian God never trumped the knotted person. Melanesian modernity has not had much to offer to village funerary practices, other than the occassional coffin, urban refrigerated morgues, and, of course, air transportation of corpses.

Capitalism and its related concepts of private property and possessive individualism (MacPherson 1962) have penetrated Murik kinship and economy. But little development has taken place. Despite chronic deficits due to lack of arable land, the Murik small-scale fishery sustains the adaptive strategy of trade and petty capitalism to feed the population and pay the costs of daily needs, such as rice and batteries, but it does not seem to enable capital accumulation. The Murik Lakes are not a space of poverty. At the same time, this intertidal commons limits development.

In the absence of aquaculture projects, the Murik Lakes are not divisible in the way land may be divided between cash cropping and subsistence production. The fishery cannot be isolated, as land may be set aside for coffee or copra production. Moreover, the Murik Lakes have not produced, and I suspect that they are not capable of producing, large-scale harvests. As such, no substantial sums of money have flooded the local-level economy (see Bainton and Macintyre, this volume). Remittances from employed kin typically take the form of outboard motors and boats. The villages have not become stratified between rich and poor peasants to any notable degree. There are subtle degrees of difference, to be sure, but not unresolvable ones that cut kinship ties.

Finally, a word about a relatively benign colonial and postcolonial history. Neither the state nor extractive industries have polluted or otherwise damaged the Sepik estuary. Nor is the comparative picture of postcolonism any more problematic in the nation as a whole. Regional networks, not to mention international ones, have only begun to advance mobility. Telecommunications have not altered the Murik sense of belonging, either to unmoor or disconnect it from the villages or to reorient or integrate national and local space into a new spectral geography.

Civil war, nuclear bombs, and ongoing, more banal, forms of violence have not forced or caused truncations of funerary practices. International migration has not shifted burial practices and created new needs or a funeral industry to fill them (see Carucci, this volume). While we have seen that funerals give rise to mortuary dialogue about personhood (see Bell, this volume), political debates over the nature of citizenship in the postcolony, for example, or forms of ethnic identity (see Wilson and Sinclair, this volume), they have not entered into, much less taken over, the Murik work of death.

Death continues to arouse love, anger, guilt, and fear. That is, death evokes the Kleinian breast and the collective project of reparation. Rather than atemporal breasts, dialogized breasts inform and are informed by Murik history and habitus as well as Melanesian modernity. Death elicits expressions of love, care, and longing from mourning kin. Mourning goes on sending men and women into possession states. Mourning gives rise to manic performances by the Female Cult. Grief goes on being cared for by tying knots. People go on being buried in sawed-off canoe hulls as well as coffins. While the Kaliai of East New Britain (Lattas 1993) criticize colonial and state-based modernity through death-related fantasies and dreams of persecution, the ghosts and ritual retaliations Murik fear remain local and nonstate in origin.

However, the dialogue between Murik death and mourning and modernity shows a weakened Male Cult and "his" canoe-body cosmology. In 1936, the male person was "knotted" and Christian. By 1982, with the end of painting canoe motifs on the dead, the end of disinterment divination practices, and the decline of death pollution fears, "he" had become somewhat less knotted. In 2010, Melanesian modernity still contested "his" voice, but although "his" voice remained unmerged, it was rather quiet.

The conjunction of Murik and modern views of death—the one processual, plural, and local, knotted, in a word, and the other punctual and irrevocable, binary and objective—remains open and unpredictable, rather than reducible to a single vision of identity that might stand above either of them. Polyphonic authorities superimpose their dialogue upon the Kleinian rage, guilt, and love that mourning revives. At these times, we encounter equivocal commentary—a both/and exchange about the person in a postcolonial world in a state of becoming.

David Lipset is Professor of Anthropology at the University of Minnesota. He has done fieldwork in the Murik Lakes region of the Sepik River in Papua New Guinea off and on since 1981. He is the author of *Gregory Bateson: Legacy of a Scientist* (1982) and *Mangrove Man: Dialogics of Culture in the Sepik Estuary* (1997) in addition to two co-edited volumes and many journal articles and book chapters.

Notes

1. The Murik are hereditary trading partners of both the Manam Islanders and the Kayan people.

2. Note that calling out the name of deceased kin at twilight draws their *nabran* close, which threatens the living rather than reviving the dead.
3. Usually erected over a grave or, at least, over a relic of an ancestor.
4. Ledoux wanted to go along but was not permitted to do so because he "smell[ed] of soap" (1936: 139).
5. Initially with Kathleen Barlow.
6. Names have been changed in this case. The company had been clear-cutting logs for at least a decade on lands adjacent to the westernmost Murik-speaking village of Kaup, where he was from.

References Cited

Abraham, Karl. 1927. *Selected Papers of Karl Abraham, M.D.* London: L. & Virginia Wolff.

Bakhtin, Mikhael. 1981. *The Dialogic Imagination: Four Essays by M. M. Bakhtin*, edited by Michael Holquist. Austin: University of Texas Press.

———. 1984. *Problems of Dostoevsky's Poetics.* Translated by Caryl Emerson. Minneapolis: University of Minnesota Press.

Barlow, Kathleen. 1985. "The Social Context of Infant Feeding in the Murik Lakes of Papua New Guinea." In *Infant Care and Feeding in the South Pacific*, edited by LB Marshall, 137–54. New York: Gordon and Breach.

———. 1992. "Dance When I Die! Context and Role in the Clowning of Murik Women." In *Clowning as Critical Practice*, edited by W. Mitchell, 58–78. Pittsburgh: University of Pittsburgh Press.

Barlow, Kathleen and David Lipset. 1997. "Dialogics of Material Culture: Male and Female in Murik Outrigger Canoes." *American Ethnologist* 24(1): 4–36.

Bloch, Maurice. 1982. "Death, Women and Regeneration." In *Death and the Regeneration of Life*, edited by M. Bloch and J. Parry, 211–30. Cambridge: Cambridge University Press.

Bourdieu, Pierre. 1977. *Outline of a Theory of Practice.* Cambridge: Cambridge University Press.

Brison, Karen. 1998. "Giving Sorrow New Words: Shifting Politics of Bereavement in a Papua New Guinea Village." *Ethos* 26(4): 363–86.

Douglas, Mary. 1966. *Purity and Danger: An Analysis of Concepts of Pollution and Taboo.* London: Routledge and Kegan Paul.

Frankel, Stephen and Gilbert Lewis. 1989. *A Continuing Trial of Treatment: Medical Pluralism in Papua New Guinea.* Boston: Kluwer Academic Publishers.

Freud, Sigmund. 1955. "The 'Uncanny.'" In *The Standard Edition of the Complete Psychological Works of Sigmund Freud (vol. 17)*, translated by James Strachey, 217–52. London: Hogarth Press.

Ingold, Tim. 2000. *The Perception of the Environment: Essays in Livelihood, Dwelling and Skill.* London: Routledge.

Klein, Melanie. 1946. "Notes on Some Schizoid Mechanisms." *International Journal of Psycho-Analysis* 27: 99–110.

———. 1975. *Love, Guilt and Reparation and Other Works, 1921–1945.* New York: Delacorte Press.

Kuchler, Suzanne. 2003. "The Knot in Pacific Imagination." *L'Homme* 165: 205–23.

Lattas, Andrew. 1993. "Sorcery and Colonialism: Illness, Dreams and Death as Political Languages in West New Britain." *Man* NS 28 (1): 51–77.

Ledoux, Louis Pierre. 1936. "Unpublished fieldnotes in author's possession."

Lewis, Gilbert. 1976. "A View of Sickness in New Guinea." In *Social Anthropology and Medicine*, edited by JB Loudon (ASA Monograph 13), 49–103. London: Academic Press.

Lipset, David. 2014. "Living Canoes: Vehicles of Moral Imagination among the Murik of Papua New Guinea." In *Vehicles: Cars, Canoes and Other Metaphors of Moral Imagination*, edited by David Lipset and Richard Handler, 21–47. New York: Berghahn Press.

MacPherson, CB. 1962. *The Political Theory of Possessive Individualism: Hobbes to Locke*. Oxford: Oxford University Press.

Manguin, Pierre-Yves. 1986. "Shipshape Societies: Boat Symbolism and Political Systems in Insular Southeast Asia." In *Southeast Asia in the 9th to 14th Centuries*, edited by David G. Marr and AC Milner, 187–214. Singapore: Institute of Southeast Asia Studies and Research School of Pacific Studies.

Mbembe, Achille. 1992. "Provisional Notes on the Postcolony." *Africa* 62(1): 3–37.

Robbins, Joel. 2007. "Continuity Thinking and the Problem of Christian Culture: Belief, Time and the Anthropology of Christianity." *Current Anthropology* 48(1): 5–38.

Schmidt, Joseph. 1922–1923. "Die Ethnographie der Nor-Papua (Murik-Kaup-Karau) bei Dallmanhafen, Neu-Guinea." Translated by K. Barlow. *Anthropos* 18–19: 700–32.

———. 1926. "Die Ethnographie der Nor-Papua (Murik-Kaup-Karau) bei Dallmanhafen, Neu-Guinea." Translated by K. Barlow. *Anthropos* 21: 38–71.

———. 1933. "Neue Beitrage zur Ethnographie der Nor-Papua (Neuguinea)." Translated by K. Barlow. *Anthropos* 28: 321–54, 663–82.

Schram, Ryan. 2007. "Sit, Cook, Eat, Full Stop: Religion and the Rejection of Ritual in Auhelawa (Papua New Guinea)." *Oceania* 77: 172–92.

Smith, M. Estellie. 1982. "The Process of Sociocultural Continuity." *Current Anthropology* 23(2): 127–42.

Somare, Michael. 1975. *Sana: An Autobiography of Michael Somare*. Hong Kong: Niugini Press.

Stephen, Michele. 1999. "Witchcraft, Grief and the Ambivalence of Emotions." *American Ethnologist* 26(3): 1–27.

Tuzin, Donald. 1997. *The Cassowary's Revenge: The Life and Death of Masculinity in a New Guinea Society*. Chicago: University of Chicago Press.

5
Mortuary Ritual and Mining Riches in Island Melanesia

NICHOLAS A. BAINTON and MARTHA MACINTYRE

In this chapter, we analyze the historical changes to mortuary ritual in the context of large-scale resource development in insular Papua New Guinea (PNG). We compare the Lihir Islands in New Ireland Province, where a gold mine is ongoing, with changes on Misima Island in Milne Bay Province, where a mine had shut down.[1] In Lihir and Misima, mortuary rituals are similarly structured around an extended series of feasts and exchanges that complete obligations toward the deceased and create renown for the hosts. Lihirians and Misimans have been quick students of development and swiftly put their newfound wealth to good use in customary feasting. The resulting efflorescence of custom has been a defining feature of their engagement with mining capitalism. At present, Lihirian mortuary rituals continue to expand in step with the growing mining economy, while the closure of the Misima gold mine in 2004 forced a reduction in Misiman ritual excess.

Our central concerns are the ways that mortuary feasting and exchange—*kastom* par excellence—have endured and transformed. More specifically, we are interested in the changes that have taken place as these customary practices are kept relevant in periods of dramatic change. This includes not only the incorporation of introduced goods but the ways in which traditions and social obligations are imagined or idealized in moments of flux. We argue that the persistence of mortuary rituals is not simply the result of cultural continuity but the deliberate and selective revival of traditions as a direct response to modernity: in mortuary rituals, local society and individual actors engage with the processes of modernity engendered through large-scale resource development. As the fluctuations in the resource economy are voiced in the ceremonial sphere, a mortuary dialogue of creative, persistent, local answers to global capitalism is taking place.

Economies of Excess

The capacity of Melanesian exchange systems to absorb new forms of wealth and adapt to changing circumstances is well documented (see Akin and Robbins 1999; Gregory 1982; Strathern 1971a). Ian Hughes's classic historical overview of the inflation and rapid decline in shell valuables in the Central Highlands during the colonial period (1978)[2] provides insight into, and perhaps an analogy of, the boom and bust conditions associated with large-scale mining and the changes unfolding in Lihir and Misima. As the colonial powers imported huge quantities of shells to pay for labor and goods, an extraordinary escalation of exchange activities resulted. With more shells in circulation, the terms of trade declined and shells were soon devalued and replaced by state-based currencies, which in some cases saw an end to entire exchange systems.

However, the recent changes to mortuary exchange in Lihir and Misima have occurred at a time when these societies were already thoroughly monetized. The onset of resource development has not replaced shell valuables with cash or eroded mortuary exchange. Rather, mining gave rise to an "exchange glut" and the chronic inflation of prestations. Instead of a mass importation of shells, there has been a massive influx of money, which has enabled Lihirians and Misimans to purchase more pigs, garden produce, and store items for mortuary exchange.[3] And as we shall see, with more money, Lihirians have acquired more shells to sustain the ceremonial cycle. In this new world of surplus, Lihirians are compelled ever increasingly to spend on sumptuary feasts in pursuit of honor and status. As Georges Bataille might have it, such "excessive exchange" is like a kind of "deliriously formed ritual poker. But the players can never retire from the game, their fortunes made; they remain at the mercy of provocation" (1985: 122–23). In this case, mine closure might offer the only exit from such interminable competition.

Phenomena associated with cultural efflorescence are hardly new or restricted to Melanesia. Similar changes have taken place around the globe as people domesticated introduced goods and wealth—a process Marshall Sahlins (1992) has termed "develop*man*," in which indigenous people use Western things for their purposes in order to become more like themselves. The inspirational heritage for Sahlins's neologism was partly derived from a quote by a Kewa big man on the meaning of development. The quote was borrowed from Lisette Josephides's ethnography, which was based on fieldwork conducted in the PNG Highlands between 1979 and 1981 (Josephides 1985).

Sahlins interprets the Kewa man as saying that their version of development is "building up the lineage, the men's house, and killing pigs." This provided the springboard to launch his concept of develop*man*, whereby development is initially understood by indigenous people to be "their culture on a bigger scale." But Josephides was quoting from an earlier publication to which Sahlins did not refer, which reveals a somewhat different context from the one that Sahlins had assumed:

> Development, in as far as it is understood at all, is seen as a unilateral evolutionary stage that inevitably will come to all, mediated by the

> government or "companies." It is monolithic, substantive even, and foreign. As one bigman once told us, "You know what *we* mean by 'development' (in Kewa, *Ada ma rekato* [to raise or awaken the village]: building a 'house line' [*neada*], a 'men's house' [*tapada*], 'killing pigs' [*yawemena*]). This we have done. Now we are talking about white people's development." (Josephides and Schiltz 1982: 82)

Notwithstanding the value of Sahlins's concept—and the kind of cultural enlargement he describes has certainly unfolded in Lihir and Misima—there is a sense in which Sahlins's interpretation rests upon a double misunderstanding of the original quote, which may serve Sahlins's purposes but only brings us part of the way toward understanding Lihirian responses to mining. The Kewa big man was contrasting a traditional (precontact) conception of development, one that had already been achieved, with the coming of the all-encompassing white man's development that they were now being drawn into.

Although mining did not introduce Lihirians or Misimans to Western development, this was the first time that the material improvements associated with development became realistically attainable. From local perspectives, Melanesian visions of development invariably include things like hospitals, roads, airports, wharves, and schools—institutions and facilities associated with the modern state. But in the postmining era, Misimans have witnessed a sudden decline in the maintenance of these services, and the subsequent reduction in the economy is mirrored in the ways that people have altered sequential mortuary exchanges.

For Lihirians, "being more like themselves" is a critical element of their ideas of development. But as we demonstrate below, the complexity of their desires and visions of development demand that they not only build upon custom and "develop" it but simultaneously acquire the material goods that "modern economic development" brings, attain "moral equivalence" with Westerners, and incorporate *new* ways of being "developed" that synthesize cultural traditions with new political and economic objectives. In this desired state of development, mortuary rituals, or *kastom*, are seamlessly interwoven with grand social projects. Cultural efflorescence emerges from not only the novel activities of the island's nouveau riche but their deliberately selective construction of culture.

Lihir Society

The Lihir Islands are composed of the main island of Aniolam and three small outer islands, Malie, Masahet, and Mahur. Throughout the colonial period there was negligible development in Lihir. The Catholic and Methodist missions and the local copra industry provided the main points of contact with the outside world (see Bainton 2008a). National independence in 1975 brought few material changes to Lihir, and it was not until the late 1980s, when mining negotiations commenced, that Lihirians were more consistently involved with the cash economy and a wider range of foreigners. The start of mining operations in 1995 on Aniolam Island brought dramatic changes as the first land compensation payments were made and residents from Putput and Kapit villages were relocated to make way for mine operations.[4]

Lihirians were soon divided between people who owned land in the mine lease areas and people who did not. The lease area landowners have since received the largest share of mining benefits through compensation, royalties, village development projects, and business contracts with the mine (see Bainton and Macintyre 2013). The majority of Lihirians were not lease area landowners and only benefited indirectly from the mine through employment, increased health and education services, and general social and economic development. Although the unequal distribution of mine-related benefits has been the source of considerable social division, the conspicuous consumption of wealth through lavish mortuary rituals has provided a crucial means for the redistribution of benefits.

Lihirians reckon descent through matrilineal clan groups that are focused on lineage men's houses. Feasting and exchange and men's house leadership have remained central to Lihirian notions of masculinity, political leadership, and land tenure. Over time, Lihirian big men utilized new avenues to acquire status and wealth through copra production, Church leadership, local government, employment, and business activities (see Bainton 2008b). Men's houses still provide the center stage for social reproduction: it is here that Lihirians socialize young males into manhood, provide nurturance and hospitality, assume leadership roles, bury their dead, and perform ritual celebrations, particularly the final large-scale mortuary rituals that complete social obligations and confirm leadership and group solidarity. In this way, men's houses provide the arena for society "to come up," as Lihirians say, and, in good L'Annee sociologique fashion, triumph over death.

There are more than twenty different feasts that mark the various stages in the life cycle and other important events in Lihirian personhood, all of which involve the exchange and consumption of pigs, garden produce, shell money, and now cash and commodities. The final three mortuary feasts are the most elaborate forms of "forgetting" and "finishing" the person in society (see Lutkehaus, this volume). In the vernacular, these three rites are glossed as the *karat* cycle, or *lugara* in New Ireland Tok Pisin. They consist of the sacred men's "taboo" feast (*hararum*), the *katkatop* feast, and the final, celebratory "cooking the deceased" feast (*tutunkanut*). Most Lihirians agree that particular stages are required to authenticate a feast but do not always agree on their correct order.

It is likely that variation is nothing new, particularly since big men are praised for their ability to innovate so an event might be made more memorable. Ideally, as a man approached seniority, his clan would host a "taboo" feast to show him respect and commemorate his status. When he died, burial feasts would be held to begin the mourning period (*barbare*). This phase would be followed by a *katkatop* feast, the penultimate mourning feast that is staged in a somber and reflective mood. Several people might be commemorated by a *katkatop* feast, preparation for which might take months or even years. Finally, after many years, the clan will mount a large *tutunkanut* feast, which confirms the mantle of leadership and the inheritance of resources and completes the cycle of obligation toward deceased clan members.

Ritual Change

The past century ushered in various changes to Lihirian burial practices and understandings of death. Secondary burial rites were once important for the completion of the full ritual sequence and these rites drew from Lihirian notions of the moral person and revolved around the social decomposition of the body, à la Hertz. The secondary handling of the bones derived from a concern over the fate of the body, whose bones were understood as "still being the person" (Hemer 2013: 94). Ideas of moral personhood are reflected in the Lihirian term *kanut*, which is used to refer to both the body of the deceased and its spirit.

Historical alterations to Lihirian burial rites are reflected in changes in ideas about death, and these changes have been mutually reinforcing. Missionaries and government administrators were instrumental in establishing common village cemeteries, encouraging deep burial and the abandonment of arcane mortuary practices, practices that were later confirmed through the adoption of Christianity. Many Lihirians have come to view the world through a classical sort of modern dualism that separates spirit from body, and postmortem practices have gradually shifted away from emphasis on the body (*kanut*) to the spirit (*a tomber/kanut*). As we demonstrate below, the emphasis has moved further toward the politics and ritual economy of death, displacing the centrality of the deceased body and the transition of the spirit to the afterlife.

The head is regarded by Lihirians as sacred because it is the repository of the spirit in life and in death. In the past, this was evidenced by a great reverence for skulls. Temporary burial was followed by elaborate mortuary rites in which the skull was unearthed and decorated for display before a secondary burial, often in caves, took place. During the final *tutunkanut* feast, the skull of the deceased was painted with lime and red ochre pigments and mounted on the ridgepole of the men's house, or it stood on a carved pole in the enclosure of the men's house where the feast was held (a feasting stage termed *pizoz kanut*, or "decoration of the skull/deceased"). Several skulls might be set up, depending upon the scale of the feast.[5] The ultimate purpose of these impressive figures (*mormor*) was to remind guests of the deceased. These figures were magically enlivened, perhaps instilling fear into guests, thus to boost the host's prestige through the display of his spiritual agency. The skulls were later interred in local caves. Here the deceased were transformed into an asset for the host clan, which was seen to help ensure that the feast was made memorable.

Mission and government concerns over the supposed sacrilegious disturbance of the dead were the main reasons for the gradual abandonment of this ritual, which was last performed on Mahur Island in 1987.[6] Some older Lihirians recall stories about the storage of bodies in the rafters of the men's house, where the deceased was dried until the body was ritually burnt in the final *tutunkanut* feast. Whether or not the skull was also used to construct *mormor* poles may have depended upon the social standing of the deceased. Remnants of long disused "hanging poles" (*kuets*) can still be found in the enclosures of several men's houses on Masahet Island. These poles remain highly taboo, and according to several informants, clan groups would also hang their battle victims from these poles to show their power. During *tutunkanut* feasts, and when *malanggan* carvings or *mormor* were being prepared, the *kuets* pole would be decorated with shell money, and pigs and victims would be killed and displayed on the pole. This terrifying sight reinforced the authority of warrior leaders.

Burial took several forms. On the outer islands, sea burial was once a common practice (see Carucci, this volume). At least for the disposal of low-status people, a large stone would be tied around the corpse. While it is unclear whether the deceased were ritually launched out to sea in canoes, it remains common to bury people in a disused canoe (Hemer 2013: 242). Community cemeteries were more frequently used during the colonial era, but in recent decades a general shift back to burying people in their men's house enclosure has occurred. One explanation offered for this change cites sorcery fears and the need to protect deceased clan members from mystical interference (see Lipset, this volume).

Catholic Missionaries reinforced, rather than suppressed, dialogue between Christianity and Lihirian custom. As Lihirians experienced Catholicism as a powerful ritual practice and strong spiritual reality, Catholic rites were incorporated into the mortuary sequence (see Wilson and Sinclair, this volume). In most cases today, a Christian funeral service is held in the hamlet of the deceased followed by burial in their men's house enclosure. During a *tutunkanut* feast held on Masahet Island in 2011, hosts were praised for reciting Christian prayers throughout its preparatory stages as well as on each feast day—prayers to God for a successful event that replaced spells cast by magicians and "weather men" to protect the day from supernatural meddling by rivals.

Notwithstanding Christian concepts of the afterlife and the division of body and soul, Lihirian cosmology is understood through a sacred topography focused on the giant Ailaya rock on Aniolam Island. This large outcrop is the centerpiece of Lihirian sacred geography and is understood as the portal to the Lihirian afterlife. Lihirians continue to practice symbolic mortuary rites that involve seating the deceased in a canoe in the men's house and singing mournful songs that chart the journey of the deceased across the landscape and the ocean to their final destination at the Ailaya. This ritual process is followed by a Christian burial. The dialogue between Christianity and custom is further reflected in the extent to which Lihirians have reconciled the idea of accessing the Christian heaven through this cosmographic portal. These mortuary rituals and the journey of the deceased are now complicated by the location of the Ailaya rock within the mining operation, signaling broader sociological and cosmological dialogues throughout Lihir (see Bainton et al. 2012).

The Early Mining Years

Mortuary feasts staged on Aniolam and Masahet islands in 1995–1996 allow us to glimpse how rituals were practiced prior to mining and the influx of money. In these times, burial rites stretched over a couple of weeks, sometimes longer. During initial mourning, while kin came and went, a few women, who were designated mourners of the deceased's lineage, stayed in a specially constructed shelter (*polpol*) for the duration (see Wilson and Sinclair, this volume). The burial itself was conducted according to Catholic rites, and subsequent feasts rarely involved more than a hundred people. The few relatives who visited from distant villages and other islands were usually closely related to the deceased as affines or kin who had moved at marriage. Variation in form and sequence largely depended on the wealth and influence of particular households.[7]

In interviews, people reported larger feasts in the past, when scores of pigs would be given and feast gardens were "ten times the size" of those prepared by then-contemporary feast givers. Even allowing for exaggeration, it does appear that the number of people who normally attended a funeral and the subsequent feasts were indeed declining in the early independence era, a decline people attributed to lack of transportation and prevailing poverty due to a collapse of copra production. At that time, while all hamlets still built men's houses, many were in an advanced state of disrepair (see Filer 1992), which meant that the feasts and rituals were concentrated in the fenced hamlet enclosure, with guests and hosts sitting and sleeping in hastily constructed shelters.

During the early phase of mine construction in 1996–1998, dramatic changes in the scale of feasts began to occur. A road around the main island was built, and the purchase of four-wheel drive vehicles and fiberglass boats enabled attendance to the point that, at least on one occasion, the host village was unprepared for a large number of guests and had to scramble to find sufficient food and pigs. This excited period of optimism gave rise to a sudden redefinition of feasts as a means of displaying a lineage's access to cash. Mine employees and recipients of compensation payments instantly became obliged to contribute to lavish feasts and the purchase of large numbers of pigs.

The increase in ritual scale was accompanied by fierce debate. Rice, cartons of canned fish, and other store-bought goods had long been seen as acceptable gifts at feasts; indeed they were expected from Lihirians employed in towns across the country. But these goods were only viewed as "help," rather than "real" feast foods. One woman explained that feasts should only offer yams and pigs raised by the lineage on their own land and gifts from affines or exchange partners. The prestation, in other words, should attest to the *local* productivity and influence of the host lineage. At the feast where she explained the sequence and meaning of various exchanges and activities to Martha Macintyre, debate ensued about the boxes of canned fish and cartons of beer brought by men who were currently employed as laborers on the road works. Some considered the canned fish a legitimate substitute for traditional feast food; others were wary of its authenticity. The beer they banished, and a group of young men vanished into the bush to consume it, returning later to disrupt activities.

Over the following months, whenever a customary feast was held, debate about the introduction of new elements associated with the cash economy went on, eventually to fizzle out as successive feasts included commodities. Pigs arrived on decorated trucks, rather than the poles and bamboo platforms of the past. Standing in the trucks, men blew conch shells to honor them. Meat and other foods bought at the supermarket became recognized as suitable substitutes for garden produce. Even beer was grudgingly accepted but was consumed only by men, either in the men's house or in the bush at the edge of villages.

Pigs retained value, as a measure both of ritual magnitude and of the wealth and influence of the host lineage. But the relocation of Putput and Kapit villages, and the ensuing disruption to pig rearing in other mine-affected villages, meant that people had to purchase pigs. The first time this occurred there was no debate about its possible impropriety. People from the relocated village of Putput, flush with money from recent compensation payments, traveled to mainland New Ireland and bought numerous pigs to give at a *hararum* feast. New Ireland villagers seized the opportunity to gain some of the money circulating in Lihir and charged high prices for pigs. Prices rose from about K100 for a mature pig to K300 in a matter of months. There was no bartering.

Lihirians, eager to flaunt their newfound wealth, often gave double the asking price as a magnanimous display of their economic superiority.

By 1998, Lihirians traveled as far afield as Rabaul town in East New Britain, hiring boats to transport pigs. At one feast, a pig from Rabaul was paraded as the "head of the feast" (*konakarat*), its donors declaring they had spent K8,000 for it. The purchasing of pigs from other islands became a means whereby Lihirians, who had long been among the poorest New Irelanders, reveled in their newfound wealth and prestige. Tales of their profligacy spread, fueling both envy and disdain from neighbors, who had always considered Lihirians as little more than backward, crass, and unsophisticated. Interviews Martha Macintyre and Simon Foale conducted in 2000 revealed not only overstated reports of Lihirian wealth but how their pig purchases had disrupted mortuary exchanges on other islands.

Villagers on the east coast of New Ireland were apparently refusing to exchange or sell pigs to locals, eager to gain from the inflated prices they could charge Lihirians. People from the Namatanai region in New Ireland, many of whom had histories of marriage and exchange with Lihirians, also benefited from prices they paid for pigs during the mine construction phase. Pigs had become one of the main forms of wealth redistribution. The centrifugal pull on regional exchange toward Lihir, and the increasing commoditization of pigs for feasts, must be viewed as an enduring regional effect of the economic changes associated with mining. In this way, Lihirian mortuary rituals became dependent upon the mine but also on the household production of pigs and garden produce throughout the region, as the domestic mode of production throughout New Ireland came to support the cultural extravagances of elite Lihirians. Commodities were readily incorporated into traditional exchange systems, and on one level these exchanges were not deprived of their precapitalist meanings.

The ease with which Lihirians moved from exchanging pigs in networks of affinal connection to simply purchasing pigs from any vendor and using them as gifts in mortuary exchanges calls into question some of the anthropological theorization about the symbolism and alienability of pigs (Macintyre 1984; Weiner 1976; Strathern 1988). Certainly the provenance of pigs ceased to hold any significance, except for the novel notion that the farther afield purchasers traveled, the greater the value of the pig when given at a feast. Prior to the mining project, Lihirians, like other Melanesians, subscribed to the view that pigs were a form of living wealth, like persons, in many respects. Rearing and nurturing pigs meant that they embodied the labor and productivity of their producers/owners, and this mutual identity made them especially appropriate as gifts that created and confirmed relationships between people. But while some misgivings had been voiced about changes in gifts of yams and the substitution of bags of rice for yams, none were raised during the short period when pigs became unequivocal commodities.

The most obvious change in mortuary feasts in the early days of the mining project was size. Both the quantity of pigs and food distributed and the number of guests who attended increased. People attributed the new ritual scale to infrastructure: now travel to all villages on Aniolam Island was easily accessible on newly acquired trucks on the recently constructed road. But another factor, of course, was the cash received from the large compensation payouts. Almost overnight, people began buying goods that were, at that stage, things that they associated with wealth and modernity. Trucks and boats were the most visible items, but clothing, sneakers, wristwatches, sunglasses, and radios proclaimed the new status of landowners and people at work for a wage. These things became signs of wealth, as young people in particular dressed in new finery at ritual events.

During the first years of mining, some Lihirians expressed concerns that customs distinctive of Lihir would be swept away as the islanders embraced modernity. A social movement called Society Reform emerged. Its leaders, Mark Soipang (then chairman of the landowners' association) and Leo Glaglas (who had been the first Papua New Guinean to gain an international pilot's license), developed an agenda whose goal was to preserve Lihirian custom while promoting engagement with entrepreneurial ventures and regional political forces (see Bainton 2010: 142–45; Macintyre 2013: 134–35). Seeking to rationalize the clan system, they produced numerous policies aimed at reforming and "purifying" cultural practices. An attempt was even made to codify mortuary ceremonies and punish departures from custom with financial penalties. None of their programs gained widespread support, but they did reflect more general anxieties about the impact of money on feasting practices.

In 1999, a *tutunkanut* feast was held for two elderly women in the village of Kunaie. This rite was one of the first really huge mortuary feasts staged on Aniolam Island (its attendance was estimated at 1,500). People from Tanga, Tabar, and Namatanai as well as the outer islands of Lihir came with drummers and dance troupes. Tabar performers provoked much discussion after the event. They all dressed in traditional valuables and body paint. Lihirian dancers were well rehearsed and wore headdresses, woven pandanus collars, and face paint, but these were mixed with a range of sarongs and shorts (Figure 5.1; see also Hemer 2013: 142).

By contrast, Tabar dancers dressed uniformly, which occasioned great praise. Henceforth, as if by decree, Lihirian dancing groups adopted uniform dress—sarongs made in cloth, the colors chosen to denote specific groups. While nobody suggested that this was mimicry, uniformity of dress and decoration became an essential feature of dancing groups at feasts and public events.

The adoption of uniform costumes was clearly dialogical: it expressed a subtle Lihirian engagement with modernity. While declaring that they could perform according to their unique traditions, they also showed they could do

Figure 5.1. Lihirian dancers. Photo: Simon Foale, 1998.

so in new clothes. Preparations for feasts always required weeks of preparation, and beginning in about 2000, rehearsals of synchronized dancing in matching outfits were added. Soipang and Glaglas's hopes to revive "correct" feasting and mortuary practices, which were rejected when presented in long-winded speeches and newsletters, were ultimately fulfilled when they became a part of the display of wealth. Throughout these years, a range of elements were reestablished as integral to the "correct" performance of mortuary ceremonies. In the process, appeals to *kastom* have transmuted into an insistence on *kalsa*—the former term now redolent of parochialism, while the latter came to express a more cosmopolitan ideal of culture as made up of a reified cluster of distinct values and practices belonging to people from a specific place.

An Innovation

In time, the changes that emerged in the early years, and that were the source of much consternation, became completely routinized. The availability of cash, modern transportation, and other resources has given rise to larger feasts, which were more frequently held. Stories of excess abound; and massive feasts invariably leave hosts broke. It is not uncommon to hear of hosts who collectively spent upward of K100,000 for a mortuary rite. Large pigs are now purchased for around K2,000 with additional shell money provided on top, and some hosts have claimed that well over 500 pigs were slaughtered over the duration of their *tutunkanut* feasts.

Bales of rice and cartons of canned meat are always included in feasts as gifts from guests and supporters, and yams are purchased at the market and given to supplement those grown by the hosts. Guests travel to feasts on the important days and no longer stay for long periods, reducing the burden on hosts. Beer is now integral to feasting: it is presented as gifts and drunk in quantity throughout the event (often disrupting a somber and respectful ethos). Hosts keep a close record of what has been given and what "commodity gift" debts they have incurred (see Wilson and Sinclair, this volume). Dancing has become more competitive, and throughout the final days of *tutunkanut* feasts, multiple dance troupes simultaneously perform in a profusion of color, excitement, and song.

No aspect of Lihirian feasting and exchange functions independently of the capitalist sector. As market goods became converted into cultural gifts, the relationship of the Lihir exchange system became more intricately dependent upon, and in dialogue with, the capitalist sector. The ideal cyclical image in which sociality is made to "come up" through the exchange of "equivalent values" is maintained; certain goods become invested with culturally valued attributes traditionally associated with gifts. However, women's contribution to mortuary feasts has been usurped by men with access to cash.

Female productive capacities have been removed from the political economy of feasting, which effectively reduces the distinction between producers and transactors. Every time commodities are used for mortuary exchange, be it pigs, shell money, market produce, or trade store food, it sustains the cyclical image of continuity; in reality, this "cycle" is cut and spliced with the cash economy. Here we differ from other authors in this section of the volume: in our view, the processes of develop*man* that reinvigorate, vitalize, and authenticate mortuary rituals merely sustain an illusion of cultural continuity and persistence.

Every time introduced goods are used and the new expansiveness is performed, this increases the inertia of this pattern of consumption, transforming a system of delayed reciprocal exchange. In the past, exchange functioned as a leveling device, providing an important avenue for dispersing wealth and resources and consolidating membership. Previously, exchange was somewhat "regulated" by human productivity. The influx of money (particularly in the form of royalties and compensation payments) destabilized egalitarian exchange, as wealth has now come to follow an upward trajectory into the hands of a minority. The unbalanced distribution of mining money has had the following consequence: mortuary feasting is now performed on uneven ground.

Transactions are now "sped up." There are expectations that gifts given by supporters and allies during mortuary feasts be reciprocated as quickly as possible. Delaying feasts creates further risks because more debts may be accumulated that must be repaid. The strains mining money have exerted on Lihirian mortuary rites have produced an extraordinary result: the final mortuary feasts are frequently held *before* the celebrated person has died. Some Lihirians claim that this practice was started on Malie Island prior to mining as a way of introducing variation and creating renown. The historical monopoly that Malie people held over the production of shell money probably provided the means to fund this innovation. Due to the access to cash and the current pressure to perform feasts, this practice of staging premortem mortuary feasts became common.

The "deceased" is still termed *kanut* (corpse). The "living dead" may not always play an active role in ritual activities, yet their presence definitely influences events. Hosts are aware of their critical gaze and will respond accordingly. Some Lihirians argue that this shift permits them to hold rites while resources are available, makes burial "simpler," and ensures that their efforts are recognized by the "deceased." Others have stated that the practice reflects the lack of trust between generations, and this is one way in which people can ensure that younger relatives perform the appropriate mortuary rituals in their honor. In some cases, however, what results is duplication; the same feasts are held again after death in order to perform custom according to "correct" procedures or, again, to take advantage of another chance to display wealth and power.[8]

Mortuary Carvings

In the literature, the cultures of New Ireland are best known for ritual practices associated with the production, form, use, and iconography of *malanggan* carvings.[9] These carvings serve as effigies of the deceased and are central icons in the mortuary process. Historically, Lihirians produced very few *malanggan*, and some Lihirians debate as to whether *mormor* carvings were simply a crude substitute for *malanggan*. However, clans with close ties to Tabar Island, where some of the most famous *malanggan* are made (see Gunn 1987), have been known to incorporate these figures into their mortuary rites. More or less since 2010, Lihirian mortuary carvings have taken on importance as part of a wider cultural renaissance.

It is now common to find carved sculptures of *tandal* spirits (Tok Pisin *masalai*) on display during the final *tutunkanut* feast. These *tandal* spirits reside throughout the landscape in animate and inanimate forms and are a source of power, identity, and connection to place (see Bainton et al. 2012: 26–27; Gillespie and Bainton 2012). *Tandal* spirits can include detailed carvings of humans and large snakes or sharks, which sometimes also appear in the central ridgepole of men's houses. These carvings embody the *tandal*-spirit, and like *malanggan*, their power is managed through strategically staged moments of concealment and revelation within the men's house.[10] They manifest spiritual power that helps bring the cosmos into being.

Nowadays, the men's house is the most prominent physical feature in every hamlet. Clan leaders use wealth to renovate previously ramshackle structures and turn them into impressive permanent edifices. However, permanent men's houses no less express the tensions and contradictions of modernity: on the one hand, they proclaim the status and wealth of the clan and require less maintenance, freeing up time for other activities; on the other hand, they reduce opportunities for collective work, which diminishes from men's house sociality and lineage solidarity.

The standardization of men's houses has prompted the revival of traditional round-roofed thatched men's houses (*balo*). These thatched men's houses provide the stage for the spectacular act of "walking on the men's house" (*roriabalo*) phase of the *tutunkanut* feast. During this event, members of allied clans mount its roof and proclaim their contribution to and support for the final stage of the *tutunkanut* feast (see Bainton 2010: 104–7). For example, in late 2011 the Lamatlik clan on Masahet Island constructed a magnificent men's house for their *tutunkanut* feast (Figure 5.2). The new building was concealed behind a thatched wall until the day of the feast. During the moment of revelation, the hosts sang inside while the "sons" of the Lamatlik clan paraded into its enclosure in matching outfits and tore down the thatched partition to unveil it to the whole community.

The men's house, which included a large carved shark's head and tail protruding from the front and back ends of the house, signified their *tandal*-spirit. It was adorned with strings of shell money and yams and bananas. This was the first time that such a spectacle had been attempted in living memory on Masahet, and it was a very deliberate assertion of cultural superiority.

Figure 5.2. Lamatlik clan members performing on the roof of the men's house during the *tuntunkanut* feast. Photo: Nicholas Bainton, 2011.

Hypertradition

Over the life of the mine, Lihirians have reified their cultural values into a form of "hypertraditionalism." Concerns over deviations from "correct" protocols and the decline of a "moral community" have been expressed through a popular discourse about custom, which also seeks to critique modern society. Notwithstanding variations in practice, this has also given rise to a remarkable standardization in the ways that Lihirians describe mortuary rituals.

Following in the footsteps of the Society Reform program, a range of individuals and institutions (including the local-level government, the landowners association, the Lihir cultural heritage association, and even Church leaders) have attempted to document and codify aspects of Lihirian custom. The inordinate amount of time that Lihirians spend memorializing their dead and debating the role and form of custom can be compared with other cult-like responses that have emerged in response to radical experiences and new social conditions. The intensification and self-conscious revival of customary activity can be seen as a direct answer to modernity and a historical preoccupation with achieving unity in the face of divisions experienced throughout colonialism and now mining.

The earlier Society Reform program specifically aimed to strengthen Lihirian society through the strict adherence to customary values and practices. This program has found new life in the "Lihir Destiny" vision, which emerged during the renegotiating of the community mining benefits package between 2000 and 2007. The architects of this vision have proposed that an ideal Lihirian society will be achieved through the maximization of social and economic opportunities provided by the mine and a strong commitment to the virtues of Lihirian culture (see Bainton 2010). Their aim is to achieve "self-reliance and financial independence" to sustain Lihir throughout the postmining era. However, this goal is complicated by its internal contradictions: as custom and capitalism are conceptually compartmentalized in order to preserve the purity of those cultural traditions that hold society together, this clashes with the daily practices of Lihirians as they attempt to convert the excesses of mining capitalism into a more customary, and therefore moral, community.

Mortuary Rites and Mine Closure on Misima Island

Given the finite nature of mining, and the lack of alternate sustainable industries in most mining areas, the question of what happens after mine closure is critical for understandings of mortuary ritual in the context of extractive industries. In the early twentieth century, people appeared to revert to former practices when mines closed and long-term effects were considered relatively minor, although nostalgia for the boom time persisted (Halvaksz 2008). On Misima Island in Milne Bay Province, where Martha Macintyre has done research since the 1980s, no fewer than sixteen mines were opened and closed during the period from the 1880s to 1986.

Exchanges of traditional valuables, pigs and yams, continued and were not much affected at all by the ebbs and flows of cash into the economy. But contemporary large open-pit mining projects, like the Misima gold mine, employed many more local people than earlier mines, so the local economy was more affected, and with it mortuary rituals. When the gold mine closed in 2004, one of the few instances took place in PNG in which a large-scale mining project was "successfully" brought to an end.[11]

Despite the long history of gold mining in Misima (Griffin et al. 1979: 25; Hess 1980; Nelson 1976), the islanders were left with very little to show for any of it. No comparable economic activities ensued after 2004. In 2012, it was estimated that at least 300 Misimans had secured work at other mining projects throughout PNG, which has helped to redirect some wealth back to the island (Sagir 2012). Attempts to establish an agricultural development center and a fishing industry as part of the preparations for closure were unsuccessful, and artisanal mining became the most viable source of income. In addition to the severe impact on services, standards of living, and community morale (as factions fought over the remaining trust accounts), the impacts of closure reverberated throughout the realm of mortuary exchange.

As elsewhere in the Massim region (Damon and Wagner 1989), mortuary exchange is foundational to an understanding of Misiman Islanders, their values, and interactions (see Lutkehaus, this volume). On Misima, the ceremonial economy revolves around a series of funeral feasts and exchanges (*bobuton*). Where mortuary exchanges were once confined to pigs, yams, stone axe blades, and shell valuables, as in Lihir, engagement with the cash economy introduced cash, clothes, and store goods. As these sequential exchanges persist, "the living are enmeshed in relations of alternating indebtedness as they mourn and honour the dead of their own clans and of the clans into which they are married" (Gerritsen and Macintyre 1986: 3.2). The mortuary cycle typically includes a collectively observed period of mourning that remains in force until the "unraveling feast" (*iwas*) signifies the lifting of mourning restrictions and the reopening of the community to outsiders.

Paternal and maternal relatives of the deceased give garden food and pigs to those who have assisted in the mourning process, and these gifts create debts that if not reciprocated must be expunged by land transfers. Widows pass through an extended liminal phase and gradually reenter society by completing various obligations to affinal relatives (see Wilson and Sinclair, this volume). While the term *hagali* is commonly used to refer to mortuary feasts in general, it also specifically refers to presentations given by female relatives of the deceased to their affines. The final event is a large-scale memorial feast (*lobek*) held by the clan of the deceased to honor their dead. Like the Lihirian *tutunkanut* feast, it can take years of planning and may include the memorialization of several deceased clan members. A *lobek* feast leaves the hosts famous but impoverished—although it also creates indebtedness that must be reciprocated in the mortuary ceremonies held by other clans.

Misiman mortuary rituals have changed over the past century. Secondary burial practices have ceased, and Christian rites have been incorporated into the burial process. *Iwas* and *lobek* ceremonies have come to involve a *simenti* (derived from the word "cement") in which a cement grave stone is built over the burial site, and feasts are often organized on Saturdays to avoid interference with employment or Church activities (see Dalton and von Poser, this volume). In her detailed ethnography of Misiman mortuary rites, Sandra Callister observes that the ideals of reciprocity and the obligation to repay continue to permeate all aspects of Misiman society and are particularly unremitting in mortuary feasting (2000: 115).

The expansion and subsequent contraction of the Misiman economy has created tensions as people struggle to reciprocate the great debts amassed throughout the mining era. The obligation to use wealth in socially significant ways meant that mortuary rituals became more lavish. More pigs were purchased and in some cases cows,[12] and store-bought goods and money were substituted for garden produce. As competition between individuals and groups escalated, the burden increased to meet new expectations and Misima society became stratified along new political and economic lines. Individuals without access to money felt great shame as they grappled to repay debts or adequately sponsor or contribute to feasts.

In the years approaching mine closure, some Misimans worried about their mine-fueled extravagancies: "People give plenty of food and goods for mortuary feasts now because there is plenty of money. But after the mine is gone how can we repay these 'debts' when there is no cash? This will cause problems between a lot of people" (Byford 2000: 32). In the postmining era, these concerns have been realized and people have been prompted to reassess the importance of the entire mortuary complex. Put simply, the cost of death is now greater than available resources.

In 2006, some men told us of plans to drop stages that were too financially burdensome and to collapse the extended sequence into a single event—the cementing of the grave. The value of delayed exchange is being recast in terms of immediate burdens and a lack of return "profit." This popular reassessment of mortuary ritual has taken the form of postmining economic rationalism. "We have five feasts for every death," a man explained. "That is too many. If we cut it back down to two feasts that would be viable." Another man decried mortuary feasts as a "waste of money on people who were already dead." In these ways, the ethics of exchange are no longer understood as paradoxical forms of keeping while giving away, but a much simpler and taxing type of "giving away for nothing."

Contemporary reflections upon past and present expenditures and expectations for the redistribution of wealth are often peppered with bitter comments upon current financial hardships and lost opportunities. In a kind of reverse logic to the Lihirian Society Reform program, some Misimans have embarked upon a project of cultural reformation that is less concerned with a return to the "true ways" than it is with appropriate and pragmatic practice. Taking inspiration from the history of the Church, an ex-school headmaster averred, "If we can change how we worship, then we can change how we make custom." Some people even mused about the possibility of eliminating *hagali* feasts altogether: "We have to draw the line," said an informant, "and tell . . . [the other clans] that this is how it is and this is how we are going to do it from now on. They just have to accept that we are not going to make custom like that anymore." But as many Misimans know, "opting out" is both difficult and risky.

Conclusion—Mortuary Rites in the Context of Two Mines

Mortuary exchanges persist in the postmining era on Misima Island in an abbreviated and contested form, but we are cautious of exaggerating the possible parallels with a postmining future in Lihir. The most significant difference lies in the duration of each venture. The Misima mine was a mere short-lived project and generated far less wealth, which meant that resource development was less economically comprehensive, and Misimans did not develop the extensive kind of ideological commitment to tradition as Lihirians have. Therefore, the potential for an "exchange crash" appears much greater in Lihir.

Some forms of develop*man*, so Sahlins notes, may turn out to be devastatingly tragic. Lihirians have a great deal at stake in the postmining era, and World Bank advisors, corporate managers, and political leaders would doubtless argue that mine-derived wealth would be better used for investment or the development of small-scale businesses that can sustain households into the future instead of "unproductive" expenditures. If develop*man* in Lihir signals the triumph of culture over economy, or at least a dialogical relationship, it might also prove to result in the dismal failure of development (Patterson and Macintyre 2011: 11), a point that the leaders of the Lihir Destiny movement evidently recognize.

As the editors of this volume observe in the Introduction, "Mourners and the dead are both subjects of, and subject to, their own signifying discourses as well as objects of the universalizing sermons of Christianity as well as the values of capitalism." The complex mutability of those discourses, historically and in the present, means that the values and moral equivalences they attempt to invoke remain unresolved. As such, the tensions between the embrace of modernity and the constant reinvention of authentic *kalsa* are perpetually dialogical.

Lihirian innovations ensure that mortuary rituals remain meaningful in the moment. Large-scale resource development has provided impetus for the revival of tradition, some of which has been creative, some carefully crafted, while others are dictated. Stylized dance troupes, dramatic revelations of reconstructed men's houses, and the revival of a carving tradition are the source of contemporary prestige and great cultural pride. Whether or not these activities are authentic remains a moot point because the greatest invention is the claim to authenticity itself. These self-conscious assertions of cultural continuity represent an attempt to demonstrate a connection to an imagined ancestral past and to a Lihirian cultural identity insulated from massive social and economic upheavals.

In order to account for the discontinuities, structural contradictions, and social changes that have arisen over the past century, we regard the persistence of Lihirian mortuary rituals in their dialogue with modernity less as a result of cultural continuity, or the strength of traditional Lihirian voices, but rather as a continued reconstruction and revalidation of the cultural present in order to stabilize, or even slow down, an awareness of the dramatic changes they are experiencing.

Nicholas A. Bainton is an honorary senior research fellow at the University of Queensland and also manages the social impact monitoring program for the Lihir gold mine in Papua New Guinea. In addition to numerous articles and book chapters, he has published a book on his earlier anthropological research called *The Lihir Destiny: Cultural Responses to Mining in Melanesia* (2010).

Martha Macintyre is an honorary principal research fellow at the University of Melbourne and adjunct professor at the Centre for Social Responsibility in Mining at the University of Queensland. She has undertaken research in the New Ireland and Milne Bay provinces. She coedited, with Mary Patterson, *Managing Modernity in the Western Pacific* (2011).

Notes

1. We draw upon our long-term research on the social impacts of resource extraction in Misima and Lihir. Macintyre was contracted to undertake the social baseline study for the Misima gold mine (see Gerritsen and Macintyre 1986), and in 2006 we undertook research on the impacts of mine closure in Misima. We draw upon a combined engagement with the Lihir gold mine that spans more than twenty years through in-

dependent research and social impact monitoring studies for the company. Macintyre was contracted to undertake social impact monitoring studies from 1994 to 2005. She also conducted independent research into social change funded by the Australian Research Council. Bainton undertook eighteen months of Ph.D. research in Lihir from 2003 to 2004, followed by further fieldwork from 2007 to 2010 as a research fellow at the University of Queensland. Since 2010 Bainton has managed the mining company's social impact monitoring program.

2. See also Dubbeldam 1964; Finney 1974; Healey 1985; Hide 1981; and Strathern 1971b.
3. This calls to mind the work by Richard Salisbury (1962) on the introduction of steel axes in the Eastern Highlands, which allowed men to clear land for gardens faster, creating a surplus of time and excess productivity that was used to expand the scope of ritual exchange activity.
4. See Bainton 2010 for a detailed discussion on these changes.
5. Gunn notes that overmodeled skulls were found throughout central New Ireland. These were sometimes used on top of carved wooden figures or incorporated into the use of large woven *vavara malanggan*. There are also instances in Tabar, recorded as late as 1984, when the bones of the deceased were incorporated in *malanggan* rituals (Gunn 1997: 84–85).
6. In April 2015 this ritual was revived as part of the *tutunkanut* feast hosted by the Nissal clan on Mahur Island. In place of traditional *mormor* poles, the hosts painted a large mural of the faces of those clan members being memorialised. The mural was placed above a large carving of the Nissal clan *tandal*-spirit that was fixed on top of the roof of the men's house.
7. The description by Susan Hemer (2013: 263–85) of events surrounding the death of a woman on Mahur Island in 1998 provides a clear picture of the flexibility and scale of many of the mortuary rituals observed during the first years of the mining project.
8. If the ceremonial economy is sustained by the ability of Lihirians to use modern goods for customary purposes, it also rests upon a certain ideological insulation of customary activity. Thus, exchange of shell money goes on in an era when most Lihirians are flush with cash. In a novel twist, Lihirians now produce more shell money to meet the demands of ceremonial exchange. On the outer islands, teams of women regularly cut, grind, and polish minute shell disks that they string together in fathoms and sell for ceremonial exchange. Older men no longer monopolize shell money, which they previously acquired through arduous interisland trade expeditions. Nowadays, young men and women can easily buy it, and this accessibility has led to inflation, as larger sums, or greater lengths, of shell money are now required for ceremonial purposes.
9. See Billings 2007; Brouwer 1980; Küchler 2002; and Lincoln 1987.
10. Many clan leaders have faces and other manifestations of their clan *tandal*, such as octopuses, sharks, and eels, carved into the protruding ends of the Y-shaped entrance stile of their men's house. The renowned German ethnologist Otto Schlaginhaufen recorded images of these carvings during his circumnavigation of the Lihir Islands in 1906. As nearly every men's house has been now renovated with permanent materials, these carvings are de rigeur statements of cultural sophistication.
11. The Mt. Kare gold rush was possibly too short-lived to generate structural changes in the regional ceremonial economy, which in any case was substantially affected by the wealth generated by the Porgera mine and the nearby oil and gas fields (Ballard 1998; Gilberthorpe 2013; Stewart and Strathern 2002). In the case of the Panguna mine in

Bougainville, it is impossible to disentangle the impacts of the civil war from that of mine closure and the loss of cash incomes or the changing role of traditional exchange items.

12. Herds of cattle were introduced into Misima in the early twentieth century, with the view to their domestic use as sources of meat and milk. They were not consistently cared for and became feral, and there are still small herds to be found in the bush. They rapidly became an acceptable substitute for pigs in feasts. Coincidentally there was a similar feral herd on Lihir that roamed Marahun, the area that was acquired by the mining company as the site for housing of employees. These animals were all shot as the land was cleared in 1996.

References Cited

Akin, D. and J. Robbins. 1999. *Money and Modernity: State and Local Currencies in Melanesia*. Pittsburgh: University of Pittsburgh Press.

Bainton, NA. 2008a. "The Genesis and the Escalation of Desire and Antipathy in the Lihir Islands, Papua New Guinea." *The Journal of Pacific History* 43: 289–312.

———. 2008b. "Men of *Kastom* and the Customs of Men: Status, Legitimacy and Persistent Values in Lihir, Papua New Guinea." *The Australian Journal of Anthropology* 19: 195–213.

———. 2010. *The Lihir Destiny: Cultural Responses to Mining in Melanesia*. Canberra: ANU E Press.

Bainton, NA. and M. Macintyre. 2013. "'My Land, My Work': Business Development and Large-Scale Mining in Melanesia." In *Engaging with Capitalism: Cases from Oceania*, edited by Fiona McCormack and Kate Barclay, 137–63. Research in Economic Anthropology 33. Bingley, U.K.: Emerald Group Publishing.

Bainton, NA., C. Ballard, and K. Gillespie. 2012. "The End of the Beginning? Mining, Sacred Geographies, Memory and Performance in Lihir." *The Australian Journal of Anthropology* 23: 22–49.

Ballard, C. 1998. "The Sun by Night: Huli Moral Topography and Myths of a Time of Darkness." In *Fluid Ontologies: Myth, Ritual and Philosophy in the Highlands of Papua New Guinea*, edited by L. Goldman and C. Ballard, 67–85. Westport: Bergin and Garvey.

Bataille, G. 1985. *Visions of Excess: Selected Writings, 1927–1939*. Edited and translated by Allan Stoekl, with Carl R. Lovitt and Donald M. Leslie Jr. Minneapolis: University of Minnesota Press.

Billings, D. 2007. "New Ireland *Malanggan* Art: A Quest for Meaning." *Oceania* 77: 257–85.

Brouwer, EC. 1980. *A Malagan to Cover the Grave: Funerary Ceremonies in Mandak*. Ph.D. dissertation. University of Queensland, St Lucia.

Byford, J. 2000. *One Day Rich: Community Perceptions of the Impact of the Placer Dome Gold Mine, Misima Island Papua New Guinea*. Unpublished Report, Australian National University, Canberra.

Callister, S. 2000. *A Cord of Three Strands Is Not Easily Broken: Birth, Death and Marriage in a Massim Society*. MA thesis. Macquarie University, Sydney.

Damon, FH. and R. Wagner, eds. 1989. *Death Rituals and Life in the Societies of the Kula Ring*. DeKalb: Northern Illinois University Press.

Dubbeldam, LFB. 1964. "The Devaluation of the Kapauku-Cowrie as a Factor of Social Disintegration." *American Anthropologist* 66: 293–303.

Filer, C. 1992. *The Lihir Hamlet Hausboi Survey: Interim Report.* Waigani: Unisearch PNG. Unpublished report for Kennecott Explorations (Australia) and PNG Department of Mining and Petroleum.

Finney, B., U. Mikave, and A. Sambumei. 1974. "Pearl Shell in Goroka: From Valuables to Chicken Feed." *Yagl-ambu* 1: 342–49.

Gerritsen, R. and M. Macintyre. 1986. *Social Impact Study of the Misima Gold Mine,* 2 Vols. Boroko, Port Moresby: Institute of Applied Social and Economic Research.

Gilberthorpe, E. 2013. "In the Shadow of Industry: A Study of Culturization in Papua New Guinea." *Journal of the Royal Anthropological Institute* 19: 216–78.

Gillespie, K. and NA. Bainton. 2012. "Coming Out of the Stone: Dangerous Heritage and the Death of the Twinhox Band." *Yearbook for Traditional Music* 44: 71–86.

Gregory, CA. 1982. *Gifts and Commodities.* London: Academic Press.

Griffin, J., H. Nelson, and S. Firth. 1979. *Papua New Guinea: A Political History.* Melbourne: Heinemann Educational Australia.

Gunn, M. 1987. "The Transfer of Malagan Ownership on Tabar." In *Assemblage of Spirits: Idea and Image in New Ireland,* edited by L. Lincoln, 74–83. New York: George Braziller.

———. 1997. *Ritual Arts of Oceania: New Ireland in the Collections of the Barbier-Muller Museum.* Milan: Skira editore.

Halvaksz, AJ. 2008. "Whose Closure? Appearances, Temporality, and Mineral Extraction in Papua New Guinea." *Journal of the Royal Anthropological Institute* 14: 21–37.

Healey, CJ. 1985. "New Guinea Inland Trade: Transformation and Resilience in the Context of Capitalist Penetration." *Mankind* 15: 127–44.

Hemer, SR. 2013. *Tracing the Melanesian Person: Emotions and Relationships in Lihir.* Adelaide: University of Adelaide Press.

Hess, M. 1980. "Misima's Umoona Gold, Milne Bay Province." *Oral History* 8: 91–98.

Hide, R. 1981. *Aspects of Pig Production and Use in Colonial Sinasina, Papua New Guinea.* Ph.D. dissertation. Colombia University, New York.

Hughes, I. 1978. "Good Money and Bad: Inflation and Devaluation in the Colonial Process." *Mankind* 11: 308–18.

Josephides, L. 1985. *The Production of Inequality: Gender and Exchange among the Kewa.* London: Tavistock.

Josephides, L. and M. Schiltz. 1982. "Beer and Other Luxuries: Abstinence in Village and Plantation by Sugu Kewas, Southern Highlands." In *Through a Glass Darkly: Beer and Modernization in Papua New Guinea,* edited by M. Marshall, 73–82. Monograph 18. Boroko: Institute of Applied Social and Economic Research.

Küchler, S. 2002. *Malanggan: Art, Memory and Sacrifice.* Oxford: Berg.

Lincoln, L. 1987. *Assemblage of Spirits: Idea and Image in New Ireland.* New York: George Braziller.

Macintyre, M. 1984. "The Problem of the Semi-Alienable Pig." *Canberra Anthropology* 7: 109–21.

———. 2013. "Instant Wealth: Visions of the Future on Lihir, New Ireland, Papua New Guinea." In *Kago, Kastom and Kalja: The Study of Indigenous Movements in Melanesia Today,* edited by M. Tabani and M. Abong, 123–46. Marseilles: Pacific-CREDO Publications.

Nelson, H. 1976. *Black, White and Gold: Goldmining in Papua New Guinea 1987–1930*. Canberra: The Australian National University Press.
Patterson, M. and M. Macintyre. 2011. "Introduction: Capitalism, Cosmology and Globalisation in the Pacific." In *Managing Modernity in the Western Pacific*, edited by M. Patterson and M. Macintyre, 1–29. St. Lucia: University of Queensland Press.
Sagir, B. 2012. *Draft Report on Artisanal and Small-Scale Mining in Misima*. Waigani: University of Papua New Guinea.
Sahlins, M. 1992. "The Economics of Develop-Man in the Pacific." *RES* 21: 13–25.
Salisbury, RF. 1962. *From Stone to Steel: Economic Consequences of a Technological Change in New Guinea*. Melbourne: Melbourne University Press.
Stewart, PJ. and AJ. Strathern. 2002. *Remaking the World: Myth, Mining, and Ritual Change among the Duna of Papua New Guinea*. Washington, D.C.: Smithsonian Institute Press.
Strathern, AJ. 1971a. "Cargo and Inflation in Mount Hagen." *Oceania* 41: 255–65.
———. 1971b. *The Rope of Moka: Big-Men and Ceremonial Exchange in Mount Hagen, New Guinea*. Cambridge: Cambridge University Press.
Strathern, M. 1988. *The Gender of the Gift*. Berkeley: University of California Press.
Weiner, A. 1976. *Women of Value, Men of Renown*. Brisbane: University of Queensland Press.

PART 2
Equivocal Voices

6

Finishing Kapui's Name

Birth, Death, and the Reproduction of Manam Society, Papua New Guinea

NANCY C. LUTKEHAUS

In July 1994, I traveled to Manam to participate in the final mortuary rites for Kapui, the former chief of Zogari village, Manam being a small volcanic island near the mouth of the Sepik River.[1] Fifteen years earlier, when I lived in Zogari doing doctoral research, Kapui had been my adoptive father and neighbor for the eighteen months I spent there. Although Kapui died in 1992 and was buried soon afterward, his son agreed to postpone the final mortuary rite called "to throw away the *galip* nuts" (*kangari rokoaki*)[2]—until I could return to participate as a member of his family.[3] When I was able to do so, I brought Sarina Pearson, a graduate student in visual anthropology, with me to film the event.

In June 2011, almost twenty years later, I was able to travel to Papua New Guinea once again in part because I wanted to show people, "Finishing Kapui's Name: Pigs, Death and Rebirth in Manam Society," the DVD we had shot in 1994. However, in 2005, a major eruption of the Manam volcano caused approximately 9,000 people, in short, everybody, to be evacuated to the mainland and take up residence in three densely populated "Care Centers" scattered along the north coast of Madang Province (Lutkehaus n.d.). From these supposedly semipermanent, jury-rigged communities the displaced Manam Islanders look out at their majestic island—as it looms on the horizon, its caldera sometimes benignly, sometimes furiously, smoking away. Because the national volcanology observatory in Rabaul remains concerned that the Manam volcano might blow up in a major explosion, the Papua New Guinea (PNG) government has not officially allowed people to return to the island. At present however (2015), 1,500 or so islanders have returned unofficially to Manam.

Like the former inhabitants of Enewetak Atoll (see Carucci, this volume), the Manam Islanders have become an internally displaced population. Even though the causes of their resettlements differ—man-made and technologically induced on the one hand and a natural disaster on the other—perhaps not surprisingly, people in both societies put great emphasis on returning "home" for burial. Moreover, in both cases, why they want to do so relates to local concepts of the person and the relationship of person to place. For the Manam Islanders, however, place is epitomized not only by a consubstantial relationship with the land but also by Zaria, the powerful, quixotic female spirit who inhabits the Manam volcano. Traditionally, the volcano was also believed to be the dwelling place of the spirits of their ancestors (Lutkehaus 1995b).[4]

In this chapter, I first describe the *kangari rokoaki* ritual and some events that took place in 1994 to honor Kapui. In doing so, I discuss aspects that I understand as characteristic of Manam mortuary practices. This account derives from research I conducted on Manam beginning in 1978; from observations made by Father Karl Böhm (1983), the resident SVD (Society of the Divine Word) Catholic missionary on the island from the 1930s through the 1950s; and from the published and unpublished fieldwork of the British anthropologist Camilla Wedgwood, who did research on Manam in 1933 (n.d., 1934).

Following Silverman and Lipset's argument that the relationship between contemporary Melanesian mortuary practices and modernity is dialogical and open-ended (see Introduction), I conclude with observations about changes in Manam mortuary rites that exemplify the islanders' ongoing dialogue with the state in PNG. This is a *rentier* state that Lipset describes as "more concerned with facilitating extraction industries than providing services for citizenry" (this volume) and, in the case of the Manam, that is more interested in pocketing foreign aid than in facilitating Manam resettlement. Interestingly enough, showing my DVD created a new context for local-level mortuary dialogue. Peoples' reactions to viewing our video in 2011 provoked in some respects a reenactment of traditional expressions of grief. However, particularly given the lack of interest the state has shown in the Manam, their abiding notions of death and grief now voice a characteristically Manam answer to modernity.

An important dimension of Manam mortuary rites is motivated by asserting a tie between personhood and place (*anua*), a claim that turns upon the relationship of chiefly lineages to the reproduction of society (Lutkehaus 1995b; see also Carucci, this volume). When displaced islanders living on the mainland and in urban centers such as Port Moresby and Lae return to bury their dead in their former homesteads on the island, not only are they ensuring that the spirits of the dead return home to their ancestors, but they are simultaneously asserting their enduring importance to Manam identity as well as their disregard for the state.

Death and Social Reproduction

Ever since Annette Weiner critiqued exchange theory and argued that "reproduction" was a more useful trope than reciprocity for interpreting social relations and ritual behavior in Melanesian societies (1979, 1992, 1995), anthropologists have applied Weiner's perspective to a range of activities in Pacific societies, and beyond (Ginsburg and Rapp 1991, 1995). In her analysis of mortuary ritual in the Trobriand Islands, Weiner argued that women play a central role in the reproduction of matrilineal descent groups there (1976, 1988; see Wilson and Sinclair, this volume). Women from the deceased's matrilineage give gifts of banana leaf bundles and banana fiber skirts, by way of squaring debts and severing ties that had previously existed between the deceased and other matrilineages.

These gifts, Weiner pointed out, demonstrated women's agency, their capacity to produce wealth and power when faced with death, but they also served to renew the identity of the deceased's matrilineal ancestors who had created the debts (1988: 161). In turn, death was also linked to birth since "the regenerative part of the *baloma* spirit re-creates human life in women, and at death, women re-create these beliefs materially by acknowledging and removing all the debts that went into the work of making a … person" (Weiner 1988: 163). Thus, Trobriand mortuary exchanges both terminated and reproduced person and group. Echoing the L'Année sociologique view of ritual, Weiner claimed that these transactions were part of a project to maintain the status quo: "The attempt to achieve a degree of permanence against everything that tends toward destruction is the driving force in the constitution of the social system" (1988: 165).

There are several parallels between Trobriand and Manam societies. Most importantly, both are Austronesian-speaking, kinship-based societies led by hereditary chiefs. In addition, death engages the deceased's descent group. And lastly, both stage Hertzian, two-stage mortuary rituals in which burial takes place soon after death and then months or years later, a big, concluding celebration is staged to honor the deceased. .

There are differences between Trobriand and Manam, however. While Trobriand descent is reckoned matrilineally, Manam trace descent patrilineally, although matrikin do play an important role in various life cycle rituals. While Trobriand culture resembles societies in the Massim region (Leach and Leach 1983), Manam, despite its island locale and Austronesian heritage of social hierarchy, possesses institutions characteristic of the Sepik region that associate it with the Murik (see Lipset, this volume), the Kayan (see von Poser, this volume), and Eastern Iatmul (see Silverman, this volume).

These include the men's house (Tokpisin *haus tambaran*), the ritual complex of male initiation, secret flutes (Tokpisin *tambaran*), as well as stylistic motifs inscribed on canoes, masks, and other ritual paraphernalia, in addition to shared culture heroes (see Lipset 1997). Given the parallels between Manam and the Trobriands on the one hand and Manam and Sepik cultures on the other, I suggest that the analysis of death rites in Sepik societies may benefit from Weiner's notion of reproduction as well as from the imbricated view of birth and death it would imply (see von Poser, this volume).

Death and Grief

Although I was not present when Kapui died in 1992 and did not witness his burial and the first stage of his mortuary rites, I did observe several deaths and subsequent burials during the course of earlier fieldwork and can report upon this process. Immediately after someone dies, a slit-drum is beaten to alert villagers of the event. The drumbeat signifies to the living that they must cease work and be quiet, stop chopping wood, laughing, and so on (see Lipset, this volume). If a chief, or an immediate kinsman, has died, this taboo (*alinga*) will also extend to neighboring villages. Moreover, as soon as the slit-drum has announced the death of a chief, all the slit drums in the men's house (*keda*) are turned over. Out of respect for the dead chief, they will not be beaten for the subsequent year.

When a commoner dies, the *alinga* taboo lasts for only one day, while for a member of the chief's family it lasts for one week. At the end of the latter interval, sacred flutes (*embeki*) will be played, calling an end to the mourning period and the *alinga* taboo. The "voices" of the flute-spirits also are meant to accompany the spirit of the deceased on his or her journey to join the other spirits of the dead. According to the missionary Böhm, if people went to their gardens, thus violating the work taboo, it was expected that pigs would break into them and destroy or eat all of the food growing there (1983: 116). Angry at the lack of respect shown it, the vengeful spirit of the deceased entered the pigs' bodies and drove them into the garden of the wrongdoer.

After the deceased's immediate kin have had a chance to cry and wail over the body, it is painted with red pigment, adorned in new clothing, and decorated with shell or dog's teeth ornaments or, in the case of a chiefly *tanepoa labalaba* such as Kapui, bird-of-paradise plumes and curved boar's tusks, insignia of his elite status (Lutkehaus 2013). The adornment of the physical body is actually meant to honor the spirit (*mariaba*) of the dead person so that it will depart from the deceased's body in a beautiful and contented condition (see Lipset, this volume). According to Manam cosmology, while the corpse disintegrates, the *mariaba*-spirit—now invisible—continues to communicate with the living through dreams, the practice of mediums, and various material signs in the environment.

Immediately upon hearing the percussion of the slit-drum heralding an individual's death, kin and friends quickly make their way to the homestead of the deceased to sit with the deceased's relatives and keep them company. Their vigil (*lili di ang*, literally "to give face") shows that the living want to please the new spirit and will not have to fear it in the future. People also do not want living relatives of the deceased left alone at this time because the new spirit, lonely for company, will return at night to try to lure its closest kin to accompany it to the place of the dead. While men sit together chewing betel nut, smoking tobacco (Tokpsin *brus*) or cigarettes, and talking in subdued voices, women gather and sing mourning songs.

This genre of songs (*tang rang*, literally "crying songs" or *mate rang*, "death songs") is characterized by slow, sorrowful cadences. Every night for the rest of the week, people bring mats and spend the night at the deceased's homestead, singing and reminiscing about the dead person. On the last night, if a chief or his female kin have died, the *tambaran* flutes, themselves the symbol of the authority of the chiefly *tanepoa* (Lutkehaus 1990), will be played and men and women will sing *tang rang* mourning songs alternatively. New songs may be composed that honor the deceased, thus adding to the repertoire of *tang rang* songs and to the community's memory of its ancestors. Their lyrics refer to events in the deceased's life, personal characteristics, and other details.

According to the missionary, the corpse used to be wrapped inside sheaths of the betel nut palm (*depa*) shaped into a canoe. The body was covered with other sheaths and bound together so that it—and the spirit of the deceased—could not travel to the mainland (Böhm 1983: 115). The bodies I saw buried during the late 1970s and 80s were placed in an old canoe-coffin (see Figure 6.1; see also Lipset, this volume; von Poser, this volume; Silverman, this volume). However, they were still bound, usually in a new *laplap* sarong, to prevent its spirit from making its way to the mainland.

Sometimes, the canoe was also lined with brightly colored cloth, and food was placed alongside the body to provide sustenance for the spirit's impending journey. Böhm also saw money put in the hands of the deceased, but both money and food were withdrawn prior to burial. People said that these provisions were removed because they were meant for the spirit of the deceased, who consumed only the intangible "spirit" of the food and the money (Böhm 1983: 115–16). Both vehicles, however, the *depa* palm and the canoe-coffin, were meant to provide a means of transportation from the physical world of the living to the invisible world of the dead deep inside the Manam crater, a world inhabited by the spirits of the dead as well as other ancestors (Tokpisin *masalai*; Manam *mariaba*). Moreover, the spirit, although invisible, was understood to have similar needs as the living for practical items. While some things are buried with the dead, tools, clothing, and even nut-bearing trees may be destroyed so that the new spirit can use them (Böhm 1983: 117).

The body of a dead chief remains unburied longer than a commoner (sometimes several days longer) so people from distant villages may come pay their respects and see the deceased leader a last time. The canoe-coffin is then buried, either in the village cemetery, an innovation introduced by the Catholic

Figure 6.1. Manam men decorate canoe-coffin. Photo: Nancy Lutkehaus, 1978.

missionaries and enforced by the Australian authorities for hygienic reasons, or on the homestead of the deceased near his former house. In the late 1970s and 1980s, many older Manam folks said that they preferred to bury the dead on their homesteads (*anua*), while younger Manam chose cemetery burials. However, all of the chiefs about whom I had information were buried either underneath or near their own houses in the late 1970s, and when Kapui died in 1992, he was also buried close to his house. Formerly, chiefs were sometimes buried in or near the men's house.

Kapui's Burial and Mourning

As is customary, when a chief such as Kapui, dies and is buried, women and children should vacate his homestead because the *tambaran* flutes are played. Indeed, in the past, the *tambaran* themselves—in other words, the *tambaran*-spirits—were said "to bury" chiefs (Böhm 1983: 117; see von Poser, this volume). After the burial, individuals who had contact with the dead body would go down to the sea and wash with special leaves. People bathed to purify their bodies of the dead body's harmful impurities (see Lipset, this volume).

However, I later found out that several things were not done correctly when Kapui died. In the first place, the individual who should have been called upon to oversee Kapui's burial, a commoner named Ngasingasi, was not asked to perform his rightful duties, for reasons I was unable to determine. Women were not prohibited from seeing the interment. And I was told that the flutes were played. Since women were present, their performance indicates an important change in beliefs about the power of the flutes (see Tuzin 1997). As recently as the late 1970s and 1980s, flutes were not played in front of women, and women believed that they would become sick or swollen if they saw them. In 1994, Kapui's grave site was marked by a rectangle made from stones and it was covered with a sheet of corrugated iron. In 2011, the corrugated iron had disintegrated and the grave was only marked by a brightly colored croton barely visible above the tangled undergrowth that had grown up around it. Nearby were newer graves of kin who had since died.

A widow in mourning ought to let her hair grow into dreadlocks; neither should a widower shave. Both paint themselves black and give up eating foods that the deceased especially liked (see Silverman, this volume).[5] Widows once dressed in long white fiber skirts (Böhm 1983: 117); now they wear black. Similarly, at the death of a chief, his entire village used to mourn for as long as a year. Sometimes, a village might decide to forego celebrating the new year's rite (*barasi*) out of respect for its deceased chief.[6] At the end of the year, the new chief should set a date to end mourning, when everyone will remove their paint (Böhm 1983: 117–18). The widow's long hair will be cut either by her brothers or sons, and she will be released from mourning taboos. However, she is not allowed to remarry. Thus, Babirom, the widow of Kapui, remained on her own in Zogari village after her husband died, tending her gardens and raising the pigs that she and Kapui used to care for together.

During the weeklong mourning period when people may not work, a steady stream of visitors visit the homestead of the deceased bearing gifts of soup (*suru*). However, unlike everyday soup people eat, a dish primarily made up of boiled sweet potatoes, taro, and cassava, *suru* soup should have some form of meat, preferably pork, in it, although a large portion of fish or canned meat will do. When a chief dies, it is expected that chiefs from other villages, but especially those on the same side of the island with whom he has the most kinship ties, will come with their entourage to "give face." In addition to bringing food, visiting women will sit and sing mourning songs. Likewise, each clan in the deceased chief's village will come as a group with its soup and songs. And each night of the mourning period, villagers will bring sleeping mats to the home of the deceased chief to spend the night together and protect the chief's wife and children from the spirit of the deceased, who will attempt to lure his living kin to join him in the afterlife.

At the end of a week, a *bobola* feast (Figure 6.2) will be held at the homestead of the deceased to thank people for having paid their respects to the dead. In the past when a chief died, the end of the weeklong (or longer) taboo interval would also have been celebrated by the performance of masked dancers (*moarupu*). The deceased's patrilineal clan, as well as his or her matrilineal kin, contributes food for the *bobola* feast, which includes taro, bananas, and at least one small pig. In the case of a chief, collective gifts of food may also be given by each and every clan in the village.

Figure 6.2. Manam women cook pork for *bobola* mortuary feast. Photo: Nancy Lutkehaus, 1978.

Members of the deceased's patrilineage will have to reciprocate in the future with gifts of food for his affines, matrilineal kin, and friends who slept at the grave site or stayed at the homestead of the deceased during this first week after the death. This is the purpose of the second mortuary ritual (*kangari rokoaki*), which is staged for commoners and elites alike, although for elites the amount of food, baskets of nuts, and number of pigs are larger.

When a chief died, the men's house was allowed to fall into disrepair, in other words, the chief and his powerful insignia (slit drums, masks, and flutes) have died and are left to decompose. It fell to the new chief to build a new men's house, a major undertaking for him that required many pigs and a lot of food, betel nuts, and tobacco to provision workers constructing the new building. Moreover, the new chief engaged masked dancers as part of the project. The dancers literally pull down the dilapidated old men's house, thus clearing a space where a new one will be erected.

They also stage a ritual attack against the former chief called the "throwing of spears at the grave" (*poda di ung*). The spears were meant to drive the spirit of the old chief out of the village and off to the land of the dead. The dancers required food and pigs for this service.[7] Kapui's successor, Yaboruru, did not build a new men's house, nor did he sponsor the performance of the *moarupu* masks. Kapui's sons, however, did decide to honor their father by organizing a *kangari rokoaki* rite. And it was Sila Watakapura, his eldest son, who agreed to postpone it until Sarina Pearson and I arrived to film it.

My Return to Manam Island, July 1994

We reached Manam the day before the mortuary rite for Kapui was to take place. Bad weather and rough seas delayed us, which meant that the food the Zogari village women had gathered from their gardens—bananas, in particular—were getting ripe and needed to be distributed and cooked immediately. After sunset, on the evening of our arrival, women gathered at the homestead where we were staying and began to sing mourning songs both to honor us and to remember Kapui. Their songs were the same, or similar to, the ones they would have sung when Kapui had died—and for me they were very evocative of events I shared with Zogari villagers when these songs were sung. As the women's soft, mournful voices gently filled the night air, I was overcome with memories of Kapui, of mornings sitting on the grounds outside our houses drinking coffee, the *kangari rokoaki* rite performed for Moinzo, his mother, and the last time I had seen him in Zogari village, a wan image of his former robust self.

Not long after women started to sing, several young men set up a gasoline-powered generator to power a couple of fluorescent lights. The garish green glow of the lamps diminished the ethereal and melancholy effect of the women's singing, an event that had been illuminated in the past by firelight and the glow of the women's pipes or cigarettes flickering in the darkness. Perhaps the women were offended too, as they started gradually to drift off, distancing themselves from the glare and disappearing into the softer darkness of the night.

Soon after they left, a group of young men, members of a village band called the *Yang Gililies,* took their place. When I first lived in Zogari village, the band members were teenagers who played acoustic guitars and competed in local and provincial string band contests. Now they played electric guitars with an amplifier powered by the generator. Their music attracted a young crowd eager to dance and entertain us. The bandleader was Moarupu, Kapui's adopted son, and other members included one of Sila's sons. Their performance was to welcome us and, perhaps, to honor Kapui, their deceased kinsman, too.

Kangari Rokoaki—"To Throw Away the Galip Nuts"

The morning that the mortuary feast began, women in Kapui's clan, myself included, brought baskets of *kangari* nuts to his widow's homestead, along with taro and bananas. The clan also provided three pigs and several kilos of imported lamb flaps (my contribution to the feast) for the feast and a later distribution of dishes of cooked food that are central to the rite.

While women cook, men crack open the hard shells of the nuts. The sound of the latter work is as salient a part of the event as any.[8] Like the banana leaf bundles central to Trobriand mortuary exchange, *kangari* nuts are so highly valued in Manam mortuary rites that people will go as far as purchasing baskets from other islanders should they lack one of their own to give.[9] Since it was imperative that as a member of Kapui's family I provide at least one basket of nuts, one of my adoptive relatives arranged for me to buy one so that I could join female kin in a procession in which each of us carried a basket atop our heads—in the manner traditional Manam women carry heavy loads—to Kapui's former homestead. There, we slammed the baskets onto the ground with as much force as we could muster in order to make sure they created as loud a thud as possible—the bigger the basket, the louder the thud. Like the singing of mourning songs and the shelling of *kangari* nuts, the percussive thuds of baskets represent the collective work of this stage of mourning in Manam culture.

While the Manam give gifts of *kangari* nuts on many occasions—including bride-wealth payments to mainland trading partners, as compensation to settle disputes, and as part of intervillage pig exchanges—this phase of mortuary ritual is the only time when the baskets are opened as part of the ritual feast itself. As Sila explained, it was necessary to empty all the baskets of nuts, shell them, and then distribute them in their entirety to guests (Figure 6.3). No nuts should be left unshelled or held back. The guests eat some of them at the mortuary feast itself, while others are wrapped up in banana leaf packets and sent along with dishes of cooked foods the hosts will deliver to their homesteads. Hosts carefully measure what size dish each guest should receive and each dish

Figure 6.3. Men eating shelled nuts at *kangari rokoaki* mortuary celebration. Photo: Nancy Lutkehaus, 1978.

must be decorated with a packet of nuts placed on top of it or it is considered incomplete.[10]

I mentioned the parallel between Trobriand banana leaf bundles given during *sagali* exchanges and Manam *kangari* nuts; this parallel is now made even more explicit by how the shelled nuts are also wrapped in baskets made from banana leaves (Lutkehaus 1995b). Like the Trobriand bundles and skirts, the nuts symbolize a relationship between givers and takers. They also represent the end of the relationship that once existed between the deceased and the recipient. The host group acknowledges a past relationship and reciprocates the work of mourning that the recipients of the nuts performed in honor of the deceased. And, like banana leaf bundles and skirts, while money cannot be used as a substitute for *kangari* nuts at the ceremony itself, money can be used to purchase the nuts.

But why *kangari* nuts? In Manam culture, the *kangari* tree—or in this case, the nuts that metonymically represent the *kangari* tree—is an apt symbol of human life and generational continuity, the loss of which, on the one hand, and the regeneration of which, on the other, are being celebrated during the mortuary ceremony (see Silverman, this volume, for another association of trees and mortuary ritual).[11] *Kangari* are some of the largest, loftiest trees that grow on the island. Significantly, unlike breadfruit, which is produced by the other type of tall tree on Manam, *kangari* nuts can be stored almost indefinitely because of their hard shell, making them a useful food as well as a valuable exchange object.

However, while baskets of *kangari* nuts are given as gifts on several other occasions, as I mentioned above, their exchange during this mortuary ceremony is the only time that baskets of nuts are slit open and nuts are cracked and distributed out of the shell, thus ensuring that they will be eaten immediately. Once shelled, the oily nuts do not last long and quickly turn rancid or moldy. Significantly, the only other gift of nuts removed from their shells I know about is made to trading partners and their kin leaving from Manam. The nuts are cracked and given to departing guests in a small bundle. In this context, it seems as though someone's departure might compare to what the French sometimes call a "small death," not in a postcoital sense, but in the sense of an undesirable occasion that invokes a momentary but nontrivial sentiment of loss. And thus, their leave-taking is marked with a quintessential symbol of the island of Manam and the Manam people but also more generally of human life and the social relationships that make life possible.

When an unopened basket of *kangari* nuts is given to someone as a gift, the nuts can be used by the recipient in a future exchange.[12] However, when the baskets are broken open and the nuts shelled, the nuts can only be consumed by the recipients and cannot be used in any subsequent transactions. Thus, the capacity of the nuts to create new social relations is denied. In this sense, the nuts—but especially the consumption of them—evoke the end of the life of the deceased. Yet, simultaneously, the nuts also symbolize regeneration and generational continuity in their metonymic capacity as "children" (*natu*), that is, the fruit of the *kangari* tree. Just as important, however, is the *kangari* nuts' symbolic association with Manam Island and the Manam people. The island is regionally famous for its production of nuts as an exchange good and for its rich, fertile volcanic soil that is conducive both to the rapid growth of the trees to great heights and to abundant yields.

The Symbolism of Sacrifice

At the *kangari rokoaki* rite for Kapui, three pigs were slaughtered, cooked, and served to guests. The pigs were no less important to the ceremony than the *kangari* nuts but, unlike the shelled nuts, pigs—both live and cooked—are part of most Manam life cycle rites as well as intervillage exchange feasts (*buleka*; Lutkehaus 2013). Two pigs were given by Kapui's children, while the third one, the largest of the three, belonged to and had been raised first by Kapui and his wife, Babirom, and then after his death by Babirom alone. This latter pig was the most significant of the three, as it conveyed aspects of both social and personal meanings that only pigs can represent in mortuary rituals. Podarua, one of Kapui's sons-in-law, explained to me that killing an especially large pig makes people want to show their respect for the animal and the life they are about to take. For Manam Islanders, pigs, like people, have a *mariaba*-spirit. The life of the pig is taken to honor the death of a person; similarly, people must show respect to the pig (Lutkehaus 2013).

An incident occurred during Kapui's mortuary rite that underscores this idea. The younger men took the pigs away to be killed and butchered. They dragged them to a spot marked by a large *moare* plant (Tokpisin *tanget; Taetsia frucitosa*), a sign indicating that the area was taboo, or off-limits because of supernatural sanctions. Ngasingasi, who had been charged with overseeing Kapui's burial, recognized their trespass and began screaming: "Sickness and sores will appear … not one man or woman will be all right!" Fearful that the inappropriate killing of the pigs would afflict the living, Ngasingasi became adamant: the pigs must be moved. The men carried the pigs a few feet away and Ngasingasi, apparently appeased, stopped ranting. The pigs were treated with esteem; particularly the largest one that had belonged to Kapui and Babriom. Because this was the chief's pig, it was honored as if it held elite status. In addition to dogs' teeth valuables, it was adorned with a bird-of-paradise plume, a symbol of chiefly authority (see Figure 6.4).

This was the first time that I had seen a pig destined for slaughter at a mortuary rite thus decorated. The fact that the rite was meant to honor the

Figure 6.4. A pig decorated as a chief with dog's teeth necklace and bird-of-paradise plume. Photo: Nancy Lutkehaus, 1978.

former chief, that it was the largest pig contributed to the rite, and that it had been raised by the former chief and his wife all seem to suggest that the pig was a symbol of the dead chief himself. A Manam man makes this very point at the beginning of our video. Other ritual contexts in which pigs are symbols of chiefs and vice versa, chiefs become symbols of pigs, could also be cited in support of this interpretation.

Pigs, of course, are also slaughtered and distributed when commoners die. If they are symbolically equated with chiefs and otherwise anthropomorphized, sacrificial pigs in mortuary rites for commoners may stand for a particular individual who has died. As we know, throughout PNG pigs are closely associated with moral identity and people often become attached to the pigs they raise. Thus it is perhaps not surprising that Babirom looked disconsolate as she watched the large pig she and her husband raised being readied to be taken off for slaughter.

In addition to the pig being a public symbol of the dead chief, the pig appears to have had a personal meaning for Babirom as Kapui's wife. A pig is a symbol of wealth in Manam, but it also served as a symbol with a particular emotional resonance for Babirom (Obeyesekere 1981: 18). In addition to its reference as a chiefly symbol, more personally, the pig seems to have represented the widow's relationship with her deceased husband. As she told us in an interview in the video, she and Kapui raised the pig together since it was a piglet, naming it and feeding it. In a sense, it was her child (as she and Kapui had no children together, the pig may have even carried more emotional salience for her). We see her cry in the video when the pig is taken away to be slaughtered because, as she explained, it reminded her of the evenings she used to spend with Kapui when they fed the pig and admired its size. Thus, not only did the death of the pig symbolize the death of a chief, but it was a tangible reference to Babirom's loss of her husband, Kapui (see also Silverman, this volume).

In the conclusion to her book *The Trobrianders of Papua New Guinea* (1988), Weiner cites an episode in Jonathan Swift's *Gulliver's Travels* when the hero learns about an experiment that will abolish words and replace them with the actual things they represent. In this incident, Weiner observes, "Swift ironically reminds us how much we use objects to make statements of our identity, goals, and even fantasies" (1988: 159). It seems that objects express feelings as well.

"Finishing Kapui's Name"

Just as the *kangari* nuts were said to be "finished" at the mortuary rite, that is, cracked open, distributed, and eaten, so too was Kapui's name "finished." However, while the shelled *kangari* nuts were given to guests, thus necessitating that they be consumed immediately, Kapui's name did not stop being used. No prohibition forbids speaking the names of the dead and names are passed down from generation to generation (see von Poser, this volume). Ideally, personal names skip a generation, thus a grandson inherits his primary name—the one used by a patriline to refer to him—from his paternal grandfather. For example, there was already a young Kapui, the son of another member of Kapui's clan, who had been born before Kapui died and was named for the chief. Thus the name itself is not "finished," and will continue to be given to other clan members in the future. What the ritual has "finished" is the relationship between a specific individual and, in the case of Kapui, his chiefly status.

At the same time, the *kangari rokoaki* rite has several status-related goals. For one thing, Kapui's patrilineal kin gave food and *kangari* nuts to people who honored their chief by sleeping at his homestead after he died—the kin who fulfilled their obligation to him and to his "name" or reputation. For another, as in Trobriand mortuary *sagali* exchanges, the Manam also use the *kangari* exchange to "finish" or "untie" and sever reciprocal relationships between Kapui and members of other clans. Lastly, when they give food to villagers who helped them mourn in other ways, they call out individual and clan names—

affirming their prestige and reputation in the face of the loss of their leader and most influential man.

Birth and death are sociologically, ritually and symbolically linked in Manam culture (see von Poser, this volume). Among kin of course, birth reproduces the clan, while death depletes it. In either event, clan members, together with matrilineal kin and affines, assemble to celebrate or console one another, sleeping and feasting together. Both birth and death occasion taboos meant to protect the body from mystical impurities arising from contact with a corpse or a birth mother and infant. In both instances, washing in the sea is required to purify the individual (see Lipset, this volume). After a death, birth and regeneration are evoked through gifts of *kangari* nuts—the fruit or "child" of a tree. At birth, death is alluded to through taboos, pollution beliefs, concealing the mother and child inside the birth house (*boaruku*) for a month to strengthen the newborn, communal sleeping outside the *boaruku* house, and even, sometimes, singing of *tang rang* mourning songs during the night.

Many people contribute to an individual's identity in Manam society, contributions that begin with the bestowal of a name of which people have several. Because names are clan property that circulate over time, not only do names reproduce clan identity through their transmission, but their use demonstrates specific social relations between the bearer of the name and the individual or individuals who gave it to him or her, as well as others who use it when addressing him or her. The sum total of personal names an individual possesses thus represents the network of social relations that defines the person in society. After death, the living perform the *kangari rokoaki* rite in part to "finish"—or end—the network of names of the deceased.

Changes in Manam Mortuary Rites (1994–2015)

Two days after the *kangari rokoaki* rite, *The Melanesian Explorer,* a ship carrying tourists, docked offshore and disgorged its passengers on the black sand beach that serves as an intervillage boundary. Imagine my surprise, and that of the villagers, when it turned out that the seventeen tourists were well-to-do African Americans from Brooklyn and Philadelphia who were visiting PNG because of their interest in imagined likenesses between Melanesian sculpture and African art. Some were collectors whose interests had expanded to include Sepik "tribal art," while others were college teachers or people who worked in the arts field. Sarina Pearson observed:

> [The] women were elaborately dressed and groomed. Some had impressive hair extensions with small cowrie shells braided in at the hairline. Others had gold flecks in their hair and long vibrantly lac-

quered fingernails. Many of the women wore clothes cut from elaborate ethnic textiles over which lay substantial amounts of intricate gold jewelry. (1995: 71)

That is to say, by contrast to the villagers—and to the two of us in our functional, rather drab, fieldwork gear—the *tourists* were an exotic "other."

Villagers were astonished, and an air of expectation swelled through them. Clearly something quite different was about to happen. While mildly curious about *our* presence in the village but totally uninterested in hearing anything about the *kangari rokoaki* rite we were filming, the tourists for their part seemed more intent on performing themselves. Making their way up to the village from the beach, they brought a boom box with them. Turning it on, one couple began to dance, to the bemused amazement of the villagers:

The music was of an urban hip hop variety and. ... the villagers immediately drew closer eager to see what was happening. ... Sweat poured off the couple as they picked up the pace and invited the villagers to join in. A few young girls attempted the complex steps but by and large most villagers were content to just watch. (Pearson 1995: 72).

While the couple danced, several village women offered other tourists bananas and pork from a pig just killed that morning in honor of our departure. As it turned out, many of the tourists were practicing Muslims and politely declined the pork, while others rather tentatively sampled a cooked banana or two. Once they had ascertained that there was relatively little "art" being produced by the islanders that was of interest to them, they retreated back to the boat awaiting them at the beach.[13]

The incident portrayed a decidedly postcolonial dilemma. On the one hand, the Manam desired to continue to conduct aspects of their lives in a culturally appropriate manner—especially, I argue, by burying their dead on the island. On the other hand, they have had to adapt to the advent of Westerners as well as the state into their lives. Unexpected events like the arrival of the tourists, although offering them the opportunity, perhaps, to sell some produce or a carving or two, as well as a serendipitous moment of entertainment, remind them how isolated they are from the world at large and how dependent they are upon external forces they do not control.

In recent years, their sense of marginality and dependency has increased (see Silverman, this volume). When I returned to Manam in 2011 to show the video Pearson and I made of Kapui's *kangari rokoaki* rite, the screenings were extraordinary. Unlike in 1994, technology had advanced to the point where it had become possible to bring a DVD and show our movie on a small computer screen. Just as in 1994, portable generators were around, but more surprising to me was the fact that villagers now had DVD players and television monitors of their own that allowed me to show the movie at night to large crowds of viewers. Indeed, movie nights on Manam had become rather commonplace (see also Iyer 1988).

Even more remarkable, and ultimately more significant than the ubiquity of media technology in a location that lacked electricity and running water, was the fact that the Manam Islanders had quit their island and resettled elsewhere. As the result of violent and frequent volcanic eruptions that began in 2004, the PNG government ordered the entire population of 9,000 to be evacuated to the mainland. There they became "Internally Displaced Persons" (IDP), a category the United Nations uses to refer to populations who have been forced to leave their homes or "habitual residence" but who have not crossed "an internationally recognized State border" (Global Displacement Cluster Working Group, 2007: 6).

In 2011, the PNG government introduced a bill that would allocate US$600,000 to relocate the Manam IDPs from temporary housing at three "Care Centers" along the north coast of Madang Province to a permanent settlement in the foothills of the Adelbert mountain range. This move would require tremendous changes in an economy that was based not only on the cultivation of rich, volcanic soils but on the exploitation of abundant marine resources, especially tuna and mackerel. And of course, relocation would spell a transformation of the *kangari rokoaki* rite we documented in 1994. As of December 2015, the bill, known as the Manam Resettlement Act, had still not been passed by the National Parliament.

Instead, upon my return in 2011 I found a few Manam living on the island, although volcanologists had predicted the possibility of another major explosion and although no schools, medical assistance, or regular transportation to and from the island were operated by the government or by any mission. Moreover, although I saw no evidence of baskets of nuts in houses, the essential element of the *kangari rokoaki* rite, the great trees had begun to bear fruit once again. I was given none to take away as a departure gift as I always had been in the past. Just as telling was their request upon learning that I would be visiting the Murik Lakes after leaving them (see Lipset, this volume). I must tell their Murik trading partners (*taoa*) how sorry they were that they had no baskets of nuts to give me to take them.

For many young Manam, especially those born on the mainland since the evacuation but also children who were infants and toddlers at that time, the *kangari rokoaki* rite they watched in the video I showed was the first they had seen of it. Some of them had never even been to the island. Nor had they seen deceased relatives and other well-known people, such as Kapui. For these children, the video was a historic document, something akin to a documentary film on PBS or the History Channel. It depicted a way of life that perhaps they had heard about from their parents or grandparents. But, with no *kangari* nut trees growing on the mainland, they certainly had not participated in a *kangari rokoaki* rite themselves.

It is significant that when Babirom, Kapui's elderly widow, died on the mainland in 2008, her body was taken back to Zogari village for burial (see Carucci, this volume). Her adopted son, Moarupu, his wife, and their family then decided to stay and together with another family, they formed the nucleus of a new Zogari village. In 2011, I saw new houses and gardens under construction by eager people wanting to harvest coconuts, as copra production had become a major source of cash income.

As Moarupu took me around the former village to visit reoccupied homesteads, people repeatedly singled out the gravesites for comment. Not only was I told who was buried where, but Moarupu also made a point to explain that people now buried the dead at homesteads rather than in the cemetery, as they had done in the past (see Bell, this volume; von Poser, this volume; Carucci, this volume). They showed me the abandoned cemetery itself quite overgrown with weeds.

There are at least two reasons Manam Islanders had become intent on homestead burials. Both I think have to do with their desire to bring back the agency they associate with custom. On the one hand, homestead burial defies the strictures of modernity and thus asserts a kind of cultural authenticity. On the other hand, and perhaps more significantly, homestead burial in the past was a gesture to please—and appease—the *mariaba*-spirit of the deceased. Now, in the aftermath of relocation to the mainland, when Manam identity with their island, their place, and their individual homesteads is under threat, the living have come to value the association of the dead with their own land and island.

In 2011, a young Manam woman living in town told me about her family's return home to bury her grandmother, who had died on the mainland in 2005. At that time, her mother explained Manam beliefs to her about how important it was for the spirit of the dead to return not just to Manam but to its homestead. Raised a Catholic on Manam and a graduate of Divine Word University in Madang, she had never heard about this value and practice until her grandmother died. The occasion of her grandmother's burial had prompted her mother to tell her about the relationship of the *mariaba*-spirit to the land. The young woman told me how very moved she felt.

There had been no *kangari rokoaki* rite staged for her grandmother. Nor had one been held for Kapui's widow, Babirom. There were no *kangari* nuts to be had, much less any surplus food to be exchanged. In the case of Bibirom, however, a few men who knew how to play the *embeki* flutes did return with her body to bury it on the island and honor her as the wife of a chief.

After viewing the video of his grandfather's *kangari rokoaki* rite, Kapui's firstborn grandson, Momai, who was in charge of the Zogari population on the mainland, asked me to send him copies so he could listen to the *embeki* flutes being played by his father's generation. When I asked him whether he knew how to play the flutes himself, he replied that he didn't. He had not been interested in learning how to play them when he was younger, and he thought that it was too late for him to learn how to play them now, especially since so many of the men who knew how to play the flutes had died.

One of the most memorable and culturally salient aspects of screening the video of Kapui's mortuary rite was the poignant, indeed sometimes gut-wrenching, reactions it aroused among some viewers, a reaction specifically to seeing images of the dead. At least three participants in the 1994 ceremony were no longer alive in 2011. The first time they appeared on the screen, their male and female kin burst into tears and started to sob and keen. More than spontaneous expressions of emotion brought about at the sight of a husband, mother, son-in-law, and so on, these outpourings were also part of a cultural script for mourning.

I had seen it before and recognized it now as both ritualized demonstrations of love and respect as well as personal expressions of sadness. As tears were not unexpected by other villagers, the rest of the audience offered little reaction but continued watching the screen. Had it been considered culturally incorrect to see images of deceased loved ones, I would not have been permitted to show the video. Instead, the screening offered the living a culturally acceptable, albeit entirely modern, opportunity to express their grief and respect for the dead.

Conclusion—Manam Burial Practice and Modernity in PNG

What else might contemporary Manam mortuary practices tell us about their dialogue with modernity? First of all, they are in flux. Many aspects of mortuary ritual on Manam have either been lost or, at the very least, temporarily suspended. Returning to Weiner's notion of reproduction and to the idea that the Manam *kangari rokoaki* mortuary ritual plays a role that is comparable to *sagali* exchange in the Trobriand Islands, we might conclude that there has been a serious rupture in the ability of Manam society to reproduce itself according to tradition. Thus, in some Manam communities the performance of sacred flutes will end with the death of the most senior generation of men who can play them. However, the current chief's request for CDs of flute music prompted by hearing them on my video indicates that there is an abiding interest in them and perhaps the potential that they may be played again in the future, as they still are in some Manam villages.

As for the years that have passed without a *kangari rokoaki* rite being staged for Babirom, the old chief's widow, it does not mean that one will never take place in the future. As I say, *kangari* trees were bearing fruit and pigs were being fed and growing fat on the island in 2011. When I returned in May 2015, even though people were still displaced, Sila's son Momai had organized the construction of a new men's house there, and people were getting ready to host several neighboring villages for a ritual attack that symbolizes the end of the old chief's reign and publicly proclaims the authority of the new one. Moreover, this time at my departure, I was given packets of *kangari* nuts to take with me as a farewell gift. Once again people will have gifts to exchange, gifts that will reproduce the social networks so vital to them and to their relationships to the dead. Ten years after their relocation from Manam, the reproduction of society goes on and is adapting to new extenuating circumstances the people now face on the mainland.

In conclusion, I return again to the connection between birth, death, and the reproduction of Manam society, in particular, to the Manam belief in the immortality of the *mariaba*-spirit and the importance of the association of the ancestors with Manam Island and place (*anua*). The term *anua* has multiple meanings. In addition to one's homestead, it can refer to one's village and to Manam Island itself. In "Death and Social Status in Melanesia" (1927), Wedgwood referred to WHR Rivers's suggestion that many immigrant groups in Melanesia desired "to send their dead to the home whence they had come" (1927: 377). Little did she know how true this would become of the Manam.

The association between the spirits of the dead and *anua*, or home, is even more salient now that the state prohibits the islanders from living on the island and the volcano itself threatens their ability to live there. What is now at stake is the very reproduction of moral community as they have known it. For the Manam, the uncertainty of life on the edge of a volcano is a condition with which they have always lived. What is different now is the decision of the state to force the Manam to relocate and its refusal to provide schools and transportation to and from the island to returnees, even though it stalls, some ten years on, in its plans to resettle them on the mainland. For some people who watched the video of Kapui's *kangari rokoaki* ceremony, their tears may have been for the death of a way of life, for others it may have been an affirmation of their culture and of the importance of burying their dead on Manam.

Undoubtedly, the most salient change I observed in 2011 in their mortuary dialogue with modernity was the revival of homestead burial. Before their resettlement on the mainland, islanders had sometimes defied the state by burying their chiefs on their homesteads; now both elites and commoners were being buried on the island. My Zogari friends agreed that this change was significant too and specifically pointed it out to me. Given the PNG government's refusal to support the return of the Manam to their island, the reappearance of homestead graves expresses defiance of the state as well as the increased importance of Manam to people who live on the mainland or who have returned to the island: the dead should be buried on their specific *anua* homesteads on their island home. Under the shadow of the volcano, the living and the dead may then work together to reproduce a moral community amid a Melanesian modernity that seems to show little or no concern for them.

Dedication

This chapter is dedicated to my Manam father, Kapui, and to Annette Weiner, who died in 1998. It is written in memory of her contributions to the ethnography of Papua New Guinea as well as of the support she provided me as a fledgling anthropologist, hiring me to teach in the Department of Anthropology at New York University just after I had defended my dissertation at Columbia. Conversations I had with her that year, personal and professional, guided me through the stress of searching for a job. Subsequently, I have introduced students at the University of Southern California to the Trobriand Islanders through her books and film.

Nancy C. Lutkehaus is professor of anthropology at the University of Southern California. She has done anthropological research on a variety of topics among the Manam Islanders in Papua New Guinea since 1979. In addition to *Zaria's Fire: Engendered Moments in Manam Island Ethnography,* she is the author of *Margaret Mead: The Making of an American Icon* as well as numerous articles and book chapters.

Notes

1. See Lutkehaus 1995b; and Wedgwood 1934.
2. *Kangari* is the Manam term for Tahitian almonds or *canarium* nuts, commonly referred to as *galip* in Tok Pisin.
3. It is not unusual for there to be an extended period of time between death and the final mortuary, as a large number of pigs and other foods must be distributed at the ceremony.
4. The Manam associate the fire in the volcano with Zaria's vagina.
5. Barlow notes that the Murik also acknowledge the rupture of a relationship by renouncing food (2000: 18).
6. See Lutkehaus (1995b). During the annual Barasi celebration the living are expected to leave gifts of food, betel nut, and tobacco at the graves of their deceased family members to please their spirits so that they will do no harm to the living in the upcoming year.
7. For more about the performance of the *moarupu* masks and the succession of chiefs, see Lutkehaus (1995b: 238–44).
8. Cracking the nuts and removing them from shells may symbolize death and regeneration/reproduction. See Valeri on breaking a receptacle of water and coconuts in

Ancient Hawai'i as a symbol of death and renewal, or at least as a symbol of transition (1985: 216, 383n49).
9. Baskets range in size and price from K3 to K10 (approximately US$2.50 to US$8.00). *Kangari* trees are inherited from both paternal and maternal relatives. The trees usually bear nuts once a year. They are harvested by men and boys who climb up the large, stately trees and shake the nuts down to the ground. Women and children gather nuts and bring them home to spread out on a rack above the hearth fire to dry. The baskets, woven out of coconut fronds, are stored in rafters above the hearth to continue to smoke.
10. Like pigs a chief receives at an intervillage exchange (*buleka*), which he distributes to villagers to eat, the distribution of pork and cooked foods at the *kangari rokoaki* rite is a gesture of care, nurture, and commensality that unites the community.
11. On the cross-cultural symbolism of trees, see Laura Rival 1998.
12. Baskets of *kangari* are so important as exchange items because, like pigs, they are never simply consumed by one's own family.
13. For a more detailed description of our encounter with this group of tourists, see Pearson 1995.

References Cited

Barlow, Kathleen. 2000. "Working Mothers and the Work of Culture in a Papua New Guinea Society." *Ethos* 29(1): 1–30.
Böhm, Karl. 1983. *The Life of Some Island People of New Guinea*. Introduction by Nancy Lutkehaus. Collectanea Instituti Anthropos No. 29. Berlin: Dietrich Reimer Verlag.
Ginsburg, Faye D. and Reyna Rapp. 1991. "The Politics of Reproduction." *Annual Review of Anthropology* 20: 311–43.
———. 1995. "Introduction." In *Conceiving the New World Order: The Global Politics of Reproduction*, edited by Faye Ginsburg and Reyna Rapp, 1–17. Berkeley: University of California Press.
Global Protection Cluster Working Group. 2007. *Handbook for the Protection of Internally Displaced Persons*. Geneva, Switzerland: Internal Displacement Monitoring Centre.
Hollan, Douglas W. and Jane C. Wellencamp. 1996. *The Thread of Life: Toraja Reflections on the Life Cycle*. Honolulu: University of Hawaii Press.
Iyer, Pico. 1988. *Video Night in Katmandu: And Other Reports from the Not-So-Far East*. New York: Knopf.
Leach, Jerry W. and Edmund Leach, eds. 1983. *The Kula: New Perspectives on Massim exchange*. Cambridge: Cambridge University Press.
Lipset, David. 1997. *Mangrove Man: Dialogics of Culture in a Sepik Estuary*. Cambridge: Cambridge University Press.
Lutkehaus, Nancy. N.d. "Lives in Limbo: The Fate of Living on a Pacific Island That Is an Active Volcano." Paper presented at the meetings of the Association for Social Anthropology in Oceania, Kona, Hawai'i. February 9, 2014.
———. 1985. "Pigs, Politics, and Pleasure: Manam Perspectives on Trade and Regional Integration." *Research in Economic Anthropology* 7: 123–141.
———. 1990. "The *Tambaran* of the *Tanepoa*: Traditional and Modern Forms of Leadership on Manam Island." In *Sepik Heritage: Tradition and Change in Papua New Guinea*, edited by Nancy Lutkehaus et al., 298–308. Durham: Carolina Academic Press.

———. 1995a. "Gender Metaphors: Female Rituals as Cultural Models in Manam." In *Gender Rituals: Female Initiation in Melanesia*, edited by Nancy Lutkehaus and Paul Roscoe, 183–204. New York: Routledge.

———. 1995b. *Zaria's Fire: Engendered Moments in Manam Ethnography*. Durham: Carolina Academic Press.

———. 2013. "Bodily Transformations: The Politics and Art of Men as Pigs and Pigs as Men on Manam Island, Papua New Guinea." *Pacific Arts* 13(1): 5–15.

Obeyesekere, Gannath. 1981. *Medusa's Hair: An Essay on Personal Symbols and Religious Experience*. Chicago: University of Chicago Press.

Pearson, Sarina. 1995. *Lamb Flaps, Tourists, Pop Music and Mortuary Rites: Post-Colonialism and Tradition on Manam Island, Papua New Guinea*. MA thesis. The University of Southern California.

Rival, Laura. 1998. "Introduction: Trees, from Symbols of Life and Regeneration to Political Artifact." In *The Social Life of Trees: Anthropological Perspectives on Tree Symbolism*, edited by Laura Rival, 1–26. Oxford: Berg.

Tuzin, Donald. 1997. *The Cassowary's Revenge: the Life and Death of Masculinity in a New Guinea Society*. Chicago: University of Chicago Press.

Valeri, Valerio. 1985. *Kingship and Sacrifice: Ritual and Society in Ancient Hawaii*. Chicago: University of Chicago Press.

Wedgwood, Camilla. N.d. Unpublished Fieldnotes. Wedgwood Archives. University of Sydney.

———. 1927. "Death and Social Status in Melanesia." *Royal Anthropological Institute of Great Britain and Ireland*. 57: 377–97.

———. 1934. "Report on Research in Manam Island, Mandated Territory of New Guinea." *Oceania* 4(4): 373–403.

Weiner, Annette. 1976. *Women of Value, Men of Renown: New Perspectives in Trobriand Exchange*. Austin: University of Texas Press.

———. 1979. "Trobriand Kinship from Another View: The Reproductive Power of Men and Women." *Man* NS 14: 328–48.

———. 1988. *The Trobrianders of Papua New Guinea*. New York: Holt, Rinehart and Winston.

———. 1992. *Inalienable Possessions: The Paradox of Keeping-While Giving*. Berkeley: University of California Press.

———. 1995. "Reassessing Reproduction in Social Theory." In *Conceiving the New World Order: The Global Politics of Reproduction*, edited by Faye D. Ginsburg and Rayna Rapp, 407–21. Berkeley: University of California Press.

7

Transformations of Male Initiation and Mortuary Rites among the Kayan of Papua New Guinea

ALEXIS TH. VON POSER

The topic of this chapter is a phenomenon that I only recognized while organizing my data about the traditional *male* life cycle in Kayan, a village and language group on the north coast of Papua New Guinea (PNG).[1] When thinking about mortuary rites in Kayan, I realized that rites performed at the end of a person's life require looking at other rites that play an important role elsewhere in the life cycle and that a clear symmetry existed between male initiation and mortuary rites.[2]

In the traditional life cycle, the social person of a Kayan man only began to emerge long after his birth and did not come to an end until long after his death. This concept differs from what Bloch calls an "'all or nothing' understanding of life and death" (1988: 15). In other words, the steps taken to ensure entry into full personhood in society (see Silverman and Lipset, this volume) had to be reversed after death to successfully end that status and set the name of the deceased free to be used once again (see Lutkehaus, this volume).[3] If identity were a unit of time in traditional Kayan thinking, then time was cyclical rather than linear. In addition, every human person possessed two souls, whose moral qualities differed. Both ideas shall be discussed in due course.

After introducing the main features of Kayan personhood, in the first part of the chapter, I present corresponding sequences of ritual becoming and ceasing to be a man. In the second part, I investigate the changes that have taken place in the two ritual cycles in reaction to missionization and, more recently, in relation to increased market integration and the nation-state. I shall show that the idea of what constitutes a person in time in these rites has changed and that new concepts of identity and temporality are emerging. Thus, the shifts in the two rituals reveal that a more fundamental phenomenon is taking place, namely, a decline of local-level autonomy in response to modernity (see Lutkehaus, this volume; Silverman, this volume; and Bell, this volume).

Kayan Personhood

Kayan is situated near the mouth of the Ramu River in PNG, more or less opposite Manam Island and just a few miles down the coast from the Murik Lakes (see Lutkehaus, this volume; Lipset, this volume). It consists of one main village and several hamlets. The Catholic Mission reached Kayan in the early 1930s, when Joseph Much, a Society of the Divine Word missionary, stayed for about one year. Prior to Much's arrival, only sporadic contact took place from Monumbo, where Father Franz Vormann had established an outpost in 1899 a few miles to the east along the coast. Only in 1938 did long-term proselytizing begin under Father Leo Meiser, who resided in Kayan until 1942, when Japanese troops arrested him. A Catholic presence continued in Kayan up to the early 1980s, when the last missionary left. In other words, by 2004, only the very eldest members of the community had firsthand experience of premission days. Most villagers were more or less influenced by Christian theology and *habitus*. My main interlocutor on traditional Kayan life was Blasius Jong (see von Poser 2010, 2014), who had learned knowledge of custom from Nagi, a man who had grown up before the first missionaries reached the area (Meiser n.d.: 8, 1955: 266). Despite the impact of Catholicism, elements of both male initiation and mortuary rites remained important in Kayan, and what is still performed does resemble how the Kayan speak of pre-Christian practices.

Kayan society consists of three main descent groups, each of which is presided over by a hereditary chief (see Lutkehaus, this volume). Before the village was created in 1947, when the Australian government demanded that all Kayan live together, these three descent groups occupied separate places (*mugum*), were patrilineal and virilocal, and were strictly exogamous. Today, the community is divided into sections that are each centered on its own men's house (*nggomor*). The men's houses are subdivided into two or three family groups (*baer*) of kin (*wisac*).

Larger social groups in Kayan society I call the "social mesocosm" (see von Poser 2014: 67–76), and I contrast them with smaller units, which I call the "social microcosm" (see von Poser 2014: 156–60). Beginning with the family (*baer*) and extending to all divisions larger than the family, the role of a person differs from the smaller divisions.[4] The idea of an individual in the sense of being or occupying a unique nexus of relational ties within a social network is what I would call "participation in the social microcosm" in Kayan society. On the larger scale of the social mesocosm, the individual is not detectable. Every member of the community on this scale serves only in a social role and is, in a way, interchangeable. On this larger scale, traditional goods, like spirit-masks, magical spears, and sacred flutes, are owned by the group.

Other, intangible property, such as copyrights to songs or carving designs, is also collectively owned. This division of the person into these two layers, large and small, is important to keep in mind when we look at the Kayan dialogue with modernity.

In order to understand male initiation and mortuary rites, it is necessary to stress that in Kayan cosmology persons did not necessarily come into being at birth. Newborns were believed to be still part of the spirit world. And only when it became clear that a baby would survive and not be taken back by the spirits would people—especially men—permit themselves to become emotionally attached and make preparations to introduce him or her into adult life (cf. Gottlieb 2004).

In Kayan, a person bears a name of an ancestor and is believed to carry certain characteristics that are connected with that name (see Silverman, this volume). Each family owns a set of these names, and a newborn child will inherit one of these, which is free for usage, that is, unless it has been already given to another living kinsman. The names are mystically connected to certain skills, such as being good at fighting, carving, flute playing or having diplomatic competence (see Meiser 1955).

In addition, the person was believed to possess two spirits, one that experiences daily life (*ngerong*) and one that dreams at night (*ndurum*). A similar subdivision of the person can be found in other groups of Melanesia as well.[5] The day-spirit was thought to be present at birth and then grew in its host without any required care.[6] The second spirit, the night-spirit, had only a rudimentary presence at the beginning of life. It only became evident after a child commenced to talk about dreams—dreams in which he would encounter ancestors. As soon as dream reporting started, parents might begin to prepare for the first stage of initiation, since from now on, the development of the night-spirit had to be nurtured by several rites that marked the child's growth into his name and social role. Thus, the ritual, the ancestor's name, and the night-spirit were linked to dreams. Upon receiving a name of an ancestor, a man also inherited a slit-drum beat, with which he could be addressed from the distance. This rhythm, connected as it was to the bearer of a name, was only used after all initiatory steps were completed.[7]

Several other names, given by family members, friends, and trading partners of the parents, individualize the person as the occupant of a unique position within a social network. These different names are related to daily activities that are brought to an end, along with the day-spirit, during mortuary rites. Meantime, the night-spirit, being connected to the ancestors and to the descent group, is part of the social mesocosm. The day-spirit, manifest in the multiple names, is part of the social microcosm that connotes relational-individual concepts of personhood (Strathern and Stewart 2000).

Traditional Male Initiation

I now turn to a discussion of the two ritual cycles and then to their relationship to each other. Elsewhere, I have described in detail the traditional steps leading to full male personhood with all its rights and duties (von Poser 2014: 131–37). Here, I shall only briefly review this process. After birth, the child grew up naked until he received the first ritual loincloth. This happened at the age of approximately 12 years, when the child was also permitted to see the *tambaran* flute-spirits perform for the first time (see Tuzin 1980, 2001; Wassmann 1988, 1991; Lipset 1997; Yamada 1997).

On this occasion, the initiate was also subjected to a heavy beating with sticks and stinging nettles. To mark the transition as a symbolic death during which he was swallowed by the spirit and then spit out again, a boy would be rubbed with black paint made from ash and coconut oil. This traumatic rite was the first phase of his movement into full male personhood. By undergoing this procedure, he left the female realm and was symbolically reborn into a completely male surrounding (Wassmann 1987: 531; see also Silverman and Lipset, this volume). He would then spend the following one or two years in a bush camp, completely set apart from the village, where classificatory mothers and sisters lived. Here he would learn secret knowledge as well as skills required in daily life.

After the end of this period of seclusion, the first scarification was performed. As opposed to novices in Sepik River initiations, who were symbolically eaten by a crocodile (Bateson 1958: 136; Wassmann 1987: 531, 1991: 33; Silverman 2001: 71), the Kayan initiates were said to be eaten by a pig. They could now return to the village and were entitled to wear a specific bark belt that marked their new status. The scarification procedure was repeated twice more, after an interval of one or more years. Only after the third and final scarification, and after the novice had taken an enemy's head, was a young man allowed to wear the bark belt and the hair tube of an adult.

He was now allowed to marry, build a house, and live there with his wife. In a final rite, he received the special decoration worn by an adult member of family and society, which consisted of family-specific color patterns rubbed on the body and distinctive arrangements of boar's tusks and bird-of-paradise plumage (see Lipset 1997). Now, a man's growth into his social role was complete and he could be addressed with the specific slit-drum beat. Moreover, his night-spirit was considered fully grown. A young man had learned about the manifold connections of his own identity to the ancestral powers that were part of him. Through the night-spirit, he was now rooted deeply in the circular time of the ancestors, simultaneously connected to past and future bearers of his name.

The whole ritual procedure consisted of five stages that ranged over several years of childhood and adolescence. That the initiatory process involved a series of discrete events is important to keep in mind when looking at mortuary rites, of which I offer only a condensed account as well.

Traditional Mortuary Rites

After death, steps that had been taken as part of the initiation ceremonies would be reversed. The purpose of this reversal was to disassemble what had been built up before, namely, the connections of the night-spirit to the ancestors and the community. The body of the deceased was washed in fragrant water and then decorated with the family-specific emblems and designs that he had received in the final step of his initiation. The closest kin would spend the night watching the corpse (see Dalton, this volume) and in the morning, a small sailing canoe would be put to sea that was thought to ferry the deceased's day-spirit to Karkar, the island of the dead (see Lipset, this volume). The relational-individual part of the person having been disposed of, the rest of the mortuary rites concerned the collective part of the person, that is, his night-spirit.

At first, the possibility that the cause of death was sorcery based would be investigated. A moot might be convened, and an oracular device that I call the "wandering coffin" might be consulted. Formerly an old canoe, the coffin holding the corpse was publicly questioned as it led its bearers to places and houses of people who were close to the deceased but also to houses of people who might have had reason to kill the deceased (see Lipset, this volume). The sorcerer might be a person in conflict with the deceased or who had been a troublemaker. The wandering coffin could also lead to a place where a fight between the deceased and someone else had taken place, or it might go to items that had been subject to dispute. The wandering coffin oracle is still practiced today (Figure 7.1).

Its procession ended at the grave of the first burial, underneath the deceased's house during prestate times, but the gravesite was later moved to separate cemeteries at the insistence of early missionaries and the colonial administration. A small house would be built over the grave that was meant to provide shelter for the night-spirit (see Figure 7.2). Now mourning taboos began for the spouse.

She had to be secluded in her house, where she was not allowed to cook or touch food. She could eat only by means of pincers made of bamboo, which remain in use for smoking and betel nut chewing today (see Figure 7.3). Besides that, the handles of cutlery and cups used by the widow are covered with leaves (see Hogbin 1996: 158). The widow was endangered because her husband's spirit was eager to reunite with her. Eventually, she was released via a ceremony (*mombour*) during which she would be washed and then painted

Figure 7.1. Questioning the "wandering coffin." Photo: Alexis von Poser, 2008.

by her in-laws with black paint that marked her as unmarriageable but now allowed to participate in regular village life again.

After the flesh decomposed, the closest kin would secretly open the grave and wash the bones with herbal oil and lay them out nicely. The skull and the jawbone would be removed from the grave and given to the widow and children (see Fortune 1935). Sometimes, a lime spatula would be made from a shinbone of the deceased. The grave would be refilled afterward. Sometimes, years later, the personal belongings of the deceased, including clothes and other personal items, would be burned up while the flute-spirits were performed by the male cult (see Lutkehaus, this volume). At this point, the black paint would be washed off the widow and new, red paint would be rubbed on her skin by in-laws. Now, she was allowed to remarry, and the ancestral name of the deceased might be bestowed upon a newborn again. When the close family decided that it was time to let go of all memory of the deceased, especially if the widow decided that she wanted to remarry, the skull would be reburied with the rest of the bones and the release of the night-spirit was completed.

Figure 7.2. A grave-house for the night-spirit. Photo: Alexis von Poser, 2008.

Figure 7.3. Bamboo pincers for cigarettes and betel nuts. Photo: Alexis von Poser, 2008.

Symmetries of Male Initiation and Mortuary Rites

Mortuary rites would span many years and would essentially end where male initiation started. The two cycles seem to mirror each other (see van Gennep 1960: 3; Roscoe 1995: 233). As I mentioned, initiation rites consisted of five major events: (1) the first loincloth and encounter with the *tambaran*, (2) the first scarification ("Pig I"), (3) the second scarification ("Pig II"), (4) the third scarification ("Pig III"), and finally (5) the decoration ceremony that was also "supervised" by the male cult's flute-spirits.[8] Likewise, the mortuary cycle consisted of five rites: (1) the exhibition of the corpse, (2) the first burial, (3) the *mombour* feast when the widow was painted with black paint, (4) the cleaning of the bones, and (5) the burning of the personal belongings of the deceased.[9] The different phases can be visualized in a graph (see Table 7.1) whose two axes are time (horizontal) and social status (vertical). This chart does not follow Kayan models, of course, but I consider it helpful to understand the connections between the two processes.

The first phase of initiation and the last public phase of mortuary rites were linked by clothing and the flute-spirits of the male cult. As I stated earlier, a young man was given his first article of clothing upon his first encounter with these spirits. This was undone in the last step of the mortuary rites, when the flute-spirit appeared again to burn the clothing of the deceased. Therefore, the idea of becoming a clothed person was subjected to a ritual reversal in this phase of the mortuary process. Before donning a loincloth, a boy was not fully human; he had not yet left the spirit world completely. Dressing and growing into adulthood coincided. Moreover, both the young boy and the spouse of the deceased were painted black, symbolizing their exit from semispiritual existence. The young boy left a maternal world of being fed and learned to cook and look after himself; the grieving spouse left the

Table 7.1. Ritual status in time (time: horizontal axis, social status: vertical axis)

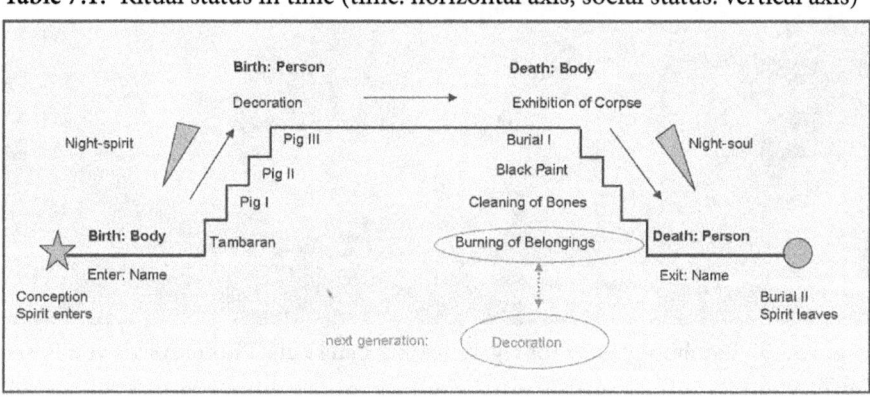

taboos inside the house, where she too was mothered, and was allowed to cook for herself again.

Symmetries between the next three initiation rituals and their corresponding steps during mortuary rites are somewhat difficult to identify due to lack of detailed reports on these practices. It seems, however, that the third initiation rite and the third mortuary rite were linked. Only after being scarified and decorated was a man allowed to marry and start to live with his wife. In reverse, a husband's corpse was separated from his widow at death and, in good Hertzian fashion, it was not until after the flesh had decomposed that his skull was brought back to her. In addition, perhaps there is an analogy between the spatial and social isolation that the spouse observed and that of initiates. Both were exiled from collective life, although for different reasons and with different results. Widows were meant to be hidden away from their husbands' spirits for their own protection, while boys were supposed to gain weight. Mothers were surprised, or at least so I was told, to see their sons emerge as big and well-built men after returning from their secret "school" in the bush camp. Their new size contrasted with the disintegrating flesh after burial.

When we compare the last phase of male initiation to the first mortuary rites, obvious symmetries appear. The final stage of the decoration ritual began with a parade of the young men through the village and ended with a presentation of their decorated bodies (see Figure 7.4). In reverse, the death rites started with an exhibition of the corpse, formerly decorated the same way.

Figure 7.4. A procession of initiated men. Photo: Alexis von Poser, 2005.

168 Alexis Th. von Poser

Then the body recreated the earlier procession through the village inside the wandering coffin.

When the young boy was sitting in the men's house in his full regalia, a spear was leaned against him pointing at his head (see Figure 7.5). This weapon marked his acquisition and possession of secret knowledge. The weapon, called "death-spear" (*yapoc*), was the property of the spirits (Meiser n.d.: 28). Now, all the old death-spears were destroyed (or sold) because of their connec-

Figure 7.5. The symbolic death. Photo: Alexis von Poser, 2005.

tion to "heathen" practices that opposed Christianity, and today a new type of spirit-spear has been substituted (*mais*). This new spear bears associations to the original, as it is still thought of as "belonging" to the spirits and of course, iconically, they still evoke warfare.

The decoration ceremony was also linked in another way to the last step in mortuary rites, the burning of personal belongings of the deceased. A son or nephew would receive the body ornaments of his dead father or uncle after the personal belongings of the latter were burned. That is to say, not only were the two processes symmetrical, they were also causally related: an event in the mortuary process of the older generation instigated a phase in the initiation process in the younger generation. They were decorated in the ornaments of the deceased.[10] One further connection can be drawn. In both rites, donations of valuables were given by kin and friends. In initiation, they were meant to support the new marriages that were now permitted to take place; in mortuary rites, they were meant to support the deceased's kin in their preparations for the next steps of the ritual.

In a sense, the whole system, consisting of the two ritual processes, implies that time moved cyclically (cf. Gell 1975, 2001).[11] Kayan kin terminology lends support to this interpretation: the word for ancestors is the same word for offspring (*ŋameir*), and one term is used for both great-grandparents and great-grandchildren (*bedrir*). If seen as part of a cyclical construction of time, the ritual concept of the person envisions him as beginning in a weak and helpless and ending in a likewise enfeebled spirit-state (see Dalton, this volume).

I suspect that more symmetries and connections existed between initiation and mortuary rites in Kayan. Those that I have been able to identify, however, are sufficient to demonstrate my general point. I shall now discuss modern versions of these rites in this society.

Modern Initiation and Mortuary Rites

The two ritual processes that I have just described are no longer performed. Only an abridged version of the first phase of initiation is still practiced. Today, a young boy is given a first grass skirt by an uncle or an aunt, the grass skirt having replaced the loincloth as an item of traditional clothing, which is then only worn during ritual occasions or dance performances. A boy might or might not then see a performance of the flute-spirits for the first time. In any case, his body will not be rubbed with black paint. Boys are no longer beaten with sticks and nettles. Neither are they scarified or secluded in the bush camp.

Today, young men marry voluntarily and do not have to wait for the decoration ceremony to start their own family. The decoration ceremony is still performed sporadically if fathers and sons wish to do so. The whole initiation process has changed considerably and obviously; cultivating the night-spirit and strengthening bonds to the ancestors is no longer seen as central to growing up. The phases of male initiation still practiced are considered optional, and their import as markers of personhood has been waived. Before discussing contemporary ways young men gain status, I shall present the modernized version of mortuary rites.

After a death, the corpse is no longer painted and decorated, nor is it washed in fragrant herbal water (see Lipset, this volume). Today, room freshener is sprayed about the body. Donations of money rather than shell valuables are made. The night watch of the deceased is still practiced. And, the next day, the wandering coffin oracle is still questioned en route to the grave. After burial, the spouse will begin to observe house taboos, which are remarkably similar to the practices mentioned above but shortened. Women now wear black clothes. Men stop shaving and cutting their hair.

The next rite combines several parts of traditional mortuary ritual. After ceremonially washing, the spouse changes out of black clothes and puts on a new colorful long and wide blouse top (Tokpisin: *meri-blaus*), which became fashionable for PNG women when PNG turned to Christianity. Men are shaven and receive a haircut. In addition, the belongings of the deceased may now be burned. The cleaning of the bones, which was done because the night-spirit of the deceased was feared as not at rest and dangerous, is no longer performed, except in rare instances. Most Kayan now dismiss it as superstitious.

A few years ago, a completely new phase of mortuary ritual was introduced: cementing the grave (see Dalton, this volume). Every family now tries to save enough money to buy cement to install a permanent marker for their beloved. Together with the demand for store-bought food, including rice, canned fish, and lamb flaps, for feasting, the new, cement graves have added to the cost of contemporary mortuary rites. A related topic of mortuary dialogue has arisen: some villagers prefer to stage what they view as Westernized rites during which a small group of kin gathers to eat when cementing the grave. Such people, who often have worked in town, argue that less elaborate mortuary rites not only save money but also time. The majority of the Kayan, however, view this kind of radically abridged kind of mortuary rite disrespectful of the dead. There is a greater issue at stake in their dialogue, of course, which has to do with contested concepts of the person. Cementing the grave constructs a lasting memorial to a specific individual. Neither individuality nor perpetuity was traditional in Kayan concepts of death.

Although initiation and mortuary rites have changed, may they still be viewed as part of a single process by which persons enter and exit society? To a certain extent, taking the sacraments of baptism, Holy Communion, and marriage have replaced initiation ritual into the Male Cult today. In addition, school graduation rites, which do not appear in Table 7.2, play an important part in the modern construction of the person.

Table 7.2. Modern status in time (time: horizontal axis, social status: vertical axis)

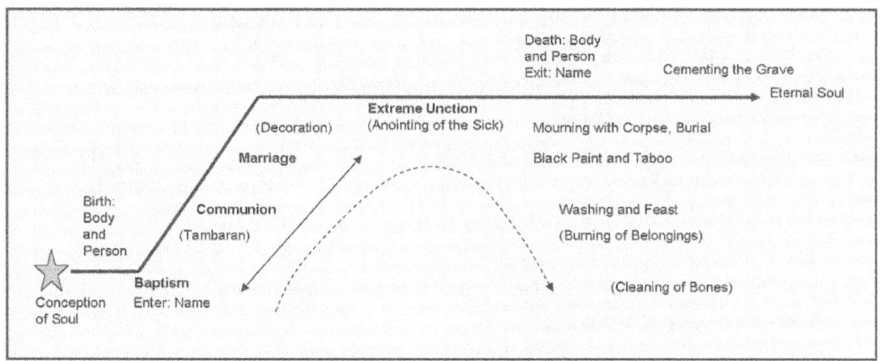

Finishing grade 6 is normal and completing high school and university are sources of prestige, as is employment in town. But traditionally-minded families still value their sons seeing a performance of the *tambaran* flute-spirits for the first time and receiving body decorations. These rites are still considered prestigious, and many young men remain keen on having their fathers and uncles prepare them on their behalf.

Broadly speaking, most contemporary Kayan view personhood in terms of baptism and Extreme Unction as well as the names of the ancestors. At death, the name of the deceased used to be freed to be given to babies. Today, a name may be bestowed upon a newborn before death (see Bainton and Macintyre, this volume), a shift that may result from the increasing population of Kayan and the consequent pressure on ancestral names. However, at the same time, many children nowadays are not given an ancestor's name at all, but either receive Christian names or names of international celebrities.

Christianity has also given rise to a fundamental change in the concept of the afterlife. An easy exchange was to replace the island of the dead—Karkar Island—with heaven, as the destination to which the day-spirit would travel after death. The concept of the night-spirit, however, had no place in Christian theology. The significance of its relationship to the ancestors diminished over time, and consequently mortuary rites came to be abridged or considered optional. Mourning taboos, while still observed, may be lifted sometimes only a few weeks after a death. Cementing the grave takes years to save for and finance, however.

Conclusion—The Last Night-Spirit

Although many phases of both initiation and mortuary rituals in Kayan have been abandoned due to incompatibility with Christian values, in those that remain, symmetries persist. Initiatory body decoration and the display of the corpse still recall each other. Today, young men still go and stay in their respective men's houses, a practice that resembles the mortuary taboos observed by the spouse or parents of the deceased, who become housebound. After the end of the seclusion of the young men and the house taboo, a ritual washing is still performed with the help of sisters' sons or maternal uncles. Decoration in initiation rites remains the central step into the adult life world, while burial remains the central step out of that life world and into the life world of the ancestors. The initiatory procession of young men through the village remains mirrored by the wandering coffin and the presentation of the decorated initiate to the whole family, who give donations that resemble the night watch of a similarly decorated deceased.

At the same time, many ritual practices have ceased to exist or have been replaced by Christian equivalents, for example, Communion has replaced scarification. The period of learning Christian values that accompanies Communion, perhaps, may be comparable to initiatory seclusion in the bush camp. The day-spirit of the deceased does not travel to Karkar Island anymore but proceeds to Christian heaven. The night-spirit may still hover around the dead body for a long time; hence cautious, or "superstitious," people still build small houses over graves. Most Kayan, however, no longer believe in the night-spirit and have replaced the two spirits with one all-encompassing Christian soul that may either reside in heaven or hell in the afterlife.

Thus, fundamental changes have taken place in Kayan. The first is in time conception. In the past, time was cyclical and local in construction. Among younger generations today, time has become linear. Changes in mortuary rites accord with this shift. The cemented grave fixes the person in a temporal continuum. Similarly, the idea of the eternal soul supports the view that ties between past and future no longer depend upon local cosmology. Under the influence of the Catholic Mission, commodities, and the media, newborns are named in ways that no longer link them to the ancestors.

With the loss of the night-spirit, the element of the person I called the social mesocosm is disappearing. One manifestation of this shift is property. In the past, every Kayan person held an interchangeable position in groups that owned ritual objects collectively, and no individual had a right to sell or destroy such a thing. Now, many people feel that they can claim sole ownership of ritual paraphernalia and have the right to dispose of them however they want to. The social microcosm, in other words, has become more important today. Families mainly look after their own affairs, an orientation senior people criticize as selfishness (Tokpisin: *mi pasin*).

In this chapter, I have shown how Kayan ritual practices and concepts of the person that derived from prestate cosmology have changed in the course of missionization and other outside influences. The village was never isolated. It was never a static community without regional relations to other groups, but the last seventy years have seen change on a larger scale than in the past, change that has occurred in a much shorter time than before. I do not lament the loss of mesocosmic personhood in Kayan. I have simply analyzed one point in time when both sides of a rapid and profound process of change in Kayan identity are still audible in mortuary dialogues about their relationship to Melanesian modernity.

The voices espousing modern concepts of the soul, time, and so on are now ascendant, and irreversibly so, I think. My adoptive father, Blasius Jong, was among the few who held the opposite view. He said that after he died he wanted his night-spirit to be ritually detached from his body by means of multiple burials and proper care for his skull and bones. No doubt, should his kin heed his wishes, his night-spirit will be the last one afforded such gestures of respect.

Alexis Th. von Poser is curator of ethnological collections at the State Museum in Hanover, Germany. He has taught anthropology at the University of Heidelberg, the Free University of Berlin, and the Divine Word University in Madang, Papua New Guinea. He is the author of *The Accounts of Jong. A Discussion of Time, Space, and Person in Kayan, Papua New Guinea* (2014).

Notes

1. I stress the word "male," since I cannot give a detailed insight into the former female initiation due to scarce information. Knowledge about these rites has been lost. Modern Kayan women do not practice menstrual seclusion anymore and mostly prefer to bear their children in the hospital in Madang, the provincial capital, rather than in birth-houses in the village. Thus, I concentrate on male initiation, even though I am certain that a ritual system comparable to the one I have found for men once existed among women. The German missionary Leo Meiser, who spent years before WWII living in Kayan, wrote, "Women have very strong secret societies" (n.d.: 47). Unfortunately but understandably he did not investigate them (see Lutkehaus and Roscoe 1995).
2. My data reflect what the Kayan themselves consider the ideal sequence in both traditional ritual cycles. Even in premission times, however, the ritual performance would follow the necessities of the moment. Practice was, so I was told, a matter of negotiation among participating parties as to how a ritual should be performed. In more recent times, the mission, money, and increased out-migration for schooling and work have all influenced Kayan ritual. My research took place over three separate visits in 2004/05, 2008, and in 2010. While I was in Kayan, deaths occurred, and I also observed different steps of mortuary rites connected to previous deaths. In 2005, I also attended the final part of a male initiation.
3. De Coppet (1981) describes similar concepts from Aré'aré on Malaita/North Solomons.
4. For instance, concepts such as "dividual" (Strathern 1988) or "fractal" person (Wagner 1991) or the idea of a "relational individual" (Strathern and Stewart 2000) have

been used to describe models that differ from individual-based conceptions. An early account of a conception of the person being only in existence through relationships, either with kin or with mythical ancestors is Leenhardt's account from New Caledonia (1984).

5. Keck describes such a division of the person among the Yupno in Papua New Guinea, where a "shadow soul" is part of every human being besides the vital energy and the breath of life (2005: 53–59). Kempf and Hermann also identify a "dream-self" among the Ngaing at the Rai Coast in Papua New Guinea (2003: 63; see also Stephen 1995; Lohmann 2003, 2007). Wilson and Sinclair (this volume) also present a concept of the Māori person being divided into three parts. Hertz writes about an idea of a split of the deceased's soul into two parts among the Olo Ngaju in Borneo as well, but here, this split only happens at the time of death (Hertz 1960: 34; cf. Parkin 1996: 89–90).
6. Some animals, such as pigs and crocodiles, that are considered social entities are similarly believed to harbor a day-spirit.
7. Kinswomen can also be called with a drumbeat but only after they are married, since the general rhythm for women is only specified by the following intonation of the respective husband's rhythm.
8. So far, I have concentrated ethnographic attention on the closest kin group and friends. But the community was also involved in the rituals since they were accompanied by feasts. Actually, the temporal spacing between the different rites was determined by the growth of pigs that were selected as piglets after one step was finished to become the required meat dish of the next feast. Depending on the status of the deceased, a smaller or larger group of Kayan villagers and of people from villages with kin affiliations to the deceased would attend each ritual and would participate in and contribute to the feasts, thus making them communal events.
9. In addition to these five rites, a secondary burial took place in secret. Like the conception of a child when a water-spirit would implant the spirit of the child in the mother's womb, thus making the new life possible, the night-spirit was believed to be present at the burial of the skull in the final step of the mourning rites. Just as conception was secret, the final burial was not a public affair. Neither event changed the social status of the person but rather marked the beginning and the end of the night-spirit. Therefore, I do not include it in the process.
10. In addition, in both cases, an image of a spirit-woman (*Sabol Meac*) would be assembled to preside over the men's house.
11. Support for such an idea might be found in local constructions of the landscape. The sun is seen to set off for its yearly journey, rising above the mainland in January. Over the first six months of the year, the position of sunrise moves toward Manam Island, then farther to the island of Boisa, and even farther into the open sea until it returns again during the second half of the year. The dry season ends, the wet season begins, and vice versa. The winds change direction. High tide precedes low tide and follows it again. The local environment is seen to move in repetitive cycles.

References Cited

Barker, John. 2008. *Ancestral Lines. The Maisin of Papua New Guinea and the Fate of the Rainforest*. Peterborough: Broadview Press.
Bateson, Gregory. 1958 [1936]. *Naven*. Stanford: Stanford University Press.

Bloch, Maurice. 1988. "Death and the Concept of Person." In *On the Meaning of Death. Essays on Mortuary Rituals and Eschatological Beliefs*, edited by Sven Cederroth, Claes Corlin and Jan Lindström, 11–29. Stockholm: Almqvist & Wiksell International.

De Coppet, Daniel. 1981. "The Life-Giving Death." In *Mortality and Immortality: the Anthropology and Archaeology of Death*, edited by Sally C. Humphreys and Helen King, 175–204. London: Academic Press.

Fajans, Jane. 1985. "The Person in Social Context: The Social Character of Baining 'Psychology.'" In *Person, Self and Experience: Exploring Pacific Ethnopsychologies*, edited by Geoffrey M. White and John Kirkpatrick, 367–97. Berkeley: University of California Press.

Fortune, Reo. 1935. *Manus Religion: an Ethnological Study of the Manus Natives of the Admiralty Islands*. Lincoln: University of Nebraska Press.

Gell, Alfred. 1975. *Metamorphosis of the Cassowaries. Umeda Society, Language and Ritual*. London: Athlone Press.

———. 2001 [1996]. *The Anthropology of Time. Cultural Construction of Mental Maps and Images*. Oxford: Berg.

Gottlieb, Alma. 2004. *The Afterlife is Where We Come From*. Chicago: University of Chicago Press.

Hertz, Robert. 1960 [1907]. *Death and the Right Hand*. Translated by R. Needham and C. Needham. Glencoe: Free Press.

Hogbin, Ian. 1996 [1970]. *The Island of Menstruating Men: Religion in Wogeo, New Guinea*. Long Grove: Waveland Press.

Keck, Verena. 2005. *Social Discord and Bodily Disorders. Healing among the Yupno of Papua New Guinea*. Durham: Carolina Academic Press.

Kempf, Wolfgang and Elfriede Hermann. 2003. "Dreamscapes: Transcending the Local in Initiation Rites among the Ngaing of Papua New Guinea." In *Dream Travelers. Sleep Experiences and Culture in the Western Pacific*, edited by Roger Ivar Lohmann, 61–85. New York: Palgrave Macmillan.

Leenhardt, Maurice. 1984 [1947]. *Do Kamo. Die Person und der Mythos in der melanesischen Welt*. Translated by Eva Brueckner-Pfaffenberger. Frankfurt/Main: Ullstein.

Lipset, David. 1997. *Mangrove Man. Dialogics of Culture in the Sepik Estuary*. Cambridge: Cambridge University Press.

Lohmann, Roger Ivar, ed. 2003. *Dream Travelers. Sleep Experiences and Culture in the Western Pacific*. New York: Palgrave Macmillan.

Lohmann, Roger Ivar. 2007. "Dreams and Ethnography." In *The New Science of Dreaming, Volume 3: Cultural and Theoretical Perspectives*, edited by Deirdre Barrett and Patrick McNamara, 35–69. Westport: Praeger.

Lutkehaus, Nancy C. and Paul B. Roscoe, eds. 1995. *Gender Rituals: Female Initiation in Melanesia*. New York: Routledge.

Meiser, Leo. N.d. (ca. 1952). *Compilation of Matter for a Description of the Tribe of the Kaean*. Unpublished typescript, situated in the Archbishop Noser Memorial Library, Madang, Papua New Guinea.

———. 1955. "The 'Platform' Phenomenon along the Northern Coast of New Guinea." *Anthropos*, 50: 265–72.

Parkin, Robert. 1996. *The Dark Side of Humanity. The Work of Robert Hertz and its Legacy*. Amsterdam: Harwood Academic Publishers.

Roscoe, Paul B. 1995. "'Initiation' in Cross-Cultural Perspective." In *Gender Rituals. Female*

Initiation in Melanesia, edited by Nancy C. Lutkehaus and Paul B. Roscoe, 219–38. New York: Routledge.
Silverman, Eric K. 2001. *Masculinity, Motherhood, and Mockery: Psychoanalyzing Culture and the Iatmul Naven Rite in New Guinea*. Ann Arbor: University of Michigan Press.
Stephen, Michele 1995. *A'aisa's Gifts. A Study of Magic and the Self*. Berkeley: University of California Press.
Strathern, Andrew and Pamela J. Stewart. 2000. *Arrow Talk. Transaction, Transition, and Contradiction in New Guinea Highlands History*. Kent: Kent State University Press.
Strathern, Marilyn. 1988. *The Gender of the Gift. Problems with Women and Problems with Society in Melanesia*. Berkeley: University of California Press.
Tuzin, Donald F. 1980. *The Voice of the Tambaran: Truth and Illusion in Ilahita Arapesh Religion*. Berkeley: University of California Press.
———. 2001. *Social Complexity in the Making. A Case Study among the Arapesh of New Guinea*. London: Routledge.
van Gennep, Arnold. 1960 [1908]. *Rites of Passage*. Translated by Monika B. Vizedom and Gabrielle L. Caffee. Chicago: University of Chicago Press.
von Poser, Alexis Th. 2010. "Blasius Jong—Ein ethnografischer Nachruf auf einen allwissenden Informanten aus Papua-Neuguinea." *Baessler Archiv* NS 58: 131–38.
———. 2011. "Der Kalender der Kayan (Papua-Neuguinea) und sein Einfluss auf Sozialordnung und Religion." *Mitteilungen der Berliner Gesellschaft für Anthropologie, Ethnologie und Urgeschichte* 32: 133–44.
———. 2014. *The Accounts of Jong. A Discussion of Time, Space, and Person in Kayan, Papua New Guinea*. Heidelberg: Universitätsverlag Winter.
von Poser, Anita. 2013. *Foodways and Empathy. Relatedness in a Ramu River Society, Papua New Guinea*. New York: Berghahn Books.
Wagner, Roy. 1991. "The Fractal Person." In *Big Men and Great Men. Personifications of Power in Melanesia*, edited by Maurice Godelier and Marilyn Strathern, 159–73. Cambridge: Cambridge University Press.
Wassmann, Jürg. 1987. "Der Biß des Krokodils: Die ordnungsstiftende Funktion der Namen in der Beziehung zwischen Mensch und Umwelt am Beispiel der Initiation, Nyaura, Mittel-Sepik." In *Neuguinea. Nutzung und Deutung der Umwelt Band 2*, edited by Mark Münzel, 511–57. Frankfurt/Main: Museum für Völkerkunde.
———. 1988. *Der Gesang an das Krokodil. Die rituellen Gesänge des Dorfes Kandingei an Land und Meer, Pflanzen und Tiere (Mittelsepik, Papua New Guinea)*. Basler Beiträge zur Ethnologie 28. Basel: Ethnologisches Seminar der Universität und Museum für Völkerkunde.
———. 1991. *The Song to the Flying Fox: The Public and Esoteric Knowledge of the Important Men of Kandingei about Totemic Songs, Names and Knotted Cords (Middle Sepik, Papua New Guinea)*. Boroko: National Research Institute.
Yamada, Yoichi. 1997. *Songs of Spirits: An Ethnography of Sounds in a Papua New Guinea Society*. Boroko: Institute of Papua New Guinea Studies.

8
Mortuary Failures
Traditional Uncertainties and Modern Families in the Sepik River, Papua New Guinea

ERIC K. SILVERMAN

Introduction

Just after sunrise in 1989, Mundjiindua, a wonderfully vibrant woman known for her good humor, seemed to be in an especially effervescent mood. A mortuary ceremony in Tambunum, an Eastern Iatmul village along the middle Sepik River in Papua New Guinea (PNG), had just ended. Upon wading ashore from a collective bath in the river that concluded the rite, Mundjiindua grinned and exclaimed in Tokpisin, the national creole, "We have cast our grief into the water. It is done." It seemed that she could not have been more pleased.

Mundjiindua never attended school. Needless to say, she was unaware of modern social theory. But her remark that morning echoed Robert Hertz (1960) and classic anthropological perspectives on the function of mortuary ritual, as outlined in the Introduction. In no uncertain terms, Mundjiindua affirmed the success of the ceremony in triumphing over death with psychosocial rejuvenation. Despite her glee, however, the wider ethos of the moment throughout the village was melancholic. Even Mundjiindua's comment seemed to reflect the *intended* outcome of the ritual, not its *actual* psychological experience. Mundjiindua spoke of what the funeral is publically said to do, not how she or anybody else honestly felt.

As Eastern Iatmul tell it, mortuary rites (*mintshanggu*, or *teva*) are meant to conclude mourning and to banish ghosts (*wundumbu*) of the newly deceased to the village of the dead. In the absence of a funeral, in fact, the dead wrongly remain "present" in the community, and grief never ends. At the level of ideology, then, the rite achieves psychic and social closure. Here, the classic paradigm established by L'Année sociologique school would seem to be vindicated. But this assertion fails to acknowledge the many expressions of cultural ambivalence and irresolution that inhere in local mortuary dialogues, especially in regard to masculine claims against the feminine. The classic view, too, elides over psychological unease and unanswerable angst after painful losses.[1]

Admittedly, I gathered little data on this anguish during my earliest periods of fieldwork in the 1980s and 1990s. In recent years, however, and perhaps in recognition of my own middle age, I delicately broached the topic with several adoptive kin, some of whom also initiated these sorrowful conversations. Overwhelmingly, they confessed to remaining in a state of deep, almost inconsolable bereavement despite their participation in all the appropriate mourning ceremonies. And thus my first argument is that mortuary ritual does *not* bring about significant psychosocial closure.

More specifically, I focus on public symbols and private emotions to show that Eastern Iatmul mortuary rites both enable *and* thwart the transformation of death into restoration. Local people respond to death in voices that are neither singular nor solidary but dialogical and irreducible.[2] In making this argument, I highlight the aesthetic elicitation of emotional, cognitive, and sensory instability during mortuary rites. Eastern Iatmul intensely value the visual and musical spectacles that comprise these ceremonies. But these performances provide participants with little opportunity to "fix" their anxieties and grief. Here, mortuary rites fail.

My second argument is that, no less than elsewhere in the Pacific today, mortuary dialogues answer modernity. The failure of mortuary ritual in Tambunum to effect psychological resolution now articulates with ongoing changes to family, marriage, and personhood in contemporary PNG. Additionally, the irreconcilable dimensions of the rite also speak to recent experiences of economic marginalization. The ethnographic cue for this component of my argument is the living room of Schola Mapat, an adoptive sister who resides and works in Wewak, the capital town of the East Sepik Province. Behind her television, computer, CD player, and electric iron and next to the clock, guitar, and kitschy plaque declaring, "We Can't … But God Can!," stands the painted wooden effigy (*melu*) of Freddie, her deceased husband (Figures 8.1 and 8.2).

Typically, men assemble these figures from fronds to serve as one of several foci during a mortuary rite. After the ceremony concludes, women burn the effigies at the riverbank and sweep the ashes into the waters to float downstream, out to sea and the place of the dead. But Freddie's effigy, carved and decorated by hereditary ritual partners, stands out as an unlikely ritual object amid an array of consumer goods in an urban woman's house. Mortuary rites in Tambunum village, I will show, have come to express thoroughly modern anguish, arising from modern notions of personhood, and anguish about modernity.

Mortuary Failures **179**

Figures 8.1 and 8.2. The *melu* effigy of Freddy in the living room of his widow in Wewak town. Photos: Eric K. Silverman, 2010.

The Quest for Wholeness

"Great social theorists," pronounced Obeyesekere (1990: 288), "like great philosophers and poets, were centrally concerned with human suffering, impermanence, and death." But anthropology, Obeyesekere continued, tended to envision culture like the "modern funeral parlor … everything is tidy, everything smells clean." Obeyesekere was writing a quarter century ago. Yet his comments remain valid, at least in regard to the reigning understanding of mortuary rites, which are still largely seen as sanitizing and neatening the social and psychological messiness of death. I propose an alternative perspective.

In a typical mourning process, according to Freud (1917), the bereaved slowly withdraws emotional attachments from the beloved. At the same time, "the grieving self finds restoration through continuous, heightened, and conscious acts of remembering" (Freud 1917: 205). Detachment and memory, in other words, together with the acceptance of the finality of death as well as the drive for self-preservation, normally compel the mourner to move on. But in the "profoundly painful depression" and "self-abasement" of melancholia, the grieving self so intensively goes on loving the deceased that the ego "shares" a deathlike fate. The bereaved, lacking in this instance some "consoling substitution" (Clewell 2004), exists only in a state of "exclusive devotion" to grief (Freud 1917: 204). Hence, "in mourning," wrote Freud (1917: 205–6), "the world has become poor and empty; in melancholia, it is the ego that has become so."

Freud revised his view of mourning in *The Ego and the Id* (1923). He now argued that the bereaved overcomes loss not by emotional withdrawal but through two other psychic processes. The grieving self must, first, identify with the deceased and, second, incorporate a mental image of the departed within his or her own identity (Clewell 2004: 61). To fully sever attachment from the deceased, as Freud initially theorized, would destroy the self. Contrary to modernist optimism, mourning does not decisively end, nor should it (see also Hagman 2001). Rather, mourning is inexhaustible.

Many anthropologists who are influenced by psychoanalysis also see various forms of loss and memory as the precondition of Pacific Island subjectivities (e.g., Maschio 1994: 193; Weiner 1995: 4). Death, like childhood separation from the mother, creates a void in the psyche that people try to fill with meaning by pursuing, as Lacan (1977) theorized, cultural goals. But the quest for wholeness must never reach completion, stressed Trawick (1990: 145), lest culture grind to a halt. To the extent that mortuary rites "work," in this view, they must fail. But this failure constitutes social life.

To some mourners, however, the inability of mortuary rites to bring about closure does not result in a renewed commitment to rebuild self and society, at least not in the contemporary Sepik. Yet these still-grieving persons are not trapped by the "indubitably pleasurable self-torment" that Freud (1917: 211) ascribed to melancholia. They are, if anything, trapped or enthralled by modern notions of marriage, parenting, and love. For Freud, moreover, melancholia partly arose from the coupling of pathological rather than normal narcissism with the ambivalent emotions the bereaved typically feels toward the deceased.

It is precisely the notion of ambivalence that is so pronounced among Eastern Iatmul mourners today, only it is directed not so much toward the deceased as toward society at large. In conversation after conversation in recent years, I heard a pervasive and lasting downhearted resignation that speaks to many kinds of losses, in particular, the absence of anticipated "development." Between the classic formulations of mourning and melancholia, I am suggesting, we can identify in Tambunum village a liminal psychosocial space in which death occasions a dialogue with modernity.

Emotion and Anxiety

Mourners in Tambunum, as in many places, temporarily step outside normal roles and occupy anomalous positions in society. They withdraw from celebrations, for example, and grow long hair and beards. This unkempt, asocial appearance symbolizes their existential proximity to death. Mourners also affix twisted cords around their bodily boundaries—limbs and necks—to contain or bind their souls, as they say, lest they lose themselves in misery and die from heartache.[3] Allegorically, these strands tether the bereaved to the world so they eventually return from mourning (see Lipset, this volume).

Death in rural PNG tends to occur with tragic suddenness. In such instances, surviving kin experience a "burning heart" (*mauwi nyingi*). These feelings, if not eventually purged through authorized mortuary rites, may erupt into wanton violence, even suicide. At this psychological level, Eastern Iatmul mortuary ritual does prove efficacious by severing, just as Freud once theorized, attachments to lost kin. But at a deeper level, we will see, the rites lead not so much to psychic closure as to ambivalence.

In addition to grief, Eastern Iatmul may also feel anger at the deceased for the sudden abandonment. Death, too, is sometimes perceived as an outright annoyance, especially when it disrupts village-wide ceremonies, such as mortuary rites. Any cooperative effort requires individuals to hold in check potentially disruptive emotions and memories, which usually pertain to past disputes. Otherwise, quarreling will thwart the very sociality that makes ritual possible and, worse, incur the wrath of spirits. In such a fraught emotional state, death may be seen as an act of hostility perpetuated by the deceased, shattering the veneer of harmony that barely conceals aggression and vulnerability.

Local mortuary rites, like all major ceremonies, present men with the opportunity to impress women by impersonating spirits. In myth, primal ancestors stole bamboo flutes and all other ceremonial paraphernalia from ancestresses (Silverman 2001: 33–40). Ever since, men exhibit the purloined sacra to women during ritual. Yet men fear that these performances might afford women an opportunity to "take back" the spirits even though women are unaware of the primal theft. To prevent this masculine nightmare, men shroud ritual with secrecy. First, they hide the flutes (*wainjiimot*) and other sound-producing objects. Thus women hear the voices of spirits but never glimpse the sources of the mysterious noises. Second, men profusely decorate the spirit carvings, and then only exhibit them in motion. As a result, women are unable to clearly see the objects. During ritual, then, men display privileges that sustain masculinity while potentially exposing themselves as the purveyors of a grand swindle that will incur, as they say, women's scorn (Tuzin 1997). Men fear similar ridicule if they err while blowing the flutes. None of these anxieties are unique to mortuary rites. But they add emotional charge to a ritual already infused with the unease of death.

For their part, women experience joy at the sights and sounds of patriclan spirits. Yet major rituals are also frightening for women. They fear the power of the spirits and the latent threats of violence that sustain men's ceremonial prerogatives. Women also report feelings of dread during the mortuary rite while gazing at the serpent spirit that represents, as I shall shortly detail, the terrifying mystery of death. This spirit may harm a woman's reproductive capacities. Yet look they must and do. For men and women alike, then, mortuary rites engender complex emotions.

Eastern Iatmul generally attribute death to moral transgression. Thus most deaths are "bad" (see Counts and Counts 2004). Additionally, wrongdoing typically provokes a contagious and capricious, often fatal form of mystical retribution called *vai*. In most cases, perpetrators are unaware of their offense. Eastern Iatmul rarely agree on what specific misdeed caused any particular death or on whom to pin the blame. The infection of *vai* dwells "in the ground" and spreads circuitously through kin networks, sometimes taking decades to strike. It had "the smell of death," reported Iatmul men to Bateson (1958: 58), "like a dead snake." Everyone in Tambunum—agnate, matrikin, and affine—is potentially connected to every trespass. Much like death and snakes, *vai* respects no boundaries.

Despite the pervasiveness of *vai*, Eastern Iatmul suffer no overwhelming sense of mistrust or moral failure (cf. Schwartz 1973; Robbins 2004: 208–9). Nor do Eastern Iatmul have a morbid obsession with death (cf. Stasch 2009: 208). Nonetheless, *vai* fosters apprehension for mourners who may think themselves somehow connected to the agent or cause of death. In such an instance, participation in mortuary rites may prove dangerous. But how much involvement is perilous? And in what activities? The answers are never clear. Some people avoid mourning obligations by redefining their normal affiliation with the deceased through alternative relationships (Silverman 2001, chap 6). But since no genealogical or social conventions differentiate safe from dangerous kin, all aspects of the mortuary rite inevitably engender angst.

According to classic social theory, as discussed in the Introduction, mortuary rites function to calm social discord and individual anxiety. Psychoanalysis advances a similar view (e.g., Gay 1980). But mortuary ritual in Tambunum elicits emotions and fears that thwart any such therapeutic outcome. The Eastern Iatmul rite, from this angle, must often be viewed as a failure.

Trees and Water

Each of the three major patriclans in the village stages an annual mortuary rite during the dry season for all of its members who passed away the previous year. One stated goal of the ceremony, to repeat, is to culminate and conclude mourning, the latter signified by a collective bath at the very end of the rite. The other goal is to send the souls of the newly deceased down the river, out to sea and the oceanic place of the dead. Both goals, it must be stressed, require immersion in water.

No group in Tambunum may enact its own rites. Thus the community divides for the mortuary rite, as it does for all rituals, into sponsors and performers. The two groups will swap food, cigarettes, and other provisions, ideally purchased in local trade stores or in town, for ritual drama. In the local idiom, performers are classificatory sisters' children (*laua-nyanggu*) and hereditary ritual partners (*tshambela*). In practice, these two groups essentially comprise the other clans of the community. Ritual thus celebrates the autonomous vitality of a descent group while admitting, as Iatmul themselves recognize, to an unsettling dependence.

A proper mortuary rite entails five days of events and preparations, culminating in a nightlong performance. The preliminary rites, some of which I describe below, include totemic recitations, nightly flute sonatas, an evening of women keening, and cursory male initiation. The entire ritual sequence begins in the afternoon. Men enclose a cult house with fronds said to restrict the gaze of women and children. But the fence also serves as one of many instances during the ceremony when men establish, only to violate, boundaries. Next, men assemble a "father-tree" (*nyait-mi*) from the tall shoots of totemic plants. This flagstaff, as it were, signifies the phallic, paternal, and ancestral endurance of the patriline (Silverman 1997). As such, the father-tree stands as a rejoinder to death and the impermanence of life.

The father-tree also represents the masculine creation of the terrestrial world. In myth, male culture heroes formed the landscape, especially villages and groves, atop a primordial feminine sea. Today, men reenact these same ancestral begettings by planting trees, cultivating gardens, and building houses—that is, by shoring up the "ground" of culture against ongoing riverine dissolution. But the river constantly erodes the landed achievements of manhood (cf. Harrison 2004). In recent years, in fact, the Sepik has dramatically swallowed vast tracts of the village, forcing much of the community to scatter. Some people now advocate relocating the *entire* village to the bush. Thus have the living, and not just the dead, surrendered to the river.

Seasonal flooding in 2009–2010 devastated the region. Water rolled through the village like the sea, I was told. Most dogs perished. Unsecured belongings floated away. The flood destroyed all food gardens. When I arrived in July 2010, villagers were dining only on sago and fish. This meal symbolizes Sepik identity. But it also now betokens destitution, specifically, the lack of money, roads, stores, and packaged foods. To escape the water, my village brother's wives and children, like nearly everybody else, sought refuge many hours away atop a hill. His youngest son wandered to play in the tall grass and was set upon by a venomous snake. The child's mother helplessly watched him die. In 2014, the community was still trying to recover from the flood. The father-tree, then, must be seen in dialogue not merely with death but also with watery dissolution and the hardships of an impoverished modernity.

The father-tree includes a stalk of bamboo. This shoot symbolizes the flutes of the male cult, which mythic men, as noted earlier, pilfered from ancestresses in order to compensate themselves, as men say, for their inability to birth children (Silverman 2001: 33–37). Bamboo that emits the finest tones must be harvested by women themselves—without their knowing the ultimate purpose of this task, of course, lest they glimpse the truth of local gender as concealed by men. At the start of the mortuary rite, I am arguing, men erect the father-tree as a phallic signifier of cosmological renewal, genealogical permanence, and, today, a vibrant modernity. That is, the father-tree stands as a symbolic claim against watery unpredictability, annihilation and impoverishment, and regression to the primal sea. But the father-tree dialogically admits to masculine subordination to uterine fertility. That the final acts of the mortuary drama all take place in the river, as I noted earlier, also exposes the futility of this arboreal message.

We can detect a similar yearning for strength and stability when men, again while preparing for the mortuary rite, tether the cult house to the father-tree. This allows them to shake the father-tree during the totemic chants, as I describe momentarily, much as they will later do to the serpent spirit. But the sight of the cult house tied to the father-tree also recalls Iatmul canoes moored to stakes along the riverbank. I vividly recall a mother screaming at her daughter one morning many years ago for failing to securely tie up her canoe the previous evening. Overnight, it had drifted downriver. The father-tree similarly seeks to prevent the edifice of culture from floating away on the waters of femininity. But it fails.

In the late afternoon, men who are learned in ritual esoterica gather beneath the father-tree. To a steady drumbeat, they chant "paths" of totemic names (*tsagi*) that plot the primordial movements of the sponsoring patriclan. These recitations, like the father-tree, celebrate the tenacity of the group, despite death. Totemic names are likened to the group's "roots." But the names themselves contradict this metaphor of stability by denoting spatiotemporal movements (Silverman 1997: 104). Similarly, the shaking of the father-tree during the chants also belies any notions of anchorage or grounding. Totemic chants reveal a world in motion.

As dusk approaches, the chanters complete their orations. They rise, face the cult house enclosure, and, as darkness falls amid a rising chorus of crickets and cicadas, shout the names of the clan's flute-spirits. Inside the building, two men begin to blow the instruments. Voices, human and numinous, blend. Shortly thereafter, the chants cease and only the graceful flute melodies flow through the darkness. Amid these acoustic eddies, we might say, the father-tree vanishes. The music ceases only at dawn.

Long flutes in Tambunum are always played in pairs. Men liken these duets to two brothers paddling a canoe. Similarly, the tunes are named for brisk currents, flowing streams, darting fish, and other idioms of aquatic flow. The melodies acoustically convey the unspoken understanding that everything in the world, as one of my village fathers, Henry Gawi, confirmed in 2014, is a material reflection of water ripples (see also Bateson 1958: 230). Airplane turbulence, for example, mirrors a canoe rocking in the river. Not by accident do Iatmul ornament nearly all forms of their material culture with motifs that evoke waves. The flutes communicate the disquieting message that reality consists of watery motion.

Even burial conveys aquatic movement. Most interments, as the result of Catholic propriety and colonial hygiene, occur in canoe-coffins (see Lipset and von Poser, this volume). Large canoes are masculine symbols of past warfare, the contemporary prestige of an outboard motor, ongoing trade, and long-distance mastery of the river. Smaller canoes evoke moral motherhood through association with women and fishing (Silverman 2001: 77). As mystical vessels, canoes embody the patrilineal spirits that are chiseled into the prows.

Canoes, too, may travel between the human and spirit worlds. Should a woman's canoe, as it is paddled in the river, suddenly roll from side to side, a ghost is said to foretell further loss. On the morning after death, young men may shoulder the deceased in a canoe-coffin. As they slip into a trancelike state, the ghost "moves" the canoe to various locations around the village, thus mapping a deadly path of mystical retribution (see von Poser and Lipset, this volume). During the final hours of the mortuary rite, moreover, mystical canoes ferry the deceased down the river and out to sea, implying a postmortem return to the womb.

To open the mortuary rite in Tambunum, I argued, men bind the cosmos to the father-tree. This arboreal axis mundi stakes a claim against death by serving as an anchor of security, stability, and prosperity. But the prevailing images of water, flow, and dissolution during the rite reveal the impotence of the father-tree to thwart the "eternal return" (Eliade 1971) to a far more powerful and pervasive primordial sea.

The Mortuary Serpent

In preparation for the all-night culmination ceremony, men remove a bundle from storage that nests the sponsoring patriclan's powerful mortuary serpent. Inside the cult house, they unwrap the wooden "snake head" (Figure 8.3). The carving exhibits ancestral figures, spirit faces, and totemic animals as well as a piscine tail, crocodilian teeth, and boars' tusks; it will later receive wings of skewered Malay apples. Other motifs suggest leaves and waves. The power of the deathly snake spirit, as my informants agreed, partly arises from its anomalous or liminal identity.

Inside the cult house, men fasten the carving to a long vine. Over the next several days, they revive the dormant spirit by meticulously applying a

Figure 8.3. The mortuary snake. Photo: Eric K. Silverman, 1989.

floral "skin" (*tsiimbe*).⁴ They also adorn the serpent with shell necklaces that represent two dimensions of social and masculine agency, namely, wealth and long-distance exchange. Today, these ornaments also convey a sense of tradition and thus further infuse the snake with ancestral potency. A long feathered tassel (*tambointsha*) dangles from its snout, an enormously exaggerated rendition of premodern homicide ornaments (see Bateson 1958, Plate XXIVA).

This tassel symbolizes the clan's martial prowess and thus serves as another retort to death, a mode of competitive swagger Bateson called "symmetrical schismogenesis" (1958: 172f). In the aftermath of a death, in other words, men do not yield but, rather, they do death one better. This collective boast also revitalizes the community since Iatmul men, Bateson reported, once attributed "prosperity" to head-hunting (1958: 14). The tassel, too, imbues the mortuary snake with the same aura of fearful admiration once accorded to warriors. And, indeed, warriors resembled snakes in their ability to stealthily cross the boundary between life and death.

Like death, snakes are wild, dangerous, often unseen, and unpredictable. Snakes represent the antithesis of proper sociality. Their presence in the village signifies careless neglect—say, by the failure to trim the grass—that allows untamed nature to intrude on culture. Too many villagers, even today, die from snakebite. Ironically, snakes also elude death. In a short Iatmul fable, an aging snake boasts that he will soon shed his skin and rejuvenate himself. But his companion, a frog, has no such talent and can only respond that his impending death is irreversible. The unfortunate moral of the story is that humans are like frogs. But the mortuary snake, despite symbolizing death, also represents the unattainable desire for immorality (see also Lohmann 2008). Each year, in fact, the mortuary snake does just that: it comes alive, through male agency, by growing a new skin, which is discarded at the end of the rite. The carving is then wrapped and stored to await rebirth the following year.

The wooden snake is likened, per Iatmul ethnophysiology and procreation beliefs, to paternal "bone" (*ava*). The ornamentation recalls maternal "skin." In this respect, the annual regeneration of the snake, hidden inside the cult house, resembles the transformative mysteries of human gestation—but in the absence of women.⁵ The mortuary rite thus argues for and against a particular vision of manhood in addition to the desire to triumph over mortality. Each year, men attempt yet acknowledge the impossibility of endless self-reproduction.

To make the decorations for the snake, men gather flowers, feathers, leaves, and other such items from around the local landscape. They bring this natural material into the cult house for cultural conversion into an ornamental "skin." Here, again, as in regard to flute music, we can discern a connection between ritual power and movement across zones and borders. Men may also attach balloons to the snake, which evidence the same aesthetic of travel. Similarly, the shell ornaments on the snake were carried from sea to village—having reversed, in fact, the final voyage of the ghosts. The layers of adornments on the snake gradually conceal the wooden "bone" that serves as the ostensible focus of the display (Figure 8.4). Slowly, the snake metamorphoses into an intentional, we will see, aesthetic of ambiguity.[6]

Nature is a chaotic, unpredictable force or realm that, like death, must be held at bay in order to sustain a village. Similarly, everyday activities "build up," in the local idiom, the ground against riverine erosion, or so it is hoped. In the male cult house, a liminal space between humanity and spirits, men prepare for the mortuary rite by inverting and combining normative distinctions. The *mintshanggu* rite resembles, much like the rural Greek funeral (Danforth 1982), an effort to mediate fundamental oppositions of middle Sepik existence, such as land/water, male/female, nature/culture, and life/death. In the end, however, the ceremony offers little resolution.

To Ferry the Dead

Inside a large house that will serve as the arena for the final, nightlong act of the mortuary proceedings, men build a temporary bamboo and frond screen,

Figure 8.4. The "bone" of the mortuary snake is decorated so thoroughly that it disappears. Photo: Eric K. Silverman, 1989.

much as they did earlier around the cult house. Behind it, they construct a tall scaffolding from which they will later, during the actual performance, tug on the snake, as I describe below, bringing the spirit alive. As the serpent twists above the ritual audience, other men, also concealed by the screen, will blow flutes. The fence will thus hide from women the fact that men impersonate the spirit's voice and movement. But the barrier also emphasizes the ritual importance of boundaries and trespass so vital to death and mortuary ritual.

In front of the fence, men erect effigies (*melu*) of each of the deceased, which they casually dress in a few items, such as shirts, skirts, and looped string bags. I recall the heartbreaking image of one deceased man, Tsuaykundmi, cradling the figure of his daughter's son, who died in infancy. After the men arrange the effigies, they abandon the house to women, who gather before the figures and weep throughout the night for their dead (Figure 8.5; see also Wilson and Sinclair, this volume). In the morning, the women leave and men return to assemble a platform, cut from a canoe, in front of the temporary screen. This podium represents the sponsoring clan's totemic *agwi*, or floating grass island, said to be the originary terrain of the world that still drifts on the primordial sea. Beneath the mortuary *agwi* men shape the gaping maw of a crocodile spirit (*wai wainjiimot*) from the pith of a banana tree. The entire ensemble is festooned with totemic and magical plants.

Atop the raft, men stack "bones" made from the shoots of wild sago palms, wrapped in coconut leaves. The "bones" are adorned with flowers, ferns, small fruits, aromatic herbs, and paint as well as balsa birds and leaf pinwheels. The latter two ornaments further symbolize the themes of flow and mobility that permeate the rite. The "bones" represent the patrilineal part of the soul, inherited from paternal semen. Yet the sago shoots themselves evoke the paradigmatic Sepik meal of maternal nurture. Hence, the "bones" are also called *kware*, or grass skirt. These objects, in other words, defy any reduction to a simple or singular meaning.

After stacking the *kware*-bones on the canoe platform, men insert the effigies.[7] Sisters' children lean clothing, canoe paddles, and money against the figures of their matrikin. During the culmination performance, dancing women will remove these gifts on behalf of the deceased and present them to mourners. They, in turn, will reciprocate by feeding the deceased's nieces and nephews. The central display, now completed, represents a floating island or raft that, resting atop a crocodile spirit, ferries the souls of the deceased down the Sepik, out to sea and the land of the dead. This tableau calls to mind culturally salient themes of movement, fluidity, and transition as well as watery dissolution. Men, recall, prepare for the mortuary ceremony by tethering the cult house to a father-tree. But the rite repeatedly detaches death from any stable semantic or psychological ground and instead draws, again and again, to watery uncertainty.

Figure 8.5. Mourning widow beside effigies. Photo: Eric K. Silverman, 1989.

An Ambivalent Meal

During one of the days of preparations, men hike to the bush to fell wild sago palms they name for each of the deceased. A tree that shatters when it hits the ground augurs further deaths in the patriline. More importantly, these trees are personified as mothers' brothers (*wau*), who feed their sisters' children (*laua*) a lifetime of meals, usually boiled chicken and fried sago. In return, these "male mothers" receive valuables and money. One night during the preparations, a few hours before dawn, women offer the ghosts bowls of sago pudding, cooked from the wild palms. Younger men, bedecked in regalia and half-possessed by the ghosts, dash out from the cult house forest. They angrily snatch the bowls from the women and swiftly disappear into the dark (see Dalton, this volume). Elder men, classed as the sisters' children of the deceased, once tasted this porridge. But people now, fearful of eating food prepared for the dead, refuse the repast. Instead, the pudding is thrown to dogs, and the plates are smashed to the ground.[8]

This meal represents a final gift of nurture from the deceased to nieces and nephews. But the event is charged with frightful edginess, as the ghost figures are liable to batter anyone who stands in their way. Additionally, the ghosts seem to repudiate the code of reciprocity by consuming a meal cooked for their nieces and nephews, who, in turn, appear prepared to devour their maternal uncles. The latter image of endocannibalism recalls the psychoanalytic perspective of Melanie Klein (see Stephen 1998). Close kin react to death by reincorporating the mother or, in this case, her mother-like brother. Yet the act of chopping down the maternal sago palms, in the context of death, also would seem to express masculine guilt and rage (see Lipset, this volume). From any angle, a meal that is normally upheld as a moral exemplar calls into question, during the mortuary rite, the ethics of everyday sociality.

If viewed through the arboreal metaphor of the father-tree discussed above, the felling of the wild palm also appears to assault the patriline (Silverman 2001: 83–84). Instead of building up society against the erosion of death, men hasten social extinction. But the transformation of this immorality into maternal nurture, however ambivalent, evokes the same trope of regeneration we saw earlier in regard to the mortuary snake. And the snake, I want to stress, no less than the ghostly meal, does not easily slot into the classic paradigm that sees mortuary ritual as fostering solidarity and order. After all, both the serpent and the spectral repast do far more to provoke rather than to becalm anxiety.

The Gender of Lifedeath

It is late in the afternoon. Inside the cult house, men tinker with the last details of the giant snake's ornamentation, which now extends for some twenty feet. After banishing women and children from the central footpath in the village, men haul the snake out of the cult house, passing through the temporary enclosure. They sprint through the village while cradling the spirit, loudly chanting "whoop, whoop, whoop," and enter the dwelling that will serve as the auditorium for the nightlong ritual performance. Above the display of canoe, crocodile spirit, and effigies, men truss the serpent to the roof and weave the long tail through the screen, back into the enclosed all-male area and atop the scaffolding they earlier erected.

These preliminaries exhibit three masculine privileges. First, men create and prepare to animate a powerful spirit. Second, men collectively traverse the village, thereby asserting "ownership" over the community (see Bateson 1958: 123). Third, the movement of the mortuary snake appears to reverse the socialization of boys. Boys transition from women and domestic houses to men and the cult house. Severed from their mothers, in other words, boys gain the phallus. During the mortuary rite, however, men bring a phallic spirit, "conceived" and "birthed" in their cult house, to women in a domestic residence. Men, that is, invert the lifecycle.

Additionally, the phallic likeness of the spirit suggests an oedipal identification of men with an omnipotent image of lethal yet regenerative potency. The mortuary serpent thus appears as a phallic mother rebirthed by men, year after year, in response to death. The mortuary dialogue in Tambunum, I am arguing, voices the unity of life and death or "lifedeath" (Weiner 1993: 238) through claims made by men in answer to female-inflected notions of birth and mortality (cf. Telban 1997). The rite, in other words, speaks no more to stable gender than it does to social and psychological comfort.

Culminating Death

Once men suspend the snake spirit from the roof, they allow women and children to meander into the dwelling and haphazardly assemble before the central display. Women keen, sway, dance, and sing personal dirges. Meanwhile, men form two "crocodile lines" at the cult house and march to the dwelling. They stream into the darkened space of the sobbing women and strut around the perimeter of the floor. By conspicuously passing behind the screen, a space forbidden to women, men dramatize yet again their capacity to trespass spatial boundaries and to master the interstitial zones of culture and death. Men, too, encompass and thus symbolically take ownership over women and the community. Yet men also subvert these privileges by positioning women at the ritual center, around which male activity, and much of their dialogue, revolves.

After circling the audience, the two "crocodile lines" stomp on the floor, shaking the house. Normally, this violence would enrage the house-spirit that dwells in the main posts. During the mortuary rite, however, the gesture summons the spirits, thus attesting yet again to masculine privilege. At this moment, flute melodies suddenly emanate from behind the partition. The magnificent snake spirit, which some liken to a dragon, awakens and contorts in the air, its long tassel swaying over the audience (Figure 8.6). Two groups of men, seated

Figure 8.6. The mortuary snake awakens. Photo: Eric K. Silverman, 1989.

on stools, start to chant the totemic "paths" of the sponsoring clan's mythic histories. This drama will continue for the next fifteen hours or so.

Lanterns, flashlights, and hearth embers flicker through a miasma of humidity, sweat, and smoke. People shuffle about. Women weep and sing. The two groups of men chant contrapuntally. Now and then, melodies from the concealed flutes bring the serpent to life. The blurring of sounds and sights exemplifies an ideal aesthetic experience, which evokes several images of unruly churning: a forest beset by a gale, ocean breakers on the shore, river waves in a storm, or a whirlwind fueled by grassland burn-offs during the dry season.[9] The snake draws the attention but is lost amid its own blurring, fluttering adornment. Likewise, the flute tones are barely audible amid the overall din. At its peaks, the ritual offers little clarity or stability.

The various motifs and ornaments on the snake carving, as noted earlier, together represent the dangerous disorder of a cosmos lacking boundaries and categories. This otherworldly message is enhanced by the snake's violent convulsions, which elicit feelings of terror. The phallic serpent would thus seem to exemplify Edmund Burke's masculine concept of the sublime, which demands reverential awe and seizes viewers in "admiring submission" (Eagleton 1990: 54). But the aesthetic reception of the serpent is best understood as a gendered dialogue, not a masculine declaration to a compliant female audience.

Women must glimpse the snake during the rite. But they may only do so when the serpent is in motion. Otherwise, men fear, the women's gaze may capture the spirit's potency. Should women view the snake "too strongly," moreover, they may go mad or harm their reproductive capacities; their male kin may also be required to compensate the cult house. Women must see the snake spirit—but not see it. The ceremony, in this sense, consists of periodic jousts between women and spirit, each having the power to "kill" the other.

Similarly, when the male chanters break into lively song, thumping their drums rapidly, the flutes respond and the snake "dances." Women may then intensify their wailing, as they report, turning their grief into an aural challenge to the masculine sounds. Both men and women enjoy these competitive climaxes, which punctuate the night. But no singular voice or vision triumphs during these conversations and thus no orthodoxy holds sway. The *mintshanggu* mortuary rite does not answer death conclusively, per Hertz and classic social theory, but like water, offering nothing stable to grasp.

A Requiem of Smoke and Water

Early in the morning, around 3:00 or 4:00 a.m., the chanters pause their totemic recitations. In a moment of intense emotion and sobbing, they sing the maternal names of the deceased in a brief poem:

> You, my child, my ancestral butterfly;
> I, your mother, feed you sago;
> It is a joyous occasion, my child, for you have eaten
> And now I send you on your way to the land of your fathers and grandfathers.

Mothers' brothers lightly tug the effigies, pulling the maternal part of the soul to the place of the dead. The precise meaning of this poem is, like a butterfly, hard to catch. Indeed, although each group refers to a unique totem such as a drifting piece of wood, and not just the butterfly, these named entities all evoke movement. Each poem, too, expresses a longing for maternal nurture and sends the souls on their final journey as matrikin. But each poem also implies that this voyage leads to ancestral patrikin. The lyrics of the song do little to alleviate its own haunting melody.

No other episode in the mortuary sequence approaches the tender emotions of the maternal parting song, with one exception. As dawn approaches, men bid farewell to the paternal part of the soul with an equally heartrending song:

> You, my father, my ancestral bamboo, your young son, not yet initiated, is going with you, father bamboo;
> You go now;
> I call the name of your stream, the stream of the dead;
> Your young son, not yet initiated, our son, you must go now.

Here, a father figure escorts the souls to the land of patrikin. As in the previous poem, each group specifies its own ancestral totem. But this narrative variation is irrelevant to the sorrowful poignancy of the moment.

The second mortuary hymn is named for an eagle. Birds evoke swift passage across topographic realms. The eagle and the butterfly, of course, symbolize the journeying soul. These images of movement also serve as meta-symbols that comment on the absence of fixed, hence comforting, messages about death. After all, the two requiems allude to conflicting destinations for the soul. Where, then, is the final resting place? Or is the soul dual or divisible? Nobody in Tambunum knows for sure (cf. Harrison 1985; Gewertz and Errington 1991: 234). Christianity only extends the uncertainty over the afterlife. There is, however, agreement that the soul initially voyages down the river, which serves as a liminal path between the living and the dead, and out to sea. Thus the soul regresses to a watery "formlessness of pre-existence" (Eliade 1958: 188; Tuzin 1977; Silverman 1997). These aquatic images call into question any stable meanings concerning death, such as that signified by the father-tree at the start of the rite.

196 Eric K. Silverman

Upon completion of the second elegy, men scamper up the walls of the house and untie the snake from the roof. Other men pull the snake backward through the frond partition. The spirit slowly disappears from view. The snake is quickly carried through the rear house door, unseen by women and children, and lugged to the forest affiliated with the male cult. There, young men strip away the "skin" and toss the ornaments aside to decay.[10] The "bone" is then wrapped and stored for the next year. Meanwhile, the audience exits the house. Female kin remove the effigies and heap each figure on the riverbank, along with a few of the deceased's possessions. Fathers' sisters kindle the piles (Figure 8.7). Rising plumes of smoke soon fill the air. Each pyre is named for ancestral grasslands that some people, evidencing yet more uncertainty, identify as the village of the dead. The ashes are swept into the river and vanish downstream.

Each dry season, as alluded to earlier, men torch the nearby grasslands. The fires envelop the region in smoke, reminding Eastern Iatmul of the mortuary bonfires and their deceased kin (cf. Harrison 2001). The world is then beclouded with bittersweet recollections and emotions. The ethereal nature of smoke connotes ghosts and the afterlife and visualizes the semantic haziness surrounding death. Smoke thus parallels the many other mortuary symbols that conjure transition, movement, and instability. Smoke, too, violates boundaries, much like water, snakes, and death. The dry season flames some-

Figure 8.7. *Melu* effigies are burned by the riverbank and their ashes are swept into the river. Photo: Eric K. Silverman, 1989.

times edge perilously close to the village and may even drive fleeing snakes to attack. Ash rains down. The fires loudly crackle. The proximity of danger serves as a reminder of the constant, frightening nearness of death.

While the mortuary piles smolder, mourners assemble at the rear of the village and slowly file down to the river. Men loudly slap the ground with leafstalks to frighten away any lingering ghosts. Each mourner grasps a small stalk, hastily tied like an effigy. Together, the clan—hundreds of people—wades into the river. Then, in a moment of exhilaration, they shout and pitch the stalks into the current to float downstream to an unknown ancestral destination.

Ritual Failure and the Persistence of Memory

Eastern Iatmul, I showed, much as Freud theorized in general, create "hyperinvested" images of the deceased during mortuary rites to assist with remembering in order to forget. Thus mourners in Tambunum shift their attention away from individual loss to a nonhuman, serpentine representation of ancestral potency and then sweep mementos of the deceased into the river. At that point, mourners can say, much like Mundjiindua, my adoptive mother whom I quoted at the beginning of this chapter, "It is done." But is mourning truly finished?

The wife of Gamboro, one of my key research assistants, died a few years ago. Her name was Pesso. "We got married a long time ago," Gamboro explained to me in 2010. Theirs, I knew, had been a marriage of companionship. "I married only one wife … since the Mission told us that God gave you only one partner," he continued, despite his disdain for Christianity. "I think about her every day, especially when I am hungry. I have no one to cook for me. My skin is loose [now]. I have become an old man." Gamboro's longing may seem coldly dispassionate. But he was drawing from culturally appropriate, masculine idioms of loneliness. It was as tender an expression of matrimonial intimacy as I ever heard in the village.

"Would you marry again," I asked? "Never," he replied. After the burial, Gamboro hung Pesso's ceremonial skirt inside their house, "just to look at," and gave her ornaments to their grown children. "Sometimes they look at her necklaces and cry." Later, Gamboro rummaged through a lifetime's collection of fading and crumbling documents within an old, tattered suitcase and finally pulled out his only photograph of Pesso. He looks at it from time to time, he told me, and grieves. "What about the mortuary rite," I asked. "Did that help?" "A joke," Gamboro said. "Inside, I still hurt."

Sometimes, Gamboro foregoes grooming. He no longer cares, he said, about his appearance. Gamboro was once a prolific woodcarver and even traveled to California in 1994 to help create the New Guinea Sculpture Garden at

Stanford University (Silverman 2003). Now he lacks any enthusiasm for his art. Anyway, with Pesso gone, who would ornament his carvings? "It is hard to do anything." Gamboro believes that he will someday reunite with Pesso upon his own death. Until then, he lives with sulking, angry grief.[11] The *mintshanggu* rite afforded Gamboro little closure, either in 2010 or four years later upon my most recent visit.

Gamboro sees Pesso in his dreams (see Bell, this volume; Tuzin 1975; Hollan 1995).[12] She tells him that she will return for a visit, aboard, as many Eastern Iatmul now report for deceased kin, a ghostly ship that resembles the tourist boat that once provided the village with its largest source of cash (Silverman 2004). But the ship ceased operation in 2006. Today, villagers tell of far greater impoverishment than two decades ago, declaring, "We are going backwards." People in Tambunum speak bitterly of neglect by provincial and national authorities and the world at large.

They also now say that their dead relatives, who periodically return at night on the otherworldly ship, want to bring them money and goods (Silverman 2013). But the magical or ancestral "road" to material plentitude remains blocked by white people and missionaries. When a local person dies, moreover, Catholic priests pray "hard" for the soul for two days; on the third day, the ghost rises from the grave and gives the priest money. Today, in other words, many Eastern Iatmul, Gamboro included, combine private grief with a collective yearning for "development" (see Bell, this volume). The response to death now includes melancholic resignation, if not anguish, about the failed promises of modernity.

My village brother, Kamboi, and one of his two wives, Kabibo, were also suffering in 2010. Their young son, as I noted earlier, had died from snakebite. But only a year earlier, their high school-aged daughter took ill and died days later. They find it impossible to end mourning. Kamboi hung their daughter's basket above his wife's bed, something I had never seen before. I also saw him occasionally chew a few leaves from the plants that adorn the daughter's grave. Kamboi and Kabibo, no less than Gamboro, mourn with what might be termed modern emotions.

Kamboi's relationship to his father, which I observed in the late 1980s, had been typical of that and earlier eras: tense, expressively cool, denied of all intimacy. When I asked Kamboi in 2010 if they ever talked, he chuckled. Dissatisfied with that style of child raising, Kamboi and many other men today self-consciously opt for a "new" model of fathering. He plays with his youngest daughter, for example, and allows her to sleep in his lap rather than passing her off to his wife. Most surprisingly, Kamboi in 2010 constantly offered patient guidance about woodcarving to his teenage son. Fathering for Kamboi entails deep emotional connections, all the more so, he said, after the death of his daughter. For Gamboro, much as for Kamboi and Kabibo, the care and love that should unite the family today renders the death of kin all the more painful. That is, modern forms of attachment, and thus the daily experiences of modernity, occasion suffering.

Not only Kamboi, Kabibo, and Gamboro but many people in Tambunum now voice anguish about modernity through mortuary dialogues that phrase death as part of a wider misery. Several times in 2010, while sitting in the evening by battery-powered lantern light, Kamboi and Kabibo spontaneously spoke to me of their grief. They ate poorly, I learned, found little pleasure in everyday work or amusements, and often awoke in the middle of the night to quietly cry and grieve. Kamboi expressed no "interest" in the affairs of the men's house or in reopening his trade store. At the same time, they all constantly lamented their poverty. "What are we doing wrong," Kamboi asked, "that we live this way?" Many people connect death to the lack of infrastructure—poor sanitation, unclean water, meager diet, and inadequate schooling as well as the absence of roads, transportation, a health clinic, and wage-paying jobs.

In 2010, Kamboi confessed to little attachment to the village. He "hates" its ground. But he is unwilling to permanently leave lest he abandon his daughter's grave, which he dug just outside the house and sealed with concrete. Almost every morning in 2010, Kamboi or Kabibo carefully trimmed the grass around the cement slab, removed fallen leaves, and primped the few remaining ornaments, including Christmas tinsel, which glistened in the sunlight (Figure 8.8). They did the same four years later. Kamboi told me that sometimes, amid a crowd, he momentarily overlooks his misery. But when alone, he slips into melancholia and finds daily life emotionally difficult. Toward the end of my stay in 2010, Kamboi said that my visit gave him and his wife something to think about other than their grief. The next morning, he asked me to copy his only photo of his daughter, a photo already fading and discolored. Gamboro made the same request about his wife. They had neither the means, nor the money, to preserve even this flimsy token of memory.

In 2014, I complied with those requests. Kamboi and Gamboro were grateful for the new photographs. Gamboro was still grieving his loss and had yet to resume the many ritual and artistic activities that were once his passion. The tinsel on the grave of Kamboi's daughter was long gone. But Kamboi had carved a large statue of Jesus to place atop the cement slab. In 2013, moreover, Kamboi had spent most of the year in the coastal town of Vanimo, near the border with Indonesian West Papua, working to carve house posts for a new governmental headquarters. But he returned to the village. Why, I asked? He pointed to his daughter's grave.

Gamboro, Kamboi, and Kabibo are not the only persons in Tambunum who now respond to death with permanent memorials. In 2014, I was surprised at the number of elaborately decorated gravesites, a recent practice that

Figure 8.8. A mother tends a homestead grave. Photo: Eric K. Silverman, 2010.

did not exist even ten years ago (see von Poser, Lutkehaus, Dalton, and Bell, this volume). Burials still occur with little ado in the raised earthen ridges that separate patrilineal residence wards. But villagers today are no longer content to allow the gravesite to fade into the landscape.[13] Indeed, the increasingly common use of commodified mortuary mementos, such as plastic flower arrangements and brightly colored prints of Jesus, together with cement slabs, wooden roofs, and metal fencing made from used water tanks, speaks to a recent desire by Eastern Iatmul to mark death as lastingly set apart from everyday life (Figure 8.9). In this Melanesian modernity, memory endures (cf. Horst 2004; Lohmann 2007).

The triumphalism of mortuary rites, according to L'Année sociologique and classic anthropology, speaks to the self-assurance of early twentieth-century social science. But mortuary ritual in Tambunum today creates no such sense of accomplishment. There is certainly little optimism. True, mourners eventually return to the tasks of everyday life. Society persists. But the pain of loss, now exacerbated by modern notions of marriage, parenting, love, and material well-being, hardly fades at the conclusion of the rites.

After the collective bath in the river, the bereaved are expected to publicly cease their grieving. Yet many mourners remain privately bound to their

Figure 8.9. The grave of John Gawi. Photo: Eric K. Silverman, 2010.

loss. The only acceptable persistence of heartache is the new practice of marking permanent graves, which are never located far from the deceased's house. With their garish, often neon-colored decoration, these modern graves stand apart from the natural, more muted hues of the village. Today, death and memory are hard to overlook. Eastern Iatmul mortuary dialogues still comment on the uncertainties about death and still raise questions about masculine agency amid motherhood. But these dialogues also encompass the woes of economic marginalization. Eastern Iatmul now grieve losses of many kinds.

Conclusion—Memory and Modernity

In 2008, during a brief visit to PNG, one of my adoptive sisters, Schola Mapat, whom I introduced at the beginning of this chapter, informed me that her husband Freddy had suddenly died not just a few years earlier but precisely on 24 April 2006. The date surprised me since most Iatmul, even today, disregard this kind of chronological precision. Schola's detail was at once banal yet touching. It was news of a modern death.

Similarly, I was struck in 2014 at the now-common practice of marking graves with impromptu crosses and placards that indicate the deceased's name, birthday, and, much as Schola volunteered, the date of death. Burial is now personalized, which also accounts for the variety of gravesite decorations and shelters. Indeed, no two graves are the same. Today, Eastern Iatmul increasingly answer death with individual and not just collective voices and expressions.

Schola clerks at the district courthouse in Wewak and earns a regular paycheck. But Schola will never ascend into the Melanesian middle class (see Gewertz and Errington 1999). After deducting taxes and repayment of educational bank loans for her children and other kin, I learned via email, Schola's fortnightly take-home pay in 2013 amounted to little more than about US$70. But her house, constructed from lumber rather than cobbled together from bush materials and discarded debris, contains several rooms and has access to municipal water and electricity. Inside are rugs, beds, a refrigerator, a computer, a telephone, and various and sundry consumer goods as well as, recall again from the opening section of this chapter, the *melu* effigy of Schola's late husband. This woodcarving, I now want to propose, materializes the emergence of modern memory.

To make this point, I need first shift my focus to the West for a moment. For centuries, the European family was "immediate, transparent, and unreflexive, unmediated by any representations of itself, [it] ... lived on a day-to-day basis" (Gillis 1996: 63–64). Thus premodern Euro-Americans generally kept their distance from the dead; they had little emotional need for contemplation or commemoration of the deceased. But during the rise of the industrial revolution in the second half of the nineteenth century, "the family" became a cardinal virtue requiring reflection and veneration. The less time Victorians actually spent *in* families, the more they pinned their sense of personal fulfillment on *the* family. People now eagerly consumed representations of domestic togetherness, such as greeting cards. Victorians also surrounded themselves with mementos of their dead, including lockets, portraits, and daguerreotypes. Death became an industry, requiring white-gloved pallbearers, hearses, and gardenlike cemeteries (Pleck 2000). The modern family found expression in the new memorialization of the dead.

Perhaps something of these attitudes about what some call the "sentimental family" are now on the rise in PNG. Today, Eastern Iatmul speak about marriage as a private, affective union between husband and wife, who unite as a "single heart" (in Tokpisin *wanbel*). Proper childcare, as in the West, is now seen to be the exclusive responsibility of parents, not other kin and village-wide institutions such as the male cult. Parents, too, should share in caretaking, and find purpose and joy, as my village brother told me, in watching their children grow. Christianity also enshrines the ideals of matrimonial sanctity and individualism, the latter by stressing personal responsibility.

Schola sometimes presents betel nuts to Freddie's effigy and asks his spirit to watch over the family. But she is afraid to touch the carving directly. Despite these magical, hence, Melanesian practices, Freddie's effigy recalls the family photographs and heirlooms that suddenly appeared in Victorian homes.

On her walls and tables Schola haphazardly displays tokens of the sentimental family: photographs, gift wrapping decorated with heart motifs, birthday and condolence cards, her children's schoolwork, Freddie's workplace awards, and countless icons of Jesus, Mary, and the Holy Family. Freddie's effigy, standing in Schola's living room, recalls the many gravesite markers that now so visibly appear here and there in the village.

In an email, Schola wrote, "I will keep it [the effigy] then pass it on to the children and … the grandchildren, sort of [as a] historical carving." Looking at it, Schola continued, "brings [me] sadness … but with that in [the] house, I also feel Fred's presence during quiet times and … nights." In June 2015, one of Schola's sons posted a blurry photograph on Facebook, writing, "Last family trip with dad its [sic] been 10 years now miss you Late Frederick Mapat." His sister commented, "Yes I miss dad" and added a sad-faced emoticon. Like the Victorians, Schola and her family find in the effigy and in photographs an expression of what it means to be a modern person, fulfilled through emotionally satisfying and tender relationships and, as on display in Schola's living room, consumer goods. This mode of personhood adds to the difficulty of letting memory drift away with the river and collective representations.

In contemporary PNG, the death of Schola's spouse, Freddie, was a modern death. I am not diminishing the anguish of death in earlier times. Not at all. Rather, my point is that Eastern Iatmul people today do not die solely as kin. They die, and are memorialized, as individuals, embedded in the nuclear family, defined by emotion in addition to their social status. Death rips a hole in society that mortuary rites, as understood by classic social theory, must mend. Today, however, death also ruptures irreparable holes in the modern "heart."

Mortuary rites in Tambunum village, I argued in this chapter, engender little resolution. They begin with an arboreal representation of stability. But as the rites unfold, imagery of flow, movement, and water wash away any such tether or ground. The collective bath that concludes the rite, as my Iatmul friends concede, fails to cleanse the pain and sorrow of memory. The rite achieves no psychosocial resolution but rather expresses the ongoing mystery of death and an inability to reground life after mourning. It is precisely this open-endedness that allows Eastern Iatmul beliefs about death to address both their modern notions of self and their contemporary anxieties.

Eric K. Silverman was professor of anthropology at Wheelock College, and is now Resident Scholar at the Women's Studies Research Center at Brandeis University in Boston. Since the late 1980s, he has conducted fieldwork among the Eastern Iatmul, studying and writing about topics including tourism, masculinity, childhood, and Facebook. He also publishes widely on Jewish Studies; his most recent book was *A Cultural History of Jewish Dress*.

Notes

1. On this point, see the moving essay by Gewertz and Errington (2002) concerning the mortuary ritual staged by another Sepik society upon the terrible death of their own daughter.
2. For the theory of cultural dialogics, drawing on Mikhael Bakhtin, see the Introduction as well as Silverman 2001; Lipset and Silverman 2005.
3. The mortuary chords exaggerate the bands tied by mothers' brothers on their sisters' children to promote health and thwart ill luck.
4. During some funerary rites, younger men blow flutes before another snake, called *ndagwi,* tied to a tree in the cult house forest. This woodcarving is never seen by women and therefore given only cursory decoration.
5. See Lipset (1997: 167–71) for mortuary birthing imagery among the Murik of the Sepik Estuary.
6. There are minor, clan-specific differences in mortuary rites. One clan, for example, decorates and displays a hornbill carving, accompanied by noises that recall the bird squawking and flapping its wings before taking flight.
7. In earlier eras, the effigies sometimes included decorated skulls (Bateson 1958, plate XXIb). Formerly, too, a deceased man's initiation cohort decorated his effigy with insignia of achievements; the opposite moiety then removed the ornaments (Bateson 1958: 155–56; see also Harrison 1990: 102–5).
8. The event concludes with a man in the cult house loudly beating a sacred plank (*wakan*), carved to resemble a fish spirit (see also Bateson 1958: 137).
9. Some say that death is followed by the East Wind, which temporarily blows the ghost out to sea (see also Bateson 1958: 230).
10. Funerary *malanggan* sculptures on New Ireland are also created to be discarded or destroyed (Küchler 2002).
11. For bereavement in the Sepik, see Gewertz and Errington (1991: chap. 4); Brison 1995; Leavitt 1995; and Tuzin 1997. More broadly, see Counts and Counts (1991).
12. Some villagers say you can ring the dead on mobile phones (see also Telban and Vávrová 2014). For the use of Ouija boards in Micronesia, see Dernbach (2005).
13. Another recent innovation in Tambunum is the *haus krai,* an importation from other regions of PNG, where kin gather for a few days at the deceased's house to sob and mourn.

References Cited

Bateson, Gregory. 1958 [1936]. *Naven: A Survey of the Problems suggested by a Composite Picture of the Culture of a New Guinea Tribe drawn from Three Points of View.* Cambridge: Cambridge University Press.

Brison, Karen J. 1995. "You Will Never Forget: Narrative, Bereavement, and Worldview among Kwanga Women." *Ethos* 23: 474–88.

Clewell, Tammy. 2004. "Mourning Beyond Melancholia: Freud's Psychoanalysis of Loss." *Journal of the American Psychoanalytic Association* 52: 43–67.

Counts, Dorothy Ayers and David R. Counts, eds. 1991. *Coping with the Final Tragedy: Cultural Variation in Dying and Grieving.* Amityville, NY: Baywood Publishing.

———. 2004. "The Good, The Bad, and The Unresolved Death in Kaliai." *Social Science & Medicine* 58: 887–97.
Danforth, Loring M. 1982. *The Death Rituals of Rural Greece*. Princeton: Princeton University Press.
Dernbach, Katherine Boris. 2005. "Spirits of the Hereafter: Death, Funerary Possession, and the Afterlife in Chuuk, Micronesia." *Ethnology* 44: 99–123.
Eagleton, Terry. 1990. *The Ideology of the Aesthetic*. London: Blackwell.
Eliade, Mircea. 1958. *Patterns in Comparative Religion*. New York: Meridian.
———. 1971. *The Myth of the Eternal Return: Cosmos and History*. Translated by WR Trask. Princeton: Princeton University Press.
Freud, Sigmund. 2005 [1917]. "Mourning and Melancholia." In *Sigmund Freud: On Murder, Mourning and Melancholia*, translated by Shaun Whiteside, 201–18. London: Penguin.
———. 1923. "The Ego and the Id." In *The Standard Edition of the Complete Psychological Works of Sigmund Freud* (vol. 19), edited and translated by J. Strachey, 12–66. London: Hogarth.
Gay, Volney P. 1980. "Death Anxiety in Modern and Pre-Modern Ritual." *American Imago* 37: 180–214.
Gewertz, Deborah B. and Frederick K. Errington. 1991. *Twisted Histories, Altered Contexts: Representing the Chambri in the World System*. Cambridge: Cambridge University Press.
———. 1999. *Emerging Class in Papua New Guinea: The Telling of Difference*. Cambridge: Cambridge University Press.
———. 2002. "Margaret Mead and the Death of Alexis Gewertz Shepard." *Amherst Magazine*, Spring 2002. Retrieved December 29, 2015, from http://www3.amherst.edu/magazine/issues/02spring/features/gewertz.html.
Gillis, John R. 1996. *A World of Their Own Making: Myth, Ritual, and the Quest for Family Values*. Cambridge: Harvard University Press.
Hagman, George. 2001. "Beyond Decathexis: Toward a New Psychoanalytic Understanding and Treatment of Mourning." In *Meaning Reconstruction & the Experience of Loss*, edited by RA Neimeyer, 13–31. Washington, D.C.: American Psychoanalytic Association.
Harrison, Simon. 1985. "Names, Ghosts and Alliance in Two Sepik River Societies." *Oceania* 56: 138–46.
———. 1990. *Stealing People's Names: History and Politics in a Sepik River Cosmology*. Cambridge: Cambridge University Press.
———. 2001. "Smoke Rising from the Villages of the Dead: Seasonal Patterns of Mood in a Papua New Guinea Society." *Journal of the Royal Anthropological Institute* NS 7: 257–74.
———. 2004. "Forgetful and Memorious Landscapes." *Social Anthropology* 12: 135–51.
Hertz, Robert. 1960 [1907]. "A Contribution to the Study of the Collective Representation of Death." In *Death and the Right Hand*, translated by R. Needham and C. Needham, 27–86, 117–54. Glencoe: Free Press.
Hollan, Douglas. 1995. "To the Afterworld and Back: Mourning and Dreams of the Dead among the Toraja." *Ethos* 23: 424–36.
Horst, Heather A. 2004. "A Pilgrimage Hone: Tombs, Burial and Belonging in Jamaica." *Journal of Material Culture* 9: 11–26.
Küchler, Suzanne. 2002. *Malanggan: Art, Memory and Sacrifice*. Oxford: Berg.

Lacan, Jacques. 1977. *Ecrits: A Selection*. Translated by Alan Sheridan. London: Tavistock.
Leavitt, Stephen. 1995. "Seeking Gifts from the Dead: Long-Term Mourning in a Bumbita Arapesh Cargo Narrative." *Ethos* 23: 453–73.
Lipset, David. 1997. *Mangrove Man: Dialogics of Culture in the Sepik Estuary*. Cambridge: Cambridge University Press.
Lipset, David and Eric K. Silverman. 2005. "Dialogics of the Body: The Moral and the Grotesque in Two Sepik River Societies." *Journal of Ritual Studies* 19: 17–52.
Lohmann, Roger Ivar. 2007. "Souvenirs des Morts: Techniques de Gestion de la Mémoire dans un village de Nouvelle-Guinée." *Journal de la Société des Océanistes* 124: 45–57.
———. 2008. "Sexual Snakes Strike Again: Immortality Expressed and Explained in a New Guinea Myth." In *Sexual Snakes, Winged Maidens and Sky Gods: Myth in the Pacific, An Essay in Cultural Transparency*, edited by Serge Dunis, 113–25. Nouméa: Le Rocher-à-la-voile and Papeete: Éditions Haere Po Tahiti.
Maschio, Thomas. 1994. *To Remember the Faces of the Dead: Plenitude of Memory in Southwestern New Britain*. Madison: University of Wisconsin Press.
Obeyesekere, Gananath. 1990. *The Work of Culture: Symbolic Transformation in Psychoanalysis and Anthropology*. Chicago: University of Chicago Press.
Pleck, Elizabeth H. 2000. *Celebrating the Family: Ethnicity, Consumer Culture, and Family Rituals*. Cambridge: Harvard University Press.
Robbins, Joel. 2004. *Becoming Sinners: Christianity and Moral Torment in a Papua New. Guinea Society*. Berkeley: University of California Press.
Schwartz, Theodore. 1973. "Cult and Context: The Paranoid Ethos in Melanesia." *Ethos* 1: 153–74.
Silverman, Eric Kline. 1997. "Politics, Gender, and Time in Melanesia and Aboriginal Australia." *Ethnology* 36: 101–21.
———. 2001. *Masculinity, Motherhood, and Mockery: Psychoanalyzing Culture and the Iatmul Naven Rite*. Ann Arbor: University of Michigan Press.
———. 2003. "High Art as Tourist Art, Tourist Art as High Art: Comparing the New Guinea Sculpture Garden at Stanford University and Sepik River Tourist Art." *International Journal of Anthropology* 18: 219–30.
———. 2004. "Cannibalizing, Commodifying, and Creating Culture: Power and Creativity in Sepik River Tourism." In *Globalization and Culture Change in the Pacific Islands*, edited by V. Lockwood, 339–57. New York: Prentice-Hall.
———. 2013. "After *Cannibal Tours*: Cargoism and Marginality in a Post-touristic Sepik River Society." *The Contemporary Pacific* 25(2): 221–57.
Stasch, Rupert. 2009. *Society of Others: Kinship and Mourning in a West Papua Place*. Berkeley: University of California Press.
Stephen, Michele. 1998. "Devouring the Mother: A Kleinian Perspective on Necrophagia and Corpse Abuse in Mortuary Ritual." *Ethos* 26: 387–409.
Telban, Borut. 1997. "Being and 'Non–Being' in Ambonwari (Papua New Guinea Ritual)." *Oceania* 67: 308–25.
Telban, Borut and Daniela Vávrová. 2014. "Ringing the Living and the Dead: Mobile Phones in a Sepik Society." *The Australian Journal of Anthropology* 25: 223–38.
Trawick, Margaret. 1990. *Notes on Love in a Tamil Family*. Berkeley: University of California Press.
Tuzin, Donald F. 1975. "The Breath of a Ghost: Dreams and the Fear of the Dead." *Ethos* 3: 555–78.

———. 1977. "Reflections of Being in Arapesh Water Symbolism." *Ethos* 5: 195–223.
———. 1997. *The Cassowary's Revenge: The Life and Death of Masculinity in a New Guinea Society*. Chicago: University of Chicago Press.
Weiner, Annette B. 1976. *Women of Value, Men of Renown: New Perspectives in Trobriand Exchange*. Austin: University of Texas Press.
Weiner, James F. 1993. "To Be at Home with Others in an Empty Place: A Reply to Mimica." *The Australian Journal of Anthropology* 4: 233–44.
———. 1995. *The Lost Drum: The Myth of Sexuality in Papua New Guinea and Beyond*. Madison: University of Wisconsin Press.

9

Everything Will Come Up Like TV, Everything Will Be Revealed
Death in an Age of Uncertainty in the Purari Delta, Papua New Guinea

JOSHUA A. BELL

On March 2002, Mailau, a prominent elder within the Aikavalavi section of Mapaio village, suddenly died at a fishing camp on the upper Purari River (Figure 9.1). Prior to his death, we spoke often and I relished our conversations. Typically, we were joined underneath his house by other Aikavalavi elders. Some four months after his passing, his wife Varia and daughter Susan invited me to eat a meal in honor of our relationships before I left for home. During that visit, we spoke about her husband's death and what followed, a sequence of events to which I will now turn.

After Mailau's body had been brought to the village, he was laid out in his house wrapped in a sheet, while close kin wailed and relatives gathered. Following a brief service by the United Church that afternoon, men from another section of Mapaio took Mailau's body, now in a coffin made from a canoe he often had used, to the graveyard and buried him, as in Murik and Kayan. Vistors stayed for a few days and then dispersed. Two months after Mailau's burial, I received a letter from Mailau's nephew, who was living in town, telling me about a recent dream in which his uncle appeared. The I'ai understand dreams to be a state in which ancestors and the recently deceased may communicate to kin. As sources of revelation, dreams are culturally significant.

Not disclosing the cause of his death, Mailau instead asked about his own funeral in the dream, what was given and who attended. To my dismay, his nephew told him that I had not attended the funeral. The dream ended with Mailau paddling back up river in his canoe. I found the letter perplexing and was reminded that despite my assistance with transportation and food during the funeral I would never be able to fully compensate community members for their hospitality. To help resolve any misunderstandings, I visited Mailua's wife and daughter. Observing I'ai mourning traditions, Varia and Susan were

Everything Will Come Up Like TV, Everything Will Be Revealed **209**

Figure 9.1. Mailau Aneane Ivia (1932–2002) on his veranda. Photo: Joshua Bell, 2002.

sleeping under their house unwashed, wearing black and lengths of braided string on ankles, wrists, and biceps (Williams 1924: 217–18).

Inhibited by my own preconceptions about mourning and overwhelmed with sadness over Mailau's death, I had been avoiding them since the funeral. Mailau's death was the first that I had experienced as an adult either in the Delta or, for that matter, at all, and his loss profoundly upset me. After admonishing me for having neglected them, the women explained how Mailau's spirit-double (*avaea*) lingered angrily in the forest and had showed them his displeasure by manipulating the food they put out for him to eat. In addition, they charged that his anger had also caused my recent illness, for which I had been hospitalized. Varia and Susan then asked me to help them with the cost of fuel and food to hold a small feast at the site of Mailau's death to help calm his restless *avaea*-spirit. Wishing to make amends, I was more than happy to oblige.

As our last meal together drew to an end, Varia and Susan allowed that while Mailau's *avaea*-spirit was no longer bothering anyone, uncertainty still hung over the reason for his death. At the time, two explanations circulated. In the one that they subscribed to, Mailau had died from "jealousy showing out because [of] every time you used to come here. His death is clearly jealousy showing out" (Susan, author's fieldnotes, June 29, 2002). They believed that rival elders, who had joined us under their house to talk, killed him.

It was true that, despite my best efforts, these meetings had often become edgy as men made tacit and overt attempts to assert customary authority, which the promise of logging royalties had made highly contested (Bell 2014). In the second account of Mailau's demise, which his paternal kin subscribed to, it was claimed that the death was retaliation for their having driven the village councillor, a suspected sorcerer (*dapu*), out of the village ten months earlier. Though motives differed, both accounts pointed to sorcery as the proximate cause of the death and each left living villagers in a state of suspicion. Regardless of the cause, his wife was confident that Mailau's *avaea*-spirit would eventually make "everything ... come up like TV, everything will be revealed."

Mailau's death highlights several issues that I explore in this chapter, that coalesce around the anxiety that death causes: death not only calls into question the moral state of the community, but by haunting the living the dead become an unpredictable source of revelation about who killed them and why (see Lipset, this volume). While these anxieties are not new, death is widely seen to have increased due to a democratization of sorcery that began in the 1950s. The moral quandries that this has caused are complicated by the new practice of homestead burial, which means the restless dead are closer and more invasive than they were during the era of cemetary burial (see Lutkehaus and von Poser and Silverman, this volume).

This view of the dead, I argue, is symptomatic of the inequalities arising from resource extraction and the failure of the postcolonial state to maintain regional infrastructure. Since the mid-1990s, descent groups have become increasingly competitive with one another, denying their mutual constitution as they struggle for legal recognition from the state to obtain royalty payments. The emergence of this bitter new arena is locally acknowledged in the phrase, "money ground" (*moni kaeou*), wherein kin relations to property are displaced by commodified relations (Bell 2006, 2009, 2015).

"Money ground" is a local idiom expressing the structural violence that communities are currently facing in the wake of resource extraction. Funerals are key events in which the moral effects of this violence becomes visible. Bringing these commentaries into view, this chapter joins other authors in this volume as well as a larger body of work that seeks to understand suffering and how globalization is embodied (see also Povinelli 2011). With the breakdown of public displays of bride-wealth (*paka aru*) due to the jealousy these exchanges can cause and the lack of other formalized institutions, funerals have become one of the last large-scale communal events involving public exchanges still practiced by the I'ai. While villages do assemble during Church events and sports tournaments, these events involve only informal interactions that are not subject to the same moral scrutiny as mortuary exchanges.

Complicating this scenario, the new practice of homestead burial overturns a hundred years of colonial mandates that bodies are buried outside the village and defies fears that the proximty of the dead may cause illness and death (see Carucci, this volume). The practice not only anoints the dead with an ongoing intravillage presence but gives mourners a platform from which they can continue to seek compensation for their loss. Perhaps most troubling for I'ai communities, the new proximity of the dead raises questions about whether living kin are drawing power from them, power through which new cycles of violence may arise. The practices, fears, and motivations that coalesce around death also point to resentments regarding the I'ai's status as less than equal members of the developing state (see Silverman, this volume; Robbins and Wardlow 2005).

Mailau's death and the discourse that followed also raised for me what was, and remains, an unnerving sense of closeness to death during and after fieldwork (Glaskin et al. 2009). This intimacy aroused "vicissitudes of empathy" (Throop 2010), feelings of loss, anger, and guilt (Rosaldo 1993; High 2011) as I struggled to understand life in the Purari Delta. Death pervaded Mapaio village during my fieldwork and has since become an integral part of my research, as elders I worked with have died and as younger friends have passed away unexpectedly (see von Poser, this volume).

As Silverman and Lipset point out in the Introduction to this volume, death and the associated mortuary rituals constitute what they call "mortuary dialogues," during which people may reflect on the state of their moral community in the historical moment. To help situate I'ai mortuary dialogues, I first discuss the colonial background of regional transformations. This involves drawing from colonial records, the work of previous anthropologists FE Williams (1922) and Robert F. Maher (1954–1955), and oral histories that I collected to reconstruct mortuary practices. I then return to the ethnographic present (2001–2010) and analyze three deaths to examine how people think about death today.

Structural Violence and the New Ambiguities of Death

How the dead haunt the living in the Purari Delta resembles other accounts both in this volume and in contexts of global inequality or regional conflict, such as the alienating conditions of Malaysian factories (Ong 1988), the wake of the Cultural Revolution in rural southwest China (Mueggler 2001), or the legacies of the Vietnam War (Kwon 2006). These varied contexts of haunting are emblematic of communities' intensely personal and cultural responses to structural violence engendered by globalization.

Building on the work of the Latin American theologian Johan Galtung (1969), Paul Farmer (2004, 2005) formulated structural violence to articulate the enduring nature of inequality in Haiti. It possesses clear parallels to the articulations of "everyday violence" (Scheper-Hughes and Bourgois 2004) and symbolic violence (Bourdieu 2000), which are equally concerned with the power dynamics of lived reality and the misrecognition of the causes of inequality. Despite critiques of its atemporality (Nixon 2011), structural violence remains an important analytic through which to understand the intersection of the biological, political, and social erasure of history and as a way to bring suffering into view. It also helps to bring into focus the social agents that disenfranchise others through the perpetuation of the status quo and through the creation of new economic and social orders (Gupta 2012).

Structural violence in the Purari Delta is exemplified in the way communities are being torn apart as companies and the state deny ancestral histories through which customary property claims are based and, more materially, how they deny the relations and histories materialized in the environment that bulldozers physically erase. The situation is the inverse of the effloresence described by Bainton and Macintyre for Lihir (see this volume) and is more akin to the abjection described by Ferguson (1999) in Zambia's Copperbelt region, where communities struggled to understand the realities behind economic decline. Instead of benefitting from resource royalties, communities in the Purari Delta are being dispossessed, which they struggle to understand (see also Silverman this volume; Robbins and Wardlow 2005; Kirsch 2006).

While death has always given rise to an ethos of moral introspection, external demands on communities exacted by resource extraction and the politics of property rights have now exacerbated this postmortem atmosphere. Armed with their own grievances and accusations, but also facing the possibility that one of their own may be responsible for the death of a loved one, increasingly families opt for homestead burials. They do so in order to assert their innocence but also to ensure that the deceased, as well as their grievances, are not forgotten in the community. The prolonged debasement that they observe becomes the grounds for claiming redress and ensures that the community does not move on. The dead literally and figuratively haunt it. Indeed, instead of a TV screen depicting the causes of a particular death, the death of a loved one plunges everyone into prolonged cycles of recrimination, a mortuary dialogue in which meaning is continually twisted rather than exposed. Doubt and uncertainty is one of the most pervasive effects of structural violence in the Purari Delta.

Living and Dying in the Purari Delta—Histories and Contexts

The I'ai are one of six linguistically and culturally related, self-identified tribes who inhabit twenty-five villages in the Delta created by the Purari River's many tributaries.[1] This rural population of 14,000 people is matched by an equal number of dispersed kin living in Papua New Guinea's (PNG's) cities, particularly Kerema and Port Moresby. Out-migration has been a defining factor of regional life since the 1950s, when the I'ai led the Tom Kabu Movement, which advocated cash cropping as a means of social transformation (Maher 1961).[2] As a result, social life across the Gulf Province became defined by farflung kin-based networks (Hitchcock and Oram 1967; Ryan 1989).

Their degree of moral integration varies, as do their views of why the region has failed to develop (Morauta 1984; Maher 1984). The anomie caused by this situation is compounded by the long regional history of European colonialism, the failure of the Kabu Movement, and the more recent repercussions of resource extraction, specifically large-scale logging (from 1995 through today), natural gas extraction (from 2002 through today), and explorations for a hydro project (see Bell 2006, 2009, 2015). This history has transformed the Purari's material culture as well as their subjectivity, and concepts of embodiment.

British (1884) and then Australian (1906) colonial rule affected Purari communities by imposing regulations of various kinds. Following the creation of administrative centers in Kerema (1906) and Kikori (1912), government patrols pacified the region. The ban on ritual headhunting and cannibalism activities that had been critical to ancestor worship and male initiation also enabled labor recruitment (Williams 1924: 107–9, 180–81). Though the London Missionary Society established a regional base on the coast in 1905, it was not until the 1930s, when Seventh-Day Adventists arrived, that Christianity began to extend its reach into villages. Even then it was not really until the 1960s that Christianity became truly widespread.

These interventions disrupted two Purari practices related to human remains. The first practice involved displaying enemies' skulls in racks within each clan's alcove in the men's longhouse (*ravi*). With pacification in 1908, pigs replaced human victims, and hunting replaced warfare as a means to demonstrate the efficacy of one's ancestors. The second practice (*kairi*) involved decorating and displaying the clan's skulls in the longhouse (Williams 1924:

65, 219–23). For this purpose, men exhumed their forebearers' skulls, overmodeled them with beeswax and mud, and then painted each with totemic and clan-specific designs before displaying them in the longhouse (Williams 1924: 92–93). Skulls were potent parts of the body that were used in making statements about gender as well as about corporate and ancestral identities (cf. Harrison 1993).

While both these displays of skulls were restricted (longhouses were off-limits to women), the *kairi* rite also involved a public feast, after which the skulls were interred in single file by the classificatory mothers' brother of each deceased person. The sponsor of the festivities then addressed the skulls, demanding that the dead's *avaea*-spirit "depart now for good and all. Never return to our village. All these bodies of pigs and dogs are for you; so, too, all these coconuts and taro. Now I bury you under the ground. You are done with forever" (Williams 1924: 223). The *kairi* rite, of course, is a Hertzian secondary burial meant to reconstitute moral community. The sponsor's declaration reflected the degree to which the dead were seen as a source of strife. According to elders the Kabu Movement ceased the practice of the *kairi* rite during the early 1950s.

As part of a program of colonial management, in 1914 Resident Magistrate HJ Ryan began requiring that villagers construct walkways between houses, build latrines, not process sago within village boundaries, and bury the dead in designated areas outside of villages (Papua 1914: 97; see Holmes 1924: 219, 225). While there is no record of local reactions to these reforms, local discontent is evident in the numerous patrol reports, in which villagers are fined or temporarily imprisoned for failing to comply (cf. Papua 1923: 53).

While precolonial burial practices are unclear, Williams was told that some bodies "were buried under ground and some in trees" (1924: 217). The former seems to have been carried out by coastal communities and required that sand be hauled into a village for the burial. Inland groups placed corpses on raised platforms and low-lying branches in order to avoid disturbance by pigs. These may have been regional patterns, although the platform/tree burial may have been a remnant of secondary burial practices. Alternatively, these varations may reflect status differences of the deceased (Holmes 1924: 225; Williams 1924: 110–16; Maher 1974). Either way, by 1922, the dead were buried under the shelter of palm leaves in designated fenced areas (Williams 1924: 217). Today, while people recall headhunting and *kairi* rites, they do not remember what burial practices were like before the arrival of the colonial government.

As part of the iconoclastic reform of the Kabu Movement, beginning in 1947 old villages were abandoned and communities resettled in new sites to facilitate shipping cash crops. In these new villages, European houses, formerly illegal under colonial rule, were built as communities attempted to embrace values the Movement promoted as modern (Maher 1961). New villages, like

Everything Will Come Up Like TV, Everything Will Be Revealed 215

Mapaio, where I worked, also helped Seventh-Day Adventists and members of the Kabu Movement establish new communities that were free of traditional connections, which they viewed as constraints. Despite relocation, longhouses remained important institutions and in Mapaio each one established its own graveyard across the Ivo branch of the Purari River.

Maher's fieldnotes depict Purari mortuary rites in the mid-1950s and provide important insight into this period of transition. On January 15, 1955, he recorded the mourning and burial of a man called Inaua in the new village of Kinipo (Figure 9.2). Women wailed, while men played drums and sang songs about the deceased's ancestors. Inaua was wrapped in a white cloth and taken to a fenced cemetary, a mile south of the village. After digging the grave, the body was placed on nipa palm leaves and covered with more leaves and sev-

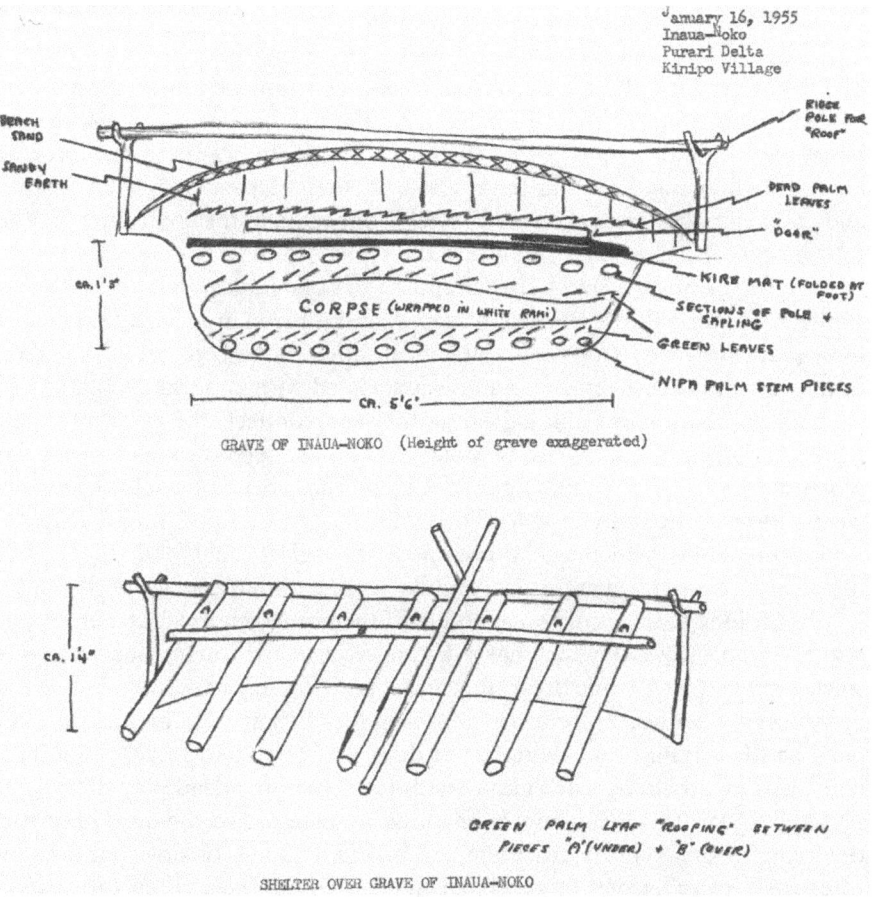

Figure 9.2. Sketch of the grave of Inaua Noko (Robert Francis Maher Papers, Box 1; courtesy of the National Anthropological Archives, Smithsonian Institution).

eral boards before being buried. A roof was then constructed over the mound. Maher noted that men complained that following European practices the deceased should have been placed in a coffin. At a time when men were striving to be modern through the Kabu Movement, such comments point to the mortuary dialogue at play. This striving for modern identities was also portrayed in the names and dates written on crosses marking graves.

Present-day burial practices do show certain continuities with what Maher observed in the 1950s. However, in order to understand them, I'ai concepts of the moral person need to be assessed in more detail. This is no easy task due to a dearth of earlier data on the topic. So I must concede that the following account must have been influenced by the region's colonial history.

Bone, Blood, Skin, and Spirit-Double

The I'ai understand the moral person to emerge from and exist within a network of paths (*kapea*) that are defined by the movement of various things: bone, blood, food, names, and knowledge. The main agents in this process are (1) the father and mother themselves, (2) their respective descent groups, and (3) their ancestors who are intimately connected to the environment. The relationship of each of these beings to the others is fluid and political (Strathern 1988). The body is said to be composed of bone (*da'aro*), blood (*aro*), and stomach (*nemu*), all of which is wrapped up by the skin or body (*kape*), or flesh (*oia*). Inherited from ego's biological father, bone connects the person to the patrilineal descent group and is associated with endurance. Blood and stomach come from ego's biological mother and connects the person to their maternal descent group. These elements evoke a gendered vision of women as nurturers and sources of life. Ego's skin or body is created by acts of feeding, which connect the individual to those that labor to produce food and to the environment from which food is obtained. Through sharing food, kin beyond the person's biological parents can and do claim children and adopt them.

In addition to their corporeal body, as I mentioned above, each person has a spirit-double (*avaea*), which has a distinctive agency.[3] During life, a person's spirit-double travels while dreaming, and it is vulnerable to sorcery. While the body decays after death, the spirit-double lingers. A spirit-double's actions depend on the actions of the living. If the dead are honored by mentioning their name and by providing one's family with food, then the dead play the role of protective guardian. While moral relations are maintained the dead may visit the living in dreams to warn them of impending harm or divert attacks by sorcerers. "If you live with them," Ke'a Aukiri told me, "clean their [graves] … they will protect you." However, should one neglect them, the dead are quick to let misfortune befall their kin.

For example, when Ke'a's daughter went out with her children to gather food, they unknowingly strayed into the family grave site and started a bush fire around the grave of a deceased brother. The daughter soon became ill and not long after, Ke'a had a dream in which his son explained his sister's malady. The following morning, Ke'a had his daughter inhale the smoke of special bark to break the power of the spirit-double bothering her. The family then gathered for a meal to appease the deceased brother.

While typically staying close to their grave site, spirit-doubles may enter the houses of living relatives. They come in either because the living still have their things or their loved ones have been mistreated. To keep the dead away, families will bury them with most of their belongings and destroy everything else. Particularly troublesome and feared are things kept as momentos that are meant to retain a connection to the deceased and that can be manipulated for the purposes of sorcery. Most commonly, it is said that the dead return to comfort beloved little children and grandchildren, aged two to five.

Up to a year after a family member has died, surviving kin are urged not to punish these children for fear that the deceased's spirit-double will return to and abduct the child's spirit-double to comfort them, resulting in the child's death. To prevent this, the dead are told that the banana stalks upon which their coffin rests are "their children" or "grandchildren." As Reverend Holmes noted reflecting on his time in the Purari Delta: "The haunting concern of ... mourning was to bid farewell to the spirit of the deceased in such a way that there would be no prospect of his returning" (1924: 227). The problem of attachment was, and remains, a central concern in I'ai cosmology.

Modernity has made these anxieties worse. The commodification of relationships and the creation of new social and economic inequalities have intensified tensions within and between communities. Resource extraction has undermined the closure mortuary rituals may once have offered and lent an acrimonious tone to the dialogues they provoke. The presence of the spirit-double now serves as a spectral reminder of conflict and jealousy (Bell 2015).

Contemporary Mortuary Rites (2001–2010)

In 2001–2002, eleven deaths in Mapaio village reverberated throughout the community (population, 650). In each case sorcery was understood to have been the cause of the death. Despite people's best intentions to renounce magic (*ivavi*) through the Kabu Movement in the 1950s, and despite subsequent purges conducted by village councillors and the Pentecostal Church in the 1970s, sorcery fears still loom large within the public imagination. The ongoing power of sorcery may be taken as another sign of the breakdown of life in the Delta and of the failures of the Church and development.

Sorcery is emblematic of the contested morality of the era of "money ground." It is the result of the structural violence of resource extraction, namely, the jealousies aroused by uneven royalty payments and struggles around the leadership of Incorporated Land Groups (ILG), under whose auspices descent groups register property with the state (Bell 2009). Despite the possibility of the dead exposing their killers, in most instances this does not happen. Instead the dialogue contemporary burial practices provoke gives rise to constant reinterpretation, mistrust, and a sense of moral failure.

As word spreads of a terminal illness or a death, kin gather at the deceased's homestead to wail. Senior family members may sing songs about the deceased's totemic affiliations (*opa*). One elder told me:

> Uncles and aunts call out [to] the father's and mother's *opa*[-totems] and [alert them that their] deceased [child] is coming. Before … one person would call out [to all of] … the deceased's [father's] *opa* [-totems] … and then go through the [other] side.

The songs foreground how the deceased is related to those gathered to mourn. While the Seventh-Day Adventists condemn totemic dimensions of the person as satanic; traditionally minded I'ai see the decline of this performance as another sign of moral decay.

As in Murik and Manam, the deceased's village section is placed under a comprehensive taboo that forbids all work other than that related to food making. Men, with less direct relations to the deceased, prepare the body for burial (washing and clothing it) and dig a grave in their longhouse's section of the village graveyard. While typically people make coffins out of an old canoe, increasingly, urban-based kin are being flown home in store-bought Western style coffins. Regardless of the coffin style, a Church service is held during which hymns are sung, the deceased's biography is read, and a sermon is given. Drawn from the community's collective knowledge of the individual, the biography details the deceased's accomplishments and schooling and may allude to other events in his life.

Once interred, the deceased's clothing and other belongings are placed around the coffin and covered up by his sleeping mat. Earth is heaped around the mat. Marked out with cut timber, the grave is invariably covered with a nylon tarp or a roof of cut sago fronds to prevent erosion. Over time, the coffin slowly sinks into the ground. A taboo marker (*vupu*) made of sago fronds is also erected to prevent disturbance (see Figures 9.3 and 9.4). In cases when the death is suspicious, a group of armed young men will watch the grave for several nights to protect it from sorcerers who in human or animal form may attempt to capture the deceased's spirit-double for their own malevolent purposes. These men are permitted without warning to shoot anything and anyone who visits the site.

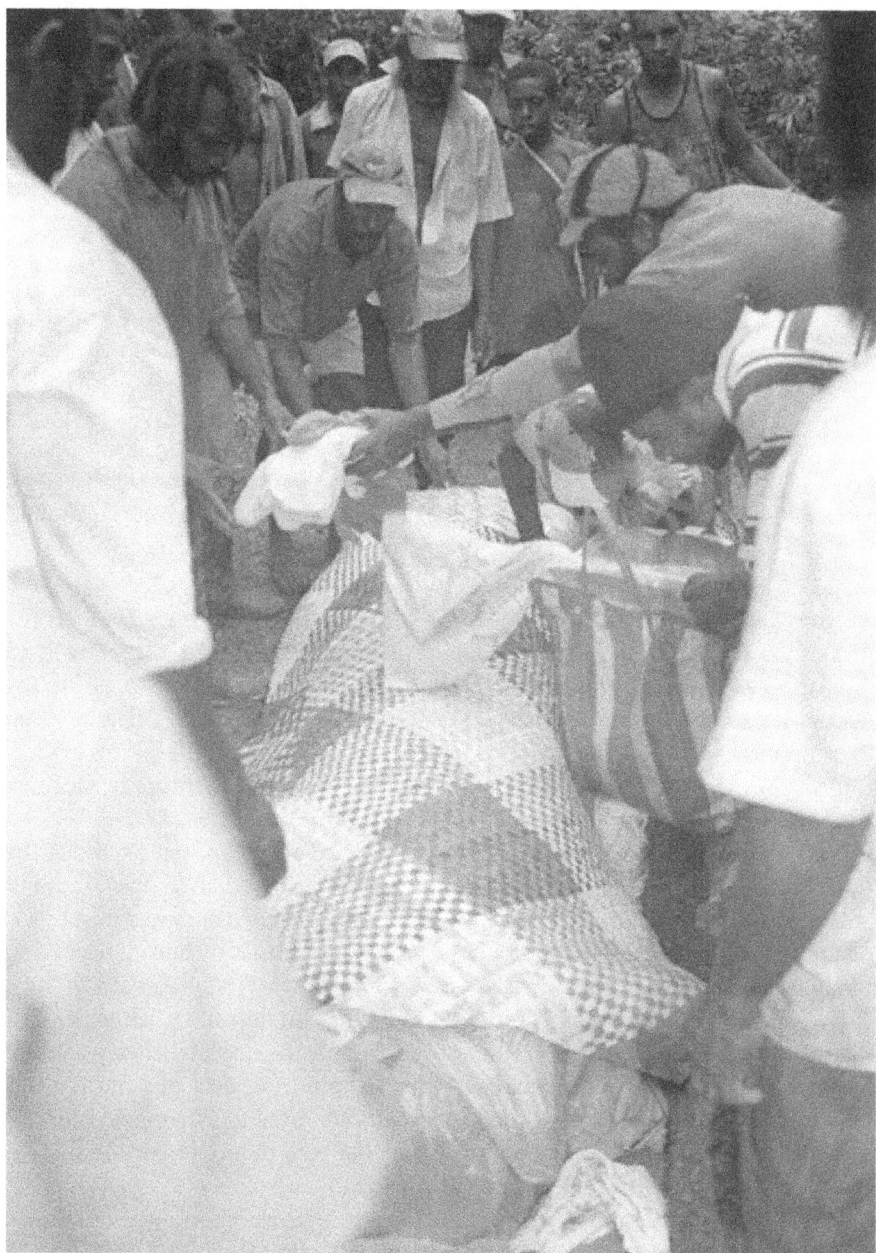

Figure 9.3. A body in a canoe-coffin is wrapped in plastic; mourners place clothes and personal effects around a nipa mat. Photo: Joshua Bell, 2001.

Figure 9.4. Woven nipa, underneath a piece of tarp, covers the burial mound while a taboo marker has been placed before the grave. Photo: Joshua Bell, 2001.

Meanwhile, another man may go off to the bush for a séance (*iviai*) with the deceased's spirit-double. The participant in this séance is said alternatively to "see" the events around the death, like watching television, or to "speak" to the deceased's spirit-double. The séance occurs immediately after a death, when its power is seen as most potent. If successful, the séance will have a critical impact on the community's discussion about the death and more broadly on their reflection about the state of their moral community.

In addition, it is common for funerals to involve discussions about the outstanding debts of the deceased. Brothers of a deceased sister may demand "head wealth" (*uku aru*), particularly if bride-wealth (*paka aru*) was never paid or the family feels that their sister was looked after poorly by her husband and his kin (see von Poser, this volume). For example, when Mailau died in 2002 (discussed at this beginning of this chapter), his agnates sent a letter demading monetary compensation from another clan for the unpaid bride-wealth of Mailau's daughter. They threatened to delay the burial until this money was paid but relented once the smell of Mailau's body grew too strong. While it is difficult to assess how these demands have changed, their current intensity is seen by many as another sign of moral decline.

During the burial, the deceased's kin begin to observe mourning taboos, which includes wearing black, not washing or cutting their hair, and, for the traditionally minded, sleeping under the house and wearing braided bands of cloth on their arms and legs. After approximately one year, the principal mourners invite kin who attended the burial to return. In the intervening time, the host kin will have planted new gardens, amassed stores of sago flour, purchased rice and so forth, and obtained fish and meat. This food is distributed to the guests, who should have also been observing mourning taboos. This event is a reciprocation of food originally brought by guests to their hosts at the burial. All the mourners will have their hair cut, and the house of the deceased's immediate kin will be cleaned (*onari laua*).

Through this feasting and cleaning, the mourners are released from their taboos, and death's disruptions are meant to come to a close. If funds allow, the family may also build a more permanent grave structure around this time or on a subsequent anniversary. This typically involves a hardwood marker and installing iron sheeting over the grave but in rare instances may consist of a concrete overlay. In doing so, the I'ai mimic periurban graves in Kerema and Port Moresby, where there is more cash and graves are used as sites of conspicuous consumption (see Silverman and Bainton, this volume).

Increasingly, the mortuary pattern described above is more an ideal than a practice. As kin disperse to the periurban centers of Kerema and Port Moresby and as the price of outboard petrol increases, the yearlong mourning is now often replaced by an abridged event around the burial. Immediate kin of the deceased may observe mourning taboos, but relatives no longer reconvene to feast and ritually clean themselves collectively. In addition, the deceased's kin must now host guests, providing food for the entire funeral (abridged or not) and at times compensate them with gifts of money. These inversions of tradition have made funerals a burden and are seen as yet another indicator of moral decline.

Homestead burials are also taking place with increased frequency in the Purari Delta, a trend found elsewhere in Papua New Guinea. In contrast to the Manam Island practices (see Lutkehaus, this volume), however, homestead burials are not meant to reconstitute the family in an ancestral place. Instead, they are in direct response to the belief that the family member's death was caused by sorcery provoked by resource extraction and uneven royalty payments. Homestead burials are a way for mourners to keep the family's grief in full view and counteract the erasure of a loved one. In Mapaio, the expression of these sentiments was particularly acute, as I'ai people struggled to be recognized as resource owners (Bell 2009). As Ke'a lamented to me:

> today we have no land. When we try and talk about it, there is always a dispute or people try to cut each other down.... That sort of attitude, competing with one another ... will [kill us all]. One can't escape death, even myself too. While in the house meeting ... we need to think of what to do and all help. But if you start gossiping, that is how we spoil our life.

Amid this ethos of rivalry and veiled antagonisms, sorcerers began to be seen to kill indiscriminately. As late as the 1970s, individuals still sought out healers who would divine the enmities behind, and cure, their illnesses. Exposing people's moral failures this way was thought to mitigate them (i.e., distribution of bride-wealth and sharing food). However, in the wake of the Kabu Movement's iconoclasm and purges by the missions, chiefs became fearful that the power of their lineages would be undercut in the post-Kabu era and were said to have taught their hereditary spells to their wives and children. New forms of magic also entered the Purari Delta, as people encountered other ethnic groups in cities. During a dispute settlement in Mapaio village, a middle-aged I'ai man called Eravu articulated the severity of the risks of the moment:

> Today, people are cut down like trees.... What is [disputed] today needs to be solved tomorrow because you and I don't know [whether] there may be someone aiming ... [to kill] you ... and you won't see your grandchildren. [This] ... is happening now. Not like before ... when someone [was] ... sick, they [would] lie down and die. Now people walk around normally and they ... [suddenly] collapse and die.

The pervasiveness of sorcery, in my view, is the local idiom for the structural violence in which I'ai people now live. The slightest dispute, they fear, will result in death.

I documented twenty-four illnesses and twenty-eight deaths that occurred between 1950 and 2001 and four illnesses and sixteen deaths that took place during 2001–2002.[4] Due to the fugitive and combustible nature of sorcery, all of these incidents were discussed privately with limited corroboration. Of the twenty-eight deaths that occurred prior to 2001, seventeen were attributed to disputes over land and leadership titles, with the remaining eleven deaths linked to a variety of reasons (e.g., adultery). Eleven of these twenty-eight cases were understood to be the action of the deceased's agnates, while the remainder were attributed to members of rival lineages within a clan. In contrast, of the sixteen deaths I documented in 2001–2002, thirteen were linked to tensions within and between clans about ILG chairmanship and resource ownership caused by the logging.

The kinship links involved in these deaths were not as clearly delineated as the older cases I recorded, because people were continuing to debate the identity of the sorcerers involved. However in each case suspicion primarily lay within the victim's descent group or longhouse. This pattern supports a general perception that threats always come from within one's community, whether one's lineage, clan, or longhouse. Among the I'ai there is an adage, "Your dog, pig, [or] chicken, you kill such a person and no one will say anything" (*Ni oroko, a'uri, kokoro nia'ane a'a mo voa mo ema kurua'aka'a*) to which people refer when speaking of sorcery. Apart from the moral autonomy of the household, another point it would seem to suggest is that the most problematic kinsmen, and thus most likely to be targets of sorcery, are agnates and affines (specifically mother's brother and sisters' son and male in-laws).

The level of stress and mistrust being what it is, funerals also become important contexts in which the behavior of both kin and nonkin are closely watched in hopes that the sorcerer will inadvertently betray themselves. While widows are particularly scruntized, nearly everyone is suspect and watched on these occassions.

The Politics of Homestead Burials

In the three case-studies to which I now turn, mortuary dialogue revolves around homestead burial and a prolonged debasement that forestalls the gradual forgetting that should occur over the course of the mortuary process. The proximity of the spirit-double, moreover, adds to the atmosphere of suspicion as people fear the possibilities of revenge.

My first case centers on a grave, a small, low-walled shelter prominently placed in front of Koivi's house in Mapaio. The grave belonged to Koivi's son, who was killed in 1999 by sorcerers following a land dispute. In a fit of grief, Koivi buried his son, and his was the first homestead burial in the village. People surmised that Koivi had harnessed powers from his son's spirit-double. He never denied it but rather acknowledged quite frankly that his son, who had been buried with a flashlight, wandered around at night flashing it. Koivi's knowledge of ancestral histories and his son's burial combined to cultivate suspicion of him, which resulted in an attack in which he was beaten for his alleged help in killing a young girl following a land dispute with the girl's father. He had assisted a sorcerer, it was said, who had pulled the girl under water and drowned her with magical fishhooks as she traveled with kin downriver on log rafts being brought to the Baimuru sawmill to sell. It was this death that led her kin to drive the suspected sorcerer, the ward councillor, who was related to the girl's mother, out of Mapaio.[5]

In response to his daughter's death, her father destroyed his house and burned or threw most of his family's possessions into the river. In addition to these displays of grief was the public debasement of the family, who slept on covered platforms around their daughter's homestead bural (Figure 9.5). Onlookers worried that the homestead burial would expose the family to sickness, which in turn threatened the wider community with contagion. This was the second homestead burial in Mapaio village.

These two homestead graves were not anomalous. In an unrelated incident, another family lost an eleven-year-old son in August 2001. Aivei, the father, attributed the death to rivalry for leadership in his ILG. When ILGs were initially formed in 1999, Aivei had been enlisted in his father's descent

Figure 9.5. Sleeping shelter around grave. Photo: Joshua Bell, 2001.

group in the longhouse Okaikenairu, despite the fact that his father had been adopted as a boy by a descent group in a different longhouse. Aivei's return to his paternal kin aroused resentment, he thought, particularly when he then began to seek his father's title. A rival who disputed his claim was seen beating his hand drum while Aivei's family waited to bury his son. Many interpreted this act as an expression of joy and thus of his role in the boy's death. This suspicion was confirmed when the old man, in another gesture of disrespect, threw a 1 kina note over Aivei's head, as the family solicited money to compensate guest-mourners. Fearing further attacks, Aivei said nothing. Instead, he quietly relinquished his leadership claims in his ILG.

Meanwhile, Aivei buried his son on his in-laws' house plot and then built a platform around it to sleep on. With the help of kin living in town, Aivei eventually constructed a new house next to his son's grave, which he marked with a cement cross. Mourning ended following a feast that was staged in honor of the cement cross (Figure 9.6).

Villagers are increasingly commemorating their loved ones with permanent markers (see von Poser, this volume). While grave markers serve as a measure of a family's ability to marshal social and financial capital, they also serve as monuments to the new geography of suffering in the region. That is, by burying the dead among the living, homestead graves increase the likelihood that some inadvertant slight will occur around the grave and that the spirit-double of the deceased will retaliate, causing further illness and conflict. By 2010, there were no fewer than eleven homestead graves in the village, and dialogue simmered around each of them.

Figure 9.6. Cement cross marking the grave of Aivei's son located next to his house. Photo: Joshua Bell, 2010.

My third and last case concerns the death of Koivi Kunu, a forty-five-year-old father of five children who was renowned for helping found the local string band Poiki Pakoni in the early 1970s. He was the son-in-law of my principal host, and we had spent time together during my first year in the community as part of the same household. While Koivi Kunu's death illustrates the perils of homestead burial, it also highlights problems caused when people die outside of the village. The dispute that ensued about his grave expressed a struggle to retain claims to land and strenghten lineage claims to resource ownership in the context of modern structural violence.

When he died in June 2002, Koivi Kunu was staying with kin in the Port Moresby settlement of Erima. Like many others, he had gotten pulled into the capitol by the 2002 national election, and it was said that he had run out of funds to come home and was enjoying himself too much to return. News of his death shocked people in the Delta and speculations as to its cause soon began. Several weeks went by as relatives secured the funds needed to charter a private plane to bring his body home (Figure 9.7). Photography having taken an increasingly important role in funerals as a means to remember the dead and of visually documenting relations with them, Koivi Kunu's affines, my principal host family, asked me to photograph events. Upset as I was by his death, I eagerly retreated behind my camera to shield myself from the sadness that erupted when his body returned.

Upon landing at the airport, kin carried his coffin to an informal settlement south of Baimuru station, where relatives lived. Though well known in Mapaio, Koivi Kunu's family lived in a settlement across the Pie River from the village. As two women called out totemic names, others clutched the coffin and wailed. Unfolding offstage, kin and affines argued over where to bury him. Koivi Kunu's adopted family had wanted to bury him in Port Moresby, while his wife desired that he be buried in Baimuru. Meanwhile, Koivi Kunu's biological father's uncles petitioned that he be buried on their land in Mapaio.

Figure 9.7. Relatives carry the coffin of Koivi Kunu to a yard in Baimuru. Photo: Joshua Bell, 2002.

The most vocal of these paternal uncles claimed he would personally care for Koivi Kunu's grave. In the end, this argument won the day and reflected the new primacy of patrilineal and biological ties.

Together with Koivi Kunu's body, a host of mourners then traveled by canoe and dinghy to Mapaio village. Upon arrival, the whole village assembled on the riverbanks in sadness. Some close kin fell out of the boats in tears. Others, waiting on shore, threw themselves into the mud. Meanwhile, others watched closely, assessing the genuiness of their displays for possible hints of who might have been involved in Koivi Kunu's death.

A tent was erected to receive the body and the coffin was brought into his father-in-law's house, where a brother-in-law, who had been in Port Moresby, explained to the assembled crowd that Koivi Kunu had been "shot" by a "magical gun" while coming home from a movie. Next morning, he awoke with a loud gasp that sounded as if someone was sitting on him. Kin tried to help but with no success. In the mortuary rites staged in Port Moresby, a young kinsman had collapsed and died. The bodies of the two men were brought to the morgue. On the way back, a young kinswoman became possessed by the deceased young man. In a séance that followed, his spirit-double revealed that he had been "shot" by a magical "slingshot" at Koivi Kunu's funeral. His death, declared the spirit-double through the voice of the young woman, was related to the same land issues that had led to Koivi Kunu's demise.

Over the next three days, as people digested these revelations, distant kin continued to arrive by canoe. Mourners slept by the coffin while a generator ran all night. When the funeral took place, the Seventh-Day Adventists deacon gave a short sermon, Koivi Kunu's biography was read, and hymns were sung by the Seventh-Day Adventists choir. The service finished, the coffin's lid was removed for final viewing. Wailing crescendoed as the body dressed in a shirt, tie, and new pants became visible under a layer of plastic. Seventh-Day Adventists deacons and youth stood around the coffin, waving away flies and spraying air freshner. Koivi Kunu's eldest son sat in a stupor at the coffin's head. Mourners filed by, hitting themselves and crying out. Many people collapsed and had to be pulled away by attendants. After a few hours, the coffin was wrapped up in a nipa mat and carried off to a grave and buried.

During the three days of debate about where Koivi Kunu should be buried, Koivi Kunu's brother-in-law, who lived in town, railed against homestead burial, dismissing it as a new custom. He worried that the powerful magic that killed Koivi Kunu still lingered around the body and could hurt others. But if and when someone died as a result of it, he said, no one should be blamed. Multiple villagers denied that homstead burial custom was unusual, observing that multiple people had been buried in Mapaio. The last word, however, went to Koivi Kunu's paternal uncle, who vouched that having "lived with Koivi Kunu, I am prepared to die with him."

Following the burial in the paternal uncle's yard, young men went fishing and hunting, and 200 kina were collected to purchase food for the funerary feast. During this time, a renowned hunter and a kinsman of the deceased somehow got lost in the rainforest. A search party found him two nights later, wandering around and exhausted. The hunter later told me privately that he had an *iviai* séance during which the spirit-doubles of both deceased men visited him. While the young man was at a loss to explain why he was killed, Koivi Kunu's spirit-double explained that numerous problems with agnates and affines as well as the death of one of his sons had caused his death.

Fearing reprisals, the hunter kept the details of his *iviai* séance quiet. For their part, many mourners reached the conclusion that Koivi Kunu was killed because of his efforts to register the ILG of his biological father's descent group. Adopted and raised by another lineage, the promise of logging and natural gas royalties had motivated him to seek to reclaim ties to his father's kin, which inflamed tensions with that group. Registering an ILG without the consent of a descent group, and thereby negating his adopted kin, exemplify the commodification of relations of the time of "money ground." The heavy rains that poured over the next several days prevented the village from assembling to discuss these revelations, and mourners dispersed.

When I returned to Mapaio in 2006, a more permanent monument had been erected on Koivi Kunu's grave. Despite his vow to look after it, the paternal uncle had neglected the grave. Instead two brothers-in-law had tended it, built a nipa palm shelter over it, and erected a wooden cross. On the cross, Koivi Kunu's name was inscribed along with his year of birth and death. Above a stylized face reminiscent of a motif in traditional I'ai carvings, a photograph of Koivi Kunu I had taken in 2001 had been glued to the top of the cross (Figure 9.8). This was an innovation in grave markers that subsequently was copied on four other graves. When I asked about the intent of the new custom, I was told that it just felt that this was the right thing to do (see Dalton, this volume).

Conclusion—A Prolonged State of Debasement

> At least I am thankful and I am happy, very happy with all my heart because
> I have lived through this year already.
> People are like the year's ripened leaves that fall noiselessly.
> But I am going to live the coming years, therefore, my name is mentioned
> and remembered, but if I die, my name and my face vanish.
> *Iri o Nepou Mo'oko* (Ripened Leaves That Fall)

Figure 9.8. Koivi Kunu's refurbished homestead grave included a photograph of him and the inscription "In loving Memory of Late Mr. David No'o Y.O.B. 1959 D.O.D. 20.06.02 RIP." Photo: Joshua Bell, 2006.

Written by Koivi Kunu in the late 1980s prior to timber concessions and resource extraction, the lyrics of this song reflect on mortality in a way that I'ai audiences still find profoundly moving. They evoke the inevitability of death and loss, the melancholy it arouses and the ephemerality of the person. They also suggest the perception that in the past the dead did slip away more readily. Today, however, the politics of resource extraction and homestead burials ensures that the dead remain close to peoples' lives, and that they are not easily forgotten. This proximity, along with the dialogue it entails, is not a space in which the I'ai find comfort, but it is one that leaves them anxious.

Despite the long-term presence of conflict linked to sorcery in the Purari Delta, the current impacts of structural violence has exacerbated local-level conflict to unprecedented heights. In addition to mortuary politics, it manifests itself in tensions related to restructuring kin groups, in domestic abuse caused by gambling, and in unexplained environmental issues (see Bell 2009, 2015). Though the timber companies involved are blamed for this sad state of affairs (see Kirsch 2006), the I'ai largely frame these deaths in terms of their own moral failings. "Money ground" is a critique of commoditization and the alienability of the Delta (see von Poser and Silverman, this volume).

Homestead burials foreground this instablity in the village. These graves demand that the community constantly acknowledge the presence of unresolved conflicts in their midst. Specifically, they also commemorate their collective inability to relenquish sorcery and that kin-based solidarity no longer characterizes their communities. Moreover, in circumventing the secondary burial (*onari laua*), when mourners were collectively cleansed of all mystical impurities of the deceased, people now live in a prolonged state of debasement. This is also an intentional affront to the rest of the village, who must now worry about exposure to the lingering dead's spirit-double, which can make them sick or kill them. Proximity to the dead weakens a fragile community.

The struggle around homstead burials in Mapaio has parallels with what Verdury (1999) described about the dead in postsocialist Eastern Europe. There, as in the Purari Delta, struggles around the dead are extensions of political claims about history and land. In the Delta, the power of the dead rests in their new and semipermanent material presence in the grave. I say semipermanent because, by 2010, Koivi Kunu's grave had fallen into neglect. The roof had collapsed and the paint on the grave marker was fading. His brothers-in-law were preoccupied with looking after their own father's grave in the wake of his suspicious death. Impermanence nowithstanding, the materiality of graves still shapes discourse about the dead and how the living deal with conflict and loss associated with them. In this sense, the dead are both "concrete, yet protean" (Verdury 1999: 28). They are morally ambivalent beings, both loved and feared. Indeed, the I'ai try to maintain a balance between being close but not too close to their dead. By doing so, they try to acknowledge community tensions without making them worse.

Failing to access the wealth flowing from regional resource extraction projects, the I'ai have not elaborated funeral rites as have Lihir people (see Bainton and Macintyre, this volume). Rather, funerals express the very problems that cause the deaths that plague them. Instead of being an opportunity for closure and renewal, people are reminded of their inability to control the externalities that beset them. Moreover, death has become a constant humiliation that demonstrates the failure of their moral community (see Silverman, this volume). Turning against themselves, I'ai are caught up in old lineage and descent group rivalries. Indeed, while the dead through their spirit-doubles continue to return and reveal the causes of deaths, these visitations add to the anxiety created by resource extraction. Collective incrimination is one of the most insidious effects of the structural violence of resource extraction.

In closing, I want to return to an issue I started to discuss at the beginning of this chapter: my moral entanglement with death during fieldwork. Given the extent to which the living try to understand and explain events, it was perhaps inevitable that I became implicated in villagers' deaths. While my disquiet was linked to my own limited experience of death in the United States, it was more intensely linked to being overwhelmed by the immediacy of death and suffering that, no doubt, relates to endemic malaria, persistent tuberculosis, the rise of HIV/AIDs, and periodic tropical diseases and parasites (see Ulijaszek 2005).

Though fifty years of sustained health care has lowered mortality rates, rural communities continue to endure these aliments. When an absence of postcolonial infrastructure had added to this picture, what might be viewed as ordinary treatment in town hospitals quickly gets bogged down in a lack of fuel or a lack of medicine in the Delta. Meanwhile, barges loaded down with supplies and highpowered boats carrying workers travel upriver. Such signs of capitalism in the hinterland demonstrate what is possible but what is not happening in villages like Mapaio.

Research in this region raises moral questions about how one can truly help. While I have always made my own medical supplies available and taken people to the regional hospital when needed, I remain keenly aware not only of my own inadequacies but also that when I am home in the United States and not in the Purari Delta, ready access to healthcare is available to me. My hope is that shedding light on the structural violence caused by resource extraction may provide at least a partial ground for compensation or at least broader acknowledgement of the region's growing inequalities. I also hope at the very least that this contribution will help the people I have come to know, as well as those who have already died, linger a little longer and leave some impression of their dignity and grace.

Joshua A. Bell is curator of globalization at the Smithsonian Institution's National Museum of Natural History. Since 2000, he has conducted field research with communities in the Purari Delta of Papua New Guinea. His latest book is a coedited volume titled *The Anthropology of Expeditions: Travel, Visualities, Afterlives* (2015).

Notes

1. The other groups are the Baroi, Kaimare, Koriki, Maipua, and Vaimuru.
2. Led by the I'ai man Tom Kabu (ca. 1920–1969), the Kabu Movement emerged in 1946 as a movement that mixed the aspirations of men who served in World War II, with the aspirations of Seventh-Day Adventist converts in the villages. Convincing villagers to destroy their ritual material culture and cease ritual practices, members of the Kabu Movement saw business as a way to transform the region. Although the Australian government stiffled the movement, it nonetheless expanded cultural horizons in the Purari Delta.
3. People also referred to the spirit-double with the untranslatable term *onomo*, which they clarified was invisible. Williams (1924: 240) makes no mention of the term *onomo*, which I am inclined to think is a local glossing of the Christian notion of soul.

4. While I undoubtedly failed to document the full range of deaths and illnesses prior to my main fieldwork, the trends exhibited in this sample are, I believe, indicative of wider regional trends for the Purari.
5. It was Mailau's involvement in the persecution of this councillor that some saw as the reason for his death.

Archival Source

Robert Francis Maher papers, National Anthropological Archives (NAAA), Smithsonian Institution; Washington, D.C., United States.

References Cited

Bell, Joshua A. 2006. "Marijuana, Guns, Crocodiles and Radios: Economies of Desire in the Purari Delta." *Oceania* 76: 220–34.
———. 2009. "Documenting Discontent: Heirlooms and Documents as Powerful Things in the Purari Delta of Papua New Guinea." *The Australian Journal of Anthropology* 20: 28–47.
———. 2014. "The Veracity of Form: Transforming Knowledges, and Their Forms in the Purari Delta of Papua New Guinea." In *Museum as Process: Translating Local and Global Knowledges,* edited by R. Silverman, 105–22. London: Routledge.
———. 2015. "Structural Violence of Resource Extraction in the Purari Delta." In *Tropical Forests of Oceania: Anthropological Perspectives,* edited by J.A. Bell, P. West, C. Filer, 127–53. Canberra: Australian National University Press.
Bourdieu, Pierre. 2000. *Pascalian Meditations.* Stanford: Stanford University Press.
Farmer, Paul. 2004. "An Anthropology of Structural Violence." *Current Anthropology* 45: 305–25.
———. 2005. *Pathologies of Power: Health, Human Rights, and the New War on the Poor.* Berkeley: University of California Press.
Ferguson, J. 1999. *Expectations of Modernity: Myths and Meanings of Urban Life on the Zambian Copperbelt.* Berkeley: University of California Press.
Galtung, Johan. 1969. "Violence, Peace, and Peace Research." *Journal of Peace Research* 6: 167–91.
Glaskin, Katie, Tonkinson, Myrna, Musharbash, Yasmine., and Burbank, Victoria eds. 2009. *Australia in Mortality, Mourning and Mortuary Practices in Indigenous Australia.* London: Ashgate.
Gupta, Akhil. 2012. *Red Tape: Bureaucracy, Structural Violence, and Poverty in India.* Durham: Duke University Press.
Harrison, Simon. 1993. *The Mask of War: Violence, Ritual, and the Self in Melanesia.* Manchester: St. Martin's Press.
High, Holly. 2011. "Melancholia and Anthropology." *American Ethnologist* 38(2): 217–33.
Hitchcock, Nancy E. and Oram, Nigel eds. 1967. *Rabia Camp and the Tommy Kabu Movement.* Canberra: The Australian National University.
Holmes, John Henry R. 1924. *In Primitive New Guinea.* London: Seeley, Service & Co.
Kirsch, Stuart. 2006. *Reverse Anthropology: Indigenous Analysis of Social and Environmental Relations in New Guinea.* Stanford: Stanford University Press.

Kwon, Heonik. 2006. *After the Massacre: Commemoration and Consolation in Ha My and My Lai*. Berkeley: University of California Press.
Maher, Robert F. 1961. *New Men of Papua: A Study in Culture Change*. Madison: University of Wisconsin Press.
———. 1974. "Koriki Chieftainship: Hereditary Status and Mana in Papua." *Ethnology* 13: 239–46.
———. 1984. "The Purari River Delta Societies, Papua New Guinea, after the Tom Kabu Movement." *Ethnology* 23: 217–27.
Morauta, Louise. 1984. *Left Behind in the Village: Economic and Social Conditions in an Area of High Outmigration*. Boroko: Institute of Applied Social and Economic Research.
Mueggler, Erik. 2001. *The Age of Wild Ghosts: Memory, Violence, and Place in Southwest China*. Berkeley: University of California Press.
Nixon, Rob. 2011. *Slow Violence and the Environmentalism of the Poor*. Cambridge: Harvard University Press.
Papua. 1914. *Papua Annual Reports for the Year 1913–14*. State of Victoria: Government Printer.
———. 1923. *Papua Annual Report for the Year 1921–22*. Government of the Commonwealth of Australia.
Povinelli, Elizabeth A. 2011. *Economies of Abandonment: Social Belonging and Endurance in Late Liberalism*. Durham: Duke University Press.
Ong, Aihwa. 1988. "The Production of Possession: Spirits and the Multinational Corporation in Malaysia." *American Ethnologist* 15: 28–42
Robbins, Joel and Holly Wardlow, eds. 2005. *The Making of Global and Local Modernities in Melanesia: Humiliation, Transformation and the Nature of Cultural Change*. Aldershot: Ashgate.
Rosaldo, Renato. 1993. "Grief and a Headhunter's Rage." In *Culture and Truth: The Remaking of Social Analysis*, 1–21. Boston: Beacon Press.
Ryan, Dawn. 1989. "Home Ties in Town: Toaripi in Port Moresby." *Canberra Anthropology* 12: 19–27.
Scheper-Hughes, Nancy and Philippe Bourgois. 2004. "Introduction: Making Sense of Violence." In *Violence in War and Peace: An Anthology*, edited by Scheper-Hughes and Bourgois, 1–31. London: Blackwell Publishing.
Strathern, Marilyn. 1988. *The Gender of the Gift*. Berkeley: University of California Press.
Throop, C. Jason. 2010. "Latitudes of Loss: On the Vicissitudes of Empathy." *American Ethnologist* 37(4): 771–82.
Ulijaszek, Stanley. 2005. "Purari Population Decline and Resurgence across the Twentieth Century." In *Population, Reproduction and Fertility in Melanesia*, edited by SJ Ulijaszek, 67–89. Oxford: Berghahn Books.
Verdury, Katherine. 1999. *The Political Lives of Dead Bodies: Reburial and Postsocialist Change*. New York: Columbia University Press.
Williams, FE. 1924. *The Natives of the Purari Delta*. Port Moresby: Government Printer.

Afterword

Mortuary Dialogues in Pacific Modernities and Anthropology

DAVID LIPSET, ERIC K. SILVERMAN, and ERIC VENBRUX

The nine ethnographic chapters in this book focus on what some Pacific Islanders say and do to try to make things right after death has shaken them out of the moral categories of daily life and thrown them into a space in which, as Hamlet put it to his father's ghost, the "time is out of joint." We call their talk and practices in such contexts "mortuary dialogues" because we observe, after Bakhtin, that they involve many shifting and contradictory voices that privilege no authoritative position, single voice, or set of meanings. In Pacific modernity, death occasions dialogues that defy resolution.

Although we have seen that dialogue goes on prior to death, especially during lapses in and out of consciousness, perhaps its most elementary form occurs between the bereaved and the deceased upon the first recognition that the loved one has passed. Death is not mute. It is a message of rejection and exclusion. In response, survivors confront the problem of moral intelligibility. In Weberian terms, death exposes a gap in meaning (2002). In their pain, mourners, Pacific women in particular, cry and wail. As they do, they ask fraught questions: Why did you leave us? Who did this to you? What will happen to us now? How will we go on? From this line of inquiry, mortuary dialogue expands outward to involve close and dispersed kin, the community at large, and even anthropological fieldworkers, as well as exponents of modern institutions and values in a widening, global gyre.

To whatever degree the ritual processes set in motion by death may or may not integrate the moral community, the grief and suffering in this elementary form of dialogue reveals that its boundaries are fragile and permeable. Spirits, possessing what are essentially mimetic human qualities, lurk about and menace mourners with their gaze and desire. Both Dalton and Lipset report instances during which funerary rites were underway when the "deceased" awoke. While they love departed kin so much that their spirits may "fly" off to be with them, Carucci reports that Marshall Islanders also fear the dead and avoid cemeteries. Mortuary rites are meant to dispatch the deceased's ghost to the afterlife and secure the boundaries of moral community, as Hertz observed so long ago. But practice and experience suggest otherwise. Their departure is rarely indisputable, much less on schedule. Ritual, so we have argued, does not resolve loss in any open-and-shut way.

Nor does it guarantee its meaning. Following Evans-Pritchard (1976), we know that death raises moral questions. Who or what society is guilty? Who and what society is innocent? As often as not, suspicion is cast widely. Oracles, through which spirits communicate about death, such as the "wandering coffin" of the Kayan or the visionary séances of the I'ai, may take place and influence dialogue in vigils and moots. What they reveal does not have the transparency of a telecast, as the I'ai wish they did. Instead, they express an ethos of doubt and angst in the midst of the current axes of conflict in communities, although perhaps not with the precision that the case studies and social dramas of the Manchester School were said to afford (Gluckman 1958; Turner 1972; Evens and Handelman 2007). As Bell put it in his chapter in this volume, instead of certainty, accusations against sorcerers made by the dead during I'ai séances give rise to "constant reinterpretation, mistrust and a sense of moral failure."

In the Introduction, we expressed theoretical qualms about the efficacy and ahistorical quality of the L'Annee sociologique view of ritual process. And many chapters did likewise. But we must concede that the "triumph or moral community" framework nonetheless appears alive and well in Pacific ethnology. However, our position remains unqualified: should ritual efforts to reproduce moral community denote anything at all, the normative relationships which they would seek to renew must be defined in whatever mix of Pacific cosmologies and modern institutions inform how they are understood in the historical moment. We do not insist that such a renewal is ever completely possible. But we do insist that Pacific peoples try to achieve moral closure in the aftermath of death and in doing so they answer Christian concepts of the soul and the afterlife as well as modern notions of community in differing, if not necessarily successful, ways. The many voices in regional mortuary dialogues advocate discrepant points of view about such issues as burial location, grave markers, and, of course, the relationship of local, cosmologically embedded concepts of the person to modernity.

During earlier eras, missionaries and colonial states banned tree-burial among the Rawa and the I'ai. Today, however, where bodies should be buried can be an open question. The answer, today as in the past, is in most instance locally self-evident: With the ancestors, of course. But where are they? In the place where the death occurred, which may be in some anonymous urban setting or among a transnational diaspora? Should the deceased be transported "home" for burial? But where is that? In a family cemetery that may have been destroyed by the construction of an American airstrip, as on Enewetak Atoll? Homestead burial seems to be undergoing a revival, particularly in Papua New Guinea. In Bell's I'ai case, in which villagers jockey for position in expectation of timber and mining royalties, homestead burial has also become a tactic, a kind of property claim through which mourners try to forestall their rivals' claims to land. On Manam Island, homestead burial answers the mismanagement of the population by Papua New Guinea authorities in the aftermath of a volcano eruption. On the one hand, the revival of homestead burial expressed a desire to return to their "place" and "ancestors." On the other, it also issued a willy-nilly challenge to the postcolonial state.

Grave markers are no less a subject of dialogue about the reproduction of moral community in the historical moment. Crosses have come to be taken for grave ornaments. But should they be inscribed with personal names or adorned with photographs or other motifs? Cement seems to be a commonplace innovation, which perhaps implies the emergence of what Silverman calls "modern memory" and the so-called sentimental family. In Carucci's case of diaspora Marshallese, cuttings from Enewetak Atoll are smuggled to the Big Island of Hawai'i to plant on gravesites by way of accentuating a connection to home. Another exemplary image might be the overturned bowls attached to the crosses Rawa people erect as grave markers, which expresses the both/and relationship of the Rawa concept of the moral person to their Christianity.

Pacific Islanders seem to combine rather than simply comply with or contest modernity in their mortuary dialogues. Bainton and Macintyre's accounts, for example, show how, in the context of extraordinary mine payments, Lihirian secondary burial rites shifted away from commemorating deceased bodies, not to forgo them but to emphasize status competition among the living through an innovation of pre-mortem celebrations. When Marshall Islanders living in Hawai'i encountered death in the context of modern bureaucracy for the first time, they went along with having to make use of the services of a funeral home. But they reject embalming because of their abiding Hertzian fear that "nothing good will come from interrupting" the processes of death. In several Papua New Guinea societies (Murik, Kayan, Manam, Eastern Iatmul and I'ai), the customary use of canoe-coffins likened the transition to the afterlife to a voyage. Today, although coffins are often purchased and not made, and this analogy seems to be on the wane, Lipset presents a case in which a spirit nevertheless has the power to communicate through its store-bought box.

Who are the principal voices in mortuary dialogues? Of course they are gendered. Eastern Iatmul men manufacture and impersonate elaborate tableaux of spirits for audiences of women and children. Manam men, for their part, stage flute performances. In addition, we have seen that men make speeches at community centers, or during vigils they debate sorcery accusations, burial sites, and grave care. But it is of interest to note the significant degree to which Pacific women do much more than serve as passive audiences for men's performances. As Wilson and Sinclair make clear, women oversee and safeguard the deceased's passage to the afterlife and in so doing play a central role in Māori mortuary rites.

Christian voices, initially of expatriate missionaries but now of Pacific Islanders, demand compliance with modern burial practices and a binary concept of the person as an eternal, individualistic soul that must be liberated from a sinful body. Today, local catechists, religious leaders, and congregants offer sermons in ways that answer, however awkwardly and with whatever tension, custom. A striking instance of this dialogue occurs the night before burial, when Catholic priests offer prayers and conduct Mass while Māori orators allude to the return of the *wairua* spirit to the ancestors. Congregants and clergy may not interpret what is taking place uniformly, however. Some Māori, according to Wilson and Sinclair, see the *wairua* spirit as a tutelary spirit, while Catholic priests understand it as a soul that moves off to the afterlife, where it has no further impact on the moral community. "Mass is ... conducted in a comfortable tone; [and] ... neither side feels the need to correct the other." Their dialogue remains unresolved, resisting, by a kind of silent agreement, any final word.

In Lihir and Misima Islands, Bainton and Macintyre report that while beneficiaries of mining royalties pour money into ever more elaborate mortuary rites, less fortunate voices in the community advocate modern labor discipline, financial accountability, and the like, or they become culturally conservative critics of how impertinent and inauthentic custom is becoming. von Poser describes a similar debate between town-dwelling Kayan and rural kin. On the one side, some people prefer a shortened version of mortuary rites at which a small group of kin assembles for a feast when the grave is cemented as both less expensive and modern. On the other, most villagers see this as nothing less than a disrespectful shortcut.

Not least, of course, voices of colonial states intrude upon Pacific mortuary dialogues. Today, the postcolonial state stakes out positions in these ongoing dialogues. Undoubtedly, the most heinous example of its intervention appears in Carucci's account of the Marshall Islanders of Enewetak Atoll. Missionaries forbade sea burials and forced people to adopt land-based interments in cemeteries. Later, the people of Enewetak became exiled from their atoll homes by ecocide caused by American nuclear testing. Eventually, some of them ended up in Hawai'i, where they continue to adapt to state-based regulations that require them to use (and pay for) funeral homes and cemetery plots.

One other voice is sometimes heard amid (rather than above) the din of mortuary dialogue: the postcolonial anthropologist, for whom the tragedy of mortality seems at least partially to dissolve the moral and professional or disciplinary boundaries between self and other, no less than it does for the kin of the deceased and the community at large. Bakhtin, analyzing relations between writers vis-a-vis their fictional characters, examined varieties of relations between what he called "author" and "hero" as turning upon the extent to which the one does or does not "coincide" with the other (1990: 242).

Under the token of tragedy and tragic heroes, in addition to analytical and scholarly voices, several ethnographers in this volume succumb to a kind of excruciating equality with their tragic heroes. From them we hear anxious autobiographical reflection and confessional self-accounting (Devereux 1967). That is to say, we hear engaged authorial voices who are not only immersed in the time and space of the other but also immersed in that time and space on behalf of the other. We do not mean to imply that colonial anthropology in the Pacific was only, or necessarily, removed from and superior to their subjects or objects of study. But the postcolonial ethos does seem to incline a subject position in which the ethnographer stands beside, rather than outside of, the tragic hero, holding common values.

Several striking examples come to mind. One thinks of Dalton's recollections of the deaths he experienced among natal kin in the United States and his account of what happened during a Rawa "watching" wake when "the deceased" opened his eyes and looked right at him. He was shaken up, needless to say, by this gaze, and all the more so when reporting what had happened and finding himself mystically implicated in causing the death.

There is also the intriguing case of a final stage of a mortuary process on Manam Island being postponed by adoptive kin for two years—until Lutkehaus, the fieldworker, returned. When she did so, Lutkehaus performed as a Manam woman ought to do by carrying a basket of almonds on her head and slamming it down to the ground as part of ceremonial exchanges between hosts and guests during a particular phase of the mortuary process. Lutkehaus also made a film of it, which she was able to screen on Manam some twenty years on to an audience of youth who had never seen anything like it and to a few adults who began to weep upon seeing images of since-deceased kin on screen. Lutkehaus expressed a strong sense of well-being at having shown her film in situ. At this moment, we might add, boundaries between self and other, local and global, anthropologists and objects, had all but dissolved.

A last remarkable instance is that of Bell among the I'ai of the Purari Delta. The widow and daughter of an informant had criticized Bell for neglecting them in their grief and even suggested that the angry spirit of their deceased husband and father had retaliated on their behalf and had made Bell ill enough to be hospitalized. What was worse, one of the explanations of the death accused Bell for having paid more attention to his deceased informant than to any of the other men in the village, thus arousing their jealousies. Reflecting that his informant's death was the very first such loss in his life, Bell comments upon the overwhelming depths to which it grieved him and the guilty sense, not only of unrepayable debt he felt to the community at large but also for his privileged access to healthcare when back home in the United States. In other words, perhaps, tragedy, in all of its proximate as well as broader-based, modern dimensions, possessed some of our authors and reduced their moral distance from it.

Having highlighted some of the issues and voices in Pacific mortuary dialogues that appear in this volume, we end by remarking on their tenacious yet equivocal tones and broader theoretical significance. The occasionally incompatible answers the dead, mourners, and others give one another and modernity portray moral personhood and moral community in a state of becoming. That is to say, the unity of their dialogue does not constitute the moral world in its entirety. And perhaps we might go as far as to propose that this lack of finality in death-related contexts is one of the defining features of postcoloniality in the insular Pacific. Or it might be that the unambiguous and conspicuous sort of inconclusiveness that characterizes death dialogues in the sample of societies presented in this volume just turns out to be part of a segment of a larger array of discourse.

The empirical reach of this part of our argument remains an open question. For now, we can affirm that we have accomplished the goal we set for this volume. We have destabilized the relationship between death ritual and moral community. More importantly, we have overheard dialogues among voices accountable both to modernity, in terms of its violence, binaries, and opportunities, and to Pacific cosmologies and moral communities, in terms of their spirits, fears, and agency, or to put it less delicately, their ancestors.

In the spirit of dialogism, we do not offer this volume as the last word on mortuary rites in the insular Pacific. Nor do we want to close the theoretical shop on mortuary ritual. Rather, we hope our volume inspires further dialogue, both empirical and conceptual.

David Lipset is Professor of Anthropology at the University of Minnesota. He has done fieldwork in the Murik Lakes region of the Sepik River in Papua New Guinea off and on since 1981. He is the author of *Gregory Bateson: Legacy of a Scientist* (1982) and *Mangrove Man: Dialogics of Culture in the Sepik Estuary* (1997) in addition to two co-edited volumes and many journal articles and book chapters.

Eric K. Silverman is former Professor of American Studies at Wheelock College, now affiliated with the Women's Studies Research Center at Brandeis University. He has worked on masculinity and art among Eastern Iatmul people in Papua New Guinea since 1989. In addition to numerous journal articles and book chapters, he is the author of three books, including *Masculinity, Motherhood and Mockery: Psychoanalyzing Culture and the Iatmul Naven Rite in New Guinea* (2001) and *A Cultural History of Jewish Dress* (2013).

Eric Venbrux is professor of comparative religion and director of the Centre for Thanatology at Radboud University, Nijmegen, The Netherlands. He is the author of *A Death in the Tiwi Islands: Ritual, Conflict and Social Life in an Australian Aboriginal Community* and coeditor of *Exploring World Art* and *Ritual, Media, and Conflict*. He has also published numerous articles on mortuary ritual in Europe and the Pacific.

References Cited

Bakhtin, MM. 1984. *Problems of Dostoevsky's Poetics*. Edited and translated by Caryl Emerson. Minneapolis: University of Minnesota Press.

———. 1990. "Author and Hero in Aesthetic Activity (ca. 1920–1923)." In *Art and Answerability: Early Philosophical Essays by M.M. Bakhtin*, edited by Michael Holquist and Vadim Liapunov and translated by Vadim Liapunov, 4–255. Minneapolis: University of Minnesota Press.

Devereux, George. 1967. *From Anxiety to Method in the Behavioral Sciences*. The Hague: Mouton.

Evans-Pritchard, EE. 1976 [1937]. *Witchcraft, Oracles and Magic among the Azande*. Oxford: Oxford University Press.

Evens, TMS and D. Handelman. 2007. *The Manchester School: Practice and Ethnographic Praxis in Anthropology*. Oxford: Berghahn.

Gluckman, Max. 1958 [1940]. *Analysis of a Social Situation in Modern Zululand*. Rhodes-Livingstone Papers, 28. New York: Humanities Press.

Turner, Victor. 1972 [1953]. *Schism and Continuity in an African Society*. Manchester: Manchester University Press.

Weber, Max. 2002 [1905]. *The Protestant Ethic and the Spirit of Capitalism*. Translated by Peter Baehr and Gordon C. Wells. London: Penguin Books.

Index

African mortuary ritual, 9–10
afterlife, 28, 49, 69, 87, 92, 116, 139, 171, 185, 186, 189, 195, 198
ancestor shrine, 75
L'Annee sociologique, 1, 3, 25, 60–61, 76, 137, 177, 200
anthropologists' subjectivity
    Bell, 209–211, 230–231
    Dalton, 61–62, 65, 64–66
    Lutkehaus, 135, 143–144, 152
    von Poser, 173
    Silverman, 178
Aries, P., 67

Bakhtin, M., 7, 83, 89
Bataille, G., 111
Bateson, G., 182, 185, 187, 192, 204n7
birth
    Marshall Islands, 29
Bloch, M., 6, 96
    and J. Parry, 5
body, 2, 29
    bathing, 55, 87, 88, 141, 178, 184, 200, 201, 204
    bones, 113, 188–189, 196
    heart, 203
    semen, 189
    skulls, 114–115, 173, 213–214
Bourdieu, P., 212
burial
    affines and, 226–227
    canoe, 28
    cemetery, 29–31, 32–33, 36–7, 54, 71, 92, 98, 163, 211, 215, 221, 223, 226, 229
    coffins, 52–53, 93, 100, 101
    canoe-coffin, 115, 139, 185, 218
    disputes, 42, 50, 226, 230
    economic change and, 30
    fears, 28, 33
    homestead, 92, 140, 153, 163, 200
    land claims and, 22
    Māori, 52–54
    money, 139
    platform, 214
    preparations for, 220
    sea, 26–29, 33, 115
    secondary, 114, 164
    tree, 214
    Western-style coffins, 218, 226

canoes, 85–87, 88, 89, 91, 107, 185, 189
capitalism, 39, 50, 106, 121
chiefs, 26, 28, 136, 138–139, 141, 147–178, 160
Christianity, 7, 8, 10, 11, 53, 54, 66, 84, 106, 114–116, 195, 197, 203
    Catholicism, 48, 51, 54, 55, 84, 95, 115, 136, 139, 160, 170, 172, 173, 185, 198
    in dialogue with tradition, 57, 72, 73, 75, 160, 170
    influence on death and burial, 12, 29, 32, 71
    Lutheran, 61
    Methodist, 113
    Seventh-Day Adventism, 84, 95, 101, 102, 106, 113, 213, 215, 218, 227
colonialism, 26, 62, 71, 83, 92, 100, 163, 213
Cook, Captain James, 48, 57

death
    ambivalence, 25, 33, 83, 90, 94, 99
    anxiety and guilt, 92, 93
    awakening from, 64, 91
    and birth, 67, 137, 150
    causes, 182
    of a chief, 139, 141–143
    and children, 217

corpse, 2, 9
  and exchange, 170, 220
  fears, 29, 211
  and feasts, 142
  Lihir, 122
  Māori, 52
  and memory, 164
  moment of, 64, 85, 87, 181
  and moral community, 138
  Murik, 87, 91, 93, 96
  and place, 136, 155–156
  pollution, 56, 84, 88, 93, 211
  and possession, 93, 102, 191, 227
  preparing the corpse, 28, 91, 138, 170
  Rawa, 63–64, 71
  resentments, 211, 223
  and resettlement, 34–35, 135–136, 152
  songs, 51, 139
  and the state, 136
  and taboos, 218, 220–221
  and uncertainties, 155
  vigil, 138–139, 218
  widows, 56, 164
  and women, 33, 48, 91, 141, 143, 154
dialogism, 7, 26, 128
diaspora, 37, 49
Douglas, M., 93
dreaming, 88
dreams, 54, 198, 209
Durkheim, E.
  collective representations, 1
  The Elementary Forms of the Religious Life, 2
  mortuary rites, 2
  social facts, 2, 76

Eliade, M., 186, 195
Enewetak and Ujelang Atolls,
exchange
  and mortuary ritual, 6, 8, 29–31, 55
  and monetization, 110–111, 125

Facebook, 203
Farmer, P., 212
feeding, 53, 55, 63
Female Cult, 89, 91, 98, 101, 107

Freud, S., 4, 88, 93, 180–181, 197
functionalism, 3
funeral homes
  Hawai'i, 38–40
funerary industry, 10–11
Frazer, JG., 25, 67

Galtung, J., 212
gender
  and fertility, 8
  Māori, 47–49, 51–52
van Gennep, A., 3, 25, 54, 55, 68
ghosts, 2, 9, 83, 87, 90, 93, 94, 98
graves
  attacking the grave, 143
  concrete, 73, 170, 173, 199, 225
  decorations, 31, 43–44, 54–55, 72, 92, 96, 98, 100, 141, 199, 200, 201, 216
  digging, 54, 100
  monuments, 228
  roofed graves, 216, 221
grief, 2, 138, 181, 198
Gulliver's Travels, 149

Hertz, R., 2, 8, 12, 39, 52, 60, 61, 68, 75, 137, 194
HIV/AIDs, 95, 105
Huntington, WR., 5
  and P. Metcalf, 67

illness, 90
individualism, 2
  and capitalism, 107
initiation societies, 89, 97–98, 101, 102, 107

joking, 89

Klein, M., 191
  breast, good and bad, 81, 82, 83, 87, 88, 90, 91, 92, 93, 95, 96, 99, 100, 104, 105, 107
  mourning, 81–83, 87, 90, 93, 107
knots, 85, 88, 89–90, 96, 100, 101, 103

Levi-Strauss, C., 5
Ledoux, LP., 90

lifedeath, 7
logging
  royalties, 210, 218

Male Cult, 89, 184, 186
male initiation, 137
Malinowski, B., 3–4
Maramatanga Movement, 48, 49, 51, 53
masculinity, 96, 99, 105
Mead, M., 90
Melanesia, 8
Men's House, 115, 123, 137, 141, 155, 213
mining, 111, 112, 113, 116
  effects of closure on mortuary ritual, 124–128
  and mortuary ritual, 117–122
modernity, 34, 57, 66, 81, 84, 105, 159, 170, 171, 178, 181, 199, 202, 203
  and ancestor shrines, 75
  concepts of death, 38–39
  and concepts of time, 173
  and death, 217
  individualism, 170
  money, 170
  and mortuary rites, 169–171
moral community, 1, 2, 39, 44, 73
mortuary rites
  ambivalence, 178, 181, 191
  birth symbolism in, 192
  and change, 120
  dongs, 195
  effigies, 189, 195, 196, 202–203
  end-of-mourning rites, 141, 143–147, 177, 183, 188, 200
  and exchange, 55
  feasting, 191
  haus krai, 204n13
  as kastom, 111
  lack of closure, 178, 194, 197
  lifedeath, 192
  Lihir Island, 113–114
  and male initiation, 159, 161–163, 166–170, 183
  men, 178, 182, 186, 187, 192–193, 196
  tree symbolism in, 183–186, 191
  serpent symbolism in, 186–189, 191–192, 194

  smoke, 195
  and women, 51–52, 54, 182, 183, 187, 194
  woodcarvings, 122–123
mourners, 2
mourning, 2, 33
  end-of-mourning rites, 141, 143–147
  Māori, 51–52
  Murik, 91, 95, 101, 102
  possession and, 191
  taboos, 52, 56, 138, 170, 181
  twisted cords, 181
  widows, 141, 153, 154, 190
mortuary dialogue, 11, 15, 26, 32, 35, 39, 44, 61, 83, 90, 91, 93, 95, 99, 100, 104, 107, 116, 199–120, 121, 136, 211, 213
mortuary feasting, 31, 113–114, 116, 120–121

Obeyesekere, G., 180

Pacific Modernity, 6, 37–9, 43–44, 74
personhood, 6
  E. Iatmul, 182, 183, 185, 187, 189, 195
  I'ai, 216–217
  Kayan, 159, 161, 173
  Lihir, 114
  Manam, 136, 138, 150
  Māori, 50, 52
  Marshallese, 26, 31
  Murik, 84–87, 88, 89, 91, 96, 107
  Rawa, 68–70, 73,
pigs, 111, 117–118, 143, 147–149, 213–214
Purari Delta, 212, 222

Radcliffe-Brown, A.R., 3
resource extraction, 210, 213
rite of rebellion, 5
ritual restoration, 4

Sahlins, M., 7, 111–112, 121, 127
sago, 92, 189, 191, 214, 218, 220
seances, oracles, divination, 63, 93, 94, 163–164, 170, 220, 228
Sepik River, 84, 189
Somare, Sir M., 84, 95

sorcery, 61, 67, 93–94, 163, 210, 218, 223, 230
spirits
    Eastern Iatmul, 177, 189, 195
    flutes, 138–139, 141, 153–154, 164, 183, 184, 185, 187, 193, 194
    I'ai, 210, 216
    Kayan, 161, 171–172
    Manam, 138–139, 143, 153, 155
    Māori, 48–49, 51, 53
    Marshall Islanders, 26, 33
    Murik, 85–88, 91
    Rawa, 63, 68–70, 76
Strathern, M., 76
structural violence, 212

subject, postcolonial, 83
Swift, J., 149

Tom Kabu Movement, 213–214, 217, 222
Trobriand Islands, 4, 8, 149
tourism, 150–151, 198

United States
    nuclear weapons testing, 34–35
Urbanism, 49

Wagner, R., 76
Wedgwood, C., 136
Weiner, A., 136–138, 149, 154
Weiner, J., 180, 192

www.ingramcontent.com/pod-product-compliance
Lightning Source LLC
Chambersburg PA
CBHW070917030426

42336CB00014BA/2446